Second Edition

Great Jobs

for

English
Majors

Julie DeGalan
Stephen Lambert

VGM Career Horizons
NTC/Contemporary Publishing Group

Library of Congress Cataloging-in-Publication Data

DeGalan, Julie.
     Great jobs for English majors / Julie DeGalan & Stephen Lambert.—2nd ed.
        p.   cm.
     Includes index.
     ISBN 0-658-00221-X
     1. Job hunting.   2. College graduates—Employment.   I. Lambert, Stephen.
II. Title.
HF5382.7 .D43 2000
650.14—dc21   99-55167
                                                                         CIP

To Barbara, Carolyn, Craig, and Bryon, with love

Published by VGM Career Horizons
A division of NTC/Contemporary Publishing Group, Inc.
4255 West Touhy Avenue, Lincolnwood (Chicago), Illinois 60712-1975 U.S.A.
Copyright © 2000 by NTC/Contemporary Publishing Group, Inc.
Printed in the United States of America
International Standard Book Number: 0-658-00221-X
   01 02 03 04 05 LB 18 17 16 15 14 13 12 11 10 9   8   7   6   5 4   3 2

CONTENTS

Acknowledgments

We want to thank the many people who directly and indirectly helped us revise and update this book, including Debra Regan and Ruth DeCotis of Plymouth State College; Jim Moran and WageWeb (Deptford, New Jersey) for providing access to the detailed wage data on their website (http://www.wageweb.com); and Marian Needham at the Newspaper Guild–CWA (www.newsguild.org) for providing salary information for guild members.

ENGLISH: A DEGREE FOR ALL SEASONS

S ometime, if you can, stop by your college or university library to see whether it holds a collection of yearbooks from the past. Perhaps they are put away for safekeeping in a special collection. Ask to see them and flip through the galleries of past graduates. Begin in the 1960s and enjoy yourself as you look at the conservative haircuts and clothes. Note, too, how mature most of these students looked, and reflect on how much less of a transition it must have been for them to pass, at least in appearance, from the world of college to the world of work.

Students of the past mimicked older adults in dress, manners, and behavior. Their closets and drawers were filled with a wardrobe that, with little change, would suffice for most adult occupations. The typical infractions of college rules that warranted discipline tended not to be behavior that rejected adult norms, but rather actions that imitated adults even more closely, such as smoking or drinking.

A DEGREE WITH A HISTORY

Of course, you'll notice each graduate's degree displayed proudly under each photograph. One thing that will immediately be apparent is how many fewer degree options there were. You'll see lots of teacher candidates and lots of science majors. History majors and some foreign language majors appear.

But, again and again, you'll see "English" boldly emblazoned under the graduates' serious but youthful mien as they stare out from a page that probably seems far more remote in time than it really is.

This was a time when, if you chose to major in English, people seldom asked, "What are you going to do with that degree?" English was the flagship of the classic undergraduate liberal arts education, and its value lay in its broad exposure to all aspects of English and the sweep and history of a culture that spoke and wrote in English. It was valued because of its history as one of the earliest degrees in the middle-class American college tradition, as well as for its emphasis on the disciplines of learning to read, write, and appreciate literature in many forms.

The English majors whose faces appear in yearbooks of the past became leaders in banking, finance, business, education, and medicine. Not only did they feel prepared for these roles by their English degrees, but society also agreed with them and valued that degree as excellent career preparation for a host of possible employment situations.

English Students Caught in Transition

Now, move through time and take a look at some yearbooks from the end of the 1970s and the early 1980s. Things were quite different for these students; there was an active rebellion against the norms of their parents' generation. The hairstyles and clothes you see in these photos are a dead giveaway of a rejection of traditional norms.

Changes were also taking place in degree programs as students sought out more esoteric majors and many seemed to delight in pursuing studies for which there seemed to be no immediate transferability to the world of work. Students were disaffected with society's power base, and rather than become part of it and manage change from within, many chose to reject it entirely.

But, in the meantime, the technical revolution was under way. Space flight was becoming a regular occurrence, and computer technology was becoming more important in nearly every sector of the economy. Society was adopting technology at an exponential rate. Everyone agreed that the more technical your background was, the greater your chances of success and your ability to master your environment would be. The press held much of this growth up for public adulation, and parents, interested in a return on their considerable investment in college, urged their sons and daughters to major in specialized technical fields.

Just as colleges and universities began offering new technical degree programs, employers, too, developed a penchant for hiring college grads with these narrowly defined degrees. They began to demand specialized graduates for specialized jobs. They only looked at business graduates or computer science majors or economists. They increased the demand for students who had some narrow skills but who did not read widely, who were not comfortable writing, and who had not been schooled in the critical analysis of ideas.

A Failure in Priorities

Many programs that emphasized technology failed to allow for teaching how to communicate this new technology in a way others could easily understand. They emphasized equipment before logical thinking, clarity of purpose, or the ability to follow through in developing an idea. Exams in these subject areas tended to emphasize the same dimensions of speed, efficiency, and economy of effort as did the subject content; tests were heavily skewed in favor of the true/false or multiple-choice exam. Students did well in selecting the correct response but proved terribly deficient in interviews with prospective employers, in completing graduate school personal essays, and in providing writing samples because they had not had the opportunity to develop their written and oral communication skills.

Both educators and employers soon realized that what they might have been gaining in depth in these subject areas, they were losing in breadth. The stage was set for the return of the English major.

A DEGREE FOR TODAY

Today's students have to leap a far wider chasm of appearance, behavior, and even idiomatic speech than did students of past decades to attain the security of permanent employment. In the contemporary youth-oriented culture, students (even older students) mimic adolescents in their language, choice of entertainment, and physical appearance. Therefore, after the long-held status of "student" is lost upon graduation from college, inexperienced job candidates must negotiate an unfamiliar terrain of language, behavior norms, and dress codes. Most students sense the enormity of these changes, and this can add to their reluctance to begin the job search.

In today's world, many new degrees further obscure the choices for first-year college students. Graphic arts, video filmography, and women's studies are examples. Business concentrations have become specialized, including marketing, advertising, and consumer behavior, all of which have enjoyed enormous growth. Although they may have peaked in popularity, they still compete for students.

Parents' Concerns

Some of this trend to such new subject areas as well as an increasing specialization of study are not the students' choices, but rather a response to their
parents' demands. Parents of college-age students tend to be keenly aware of
how their own employment prospects have or have not been fulfilled and
which of their peers has found success in a career. College places a difficult
financial burden on families today, and parents naturally want to ensure a
return on their investment in a college education. They have continued to
stress new degree choices to their children, and some colleges have responded
by creating curriculums around these demands. Although the tide seems to
be again turning away from that stage in the continuing cycle that favors specialization and pragmatism, the English degree is not often termed "hot."

Employers' Needs

Employers, however, are once again realizing that the English major not only
already has an expertise employers need desperately, but also that English
majors have had, in their academic training, the kind of solid preparation
needed to learn the ins and outs of any new environment. The world of work
is filled with communications, made both easier and faster through technology. The proliferation of communications has for many firms created a
quality crisis. Management now realizes through costly errors that businesses
need employees who can use language correctly and effectively in this technological era.

English as a major is now enjoying another in a continuing series of redis-
coveries by both students and employers. This process of constant reevalu-
ation of the English degree is one of the principle reasons it maintains its
viability in the curriculum. Its current popularity came about because of the
failure of other programs to emphasize a bedrock need of the world outside
of college: solid, effective communication skills.

Why a Degree in English Is So Important Now

So how do we account for the longevity of English as an attractive major?
Is it only for the sake of the grandeur of the language and its employment
throughout history? Might it also be because it is an educational preparation
that works for almost any field of endeavor? The answer is disarmingly
simple and yet also easily overlooked.

Human interaction is all about communication, including body language
and nonverbal communication. But the communications that we rely on for
messages and return to again and again are those that are spoken or written.
Whether you are trying to outline to a computer specialist the kind of database you need constructed or are attempting to convey to an executive caterer

the ambiance a business function needs to achieve, you must rely on your understanding, appreciation, and mastery of the English language.

Work, be it teaching at a prestigious university or rigging an offshore oil derrick, is about people communicating. It is the stuff of people explaining, arguing, expostulating, describing, elaborating, defining, agreeing, questioning, probing, clarifying, and even obscuring meaning as we come together to get work done. Regardless of the project at hand, the cost, or the technology involved, almost all projects come down to the exchange of meaning between individuals through language.

The staying power of English as a major is based on its ability to meet our basic need for communication, for clarity, for the exchange of meaning to get our work done correctly, efficiently, and with some degree of harmony. Yes, we forget this need sometimes in our fascination with technology, but eventually we realize that workers who understand and appreciate how to use language—how to make it say what we want, how to refine it, and demystify it—are urgently needed in today's workplace. This is why the English major will always be a welcome job candidate.

How does the English major acquire this skill with language? What do you study that helps you develop these abilities? Although college English departments vary dramatically and their offerings expand and contract depending on the size of the faculty and student body, we can make several solid generalizations about them.

Most English departments try to provide students with a comprehensive acquaintance with English literature from at least Chaucer's time until our own, and with American literature of the nineteenth and twentieth centuries. You may wonder what relevance Chaucer could possibly have for the modern age. Historians have long said, "If you want to know the future, read history." A study of the English language is a study of ideas, cultures, mores, and concepts through time. We study English to be truly educated, and the English major brings to his or her employment setting a high level of general information about the ideas of people and how those ideas have been expressed.

Chaucer may be the demarcation point for a study of English literature, but the author of *The Canterbury Tales* reappears in this career text as a contemporary technical writer! Six hundred years ago, Geoffrey Chaucer wrote "A Treatise on the Astrolabe," now recognized as an early and quite competitive piece of technical writing. What's more, it has reappeared in scientific journals as a model for infusing technical writing, which is often dense and turgid, with style, grace, and rhetoric. No one anecdote could better prove the point of the resiliency and potential application of an English degree.

English study expands your vocabulary, enriches your idiomatic expressions, and provides you with a never-ending set of alternatives in both oral and written communications that allows you to avoid triteness and hackneyed phrases. The writing practice you've received has allowed you to enjoy the challenge of writing, not avoid it. You've grown to appreciate the importance of editing, proofreading, and clarifying written text to ensure the most impact and the best presentation of your ideas.

Employers hope you'll consider putting these valuable skills to use in their workplace. Your reading skills will be of inestimable aid in mastering the technical jargon of whatever environment you select. You'll find yourself understanding policies and procedures and building a new vocabulary around your workplace. Even advanced technical subjects are not beyond the scope of the well-prepared English major, who can read for content and use a dictionary.

A DEGREE FOR THE FUTURE

Just as Chaucer has proved remarkably current and long-lived, so will the English degree prove important, versatile, and supremely applicable to life in an ever more complicated world. Other academic subjects may move in and out of favor, but English will continue to maintain its hold on successive generations of students and employers because it prepares students well for life and work in innumerable settings.

Look at some of the issues waiting for English majors in the workplace. An increasing reliance on technology to "enhance" communication, from voice mail to electronic mail, has left many bemoaning the deterioration of language into shorter and more meaningless "sound bites." A subject of a continuing dialogue in workplaces across the country is the growing schism between techno-language and traditional language. The English major can help establish better norms for electronic communication, demonstrating that condensation of language for reasons of cost or technology does not have to sacrifice clarity, grace, or style.

Hiring a generation of specialists has produced another startlingly embarrassing problem. Communications, even public communications, in the workplace have deteriorated in the quality of their spelling, composition, and syntax. Both internal and external communications are filled with errors that undermine the effectiveness and prestige of an organization and can do serious harm if miscommunication results. The English majors working in these environments, regardless of their work role, can help to reestablish quality writing through the high standards they maintain in their own writing and the editing and proofreading they contribute to those around them.

Planning what you want to say, outlining main points, providing effective visual aids, and ensuring that what you have to say is of interest to your audience all come naturally to English majors. They understand how to take complex material and make it clearer to a wider audience. The opportunity to improve the effectiveness of a sales presentation, the clarity and structure of training and development programs, or the impact of public relations efforts are all fruitful vineyards for the English major who wonders, "What can I bring to the workplace?"

English majors might be surprised that their talents can be both so noticeable and so needed in the workplace. "How bad can it be?" they ask. The situation is quite poor, and many employers continue to insist in interviews and articles that many of their administrative problems would be eased if they could find management staff with solid writing and speaking competencies.

No one need worry about the future of the English major in college. Though its popularity has waxed and waned, it remains a solid choice for good reasons. Other majors may appear on the scene, only to fade as student interest shifts to something else, but English remains because it is timeless, has broad applications, and contains infinite pathways for exploration. English connects us through clarity of meaning and expression; it moves us through poetry, drama, and prose; and be it an ancient Valentine card or a high school commencement address, it is the stuff of memory.

PART ONE

THE JOB SEARCH

CHAPTER ONE

THE SELF-ASSESSMENT

S elf-assessment is the process by which you begin to acknowledge your own particular blend of education, experiences, values, needs, and goals. It provides the foundation for career planning and the entire job search process. Self-assessment involves looking inward and asking yourself what can sometimes prove to be difficult questions. This self-examination should lead to an intimate understanding of your personal traits, your personal values, your consumption patterns and economic needs, your longer-term goals, your skill base, your preferred skills, and your under-developed skills.

You come to the self-assessment process knowing yourself well in some of these areas, but you may still be uncertain about other aspects. You may be well aware of your consumption patterns, but have you spent much time specifically identifying your longer-term goals or your personal values as they relate to work? No matter what level of self-assessment you have undertaken to date, it is now time to clarify all of these issues and questions as they relate to the job search.

The knowledge you gain in the self-assessment process will guide the rest of your job search. In this book, you will learn about all of the following tasks:

- Writing resumes
- Exploring possible job titles
- Identifying employment sites
- Networking
- Interviewing
- Following up
- Evaluating job offers

In each of these steps, you will rely on and return often to the understanding gained through your self-assessment. Any individual seeking employment must be able and willing to express these facets of his or her personality to recruiters and interviewers throughout the job search. This communication allows you to show the world who you are so that together with employers you can determine whether there will be a workable match with a given job or career path.

HOW TO CONDUCT A SELF-ASSESSMENT

The self-assessment process goes on naturally all the time. People ask you to clarify what you mean, or you make a purchasing decision, or you begin a new relationship. You react to the world and the world reacts to you. How you understand these interactions and any changes you might make because of them are part of the natural process of self-discovery. There is, however, a more comprehensive and efficient way to approach self-assessment with regard to employment.

Because self-assessment can become a complex exercise, we have distilled it into a seven-step process that provides an effective basis for undertaking a job search. The seven steps include the following:

1. Understanding your personal traits

2. Identifying your personal values

3. Calculating your economic needs

4. Exploring your longer-term goals

5. Enumerating your skill base

6. Recognizing your preferred skills

7. Assessing skills needing further development

As you work through your self-assessment, you might want to create a worksheet similar to the one shown in Exhibit 1.1 on the following page. Or you might want to keep a journal of the thoughts you have as you undergo this process. There will be many opportunities to revise your self-assessment as you start down the path of seeking a career.

STEP 1 Understanding Your Personal Traits
Each person has a unique personality that he or she brings to the job search process. Gaining a better understanding of your personal traits can help you

---

Exhibit 1.1

Self-Assessment Worksheet

STEP 1. Understand Your Personal Traits
The personal traits that describe me are:
(Include all of the words that describe you.)

The ten personal traits that most accurately describe
me are: *(List these ten traits.)*

STEP 2. Identify Your Personal Values
Working conditions that are important to me include:
*(List working conditions that would have to exist for
you to accept a position.)*

The values that go along with my working conditions
are:
*(Write down the values that correspond to each
working condition.)*

Some additional values I've decided to include are:
*(List those values you identify as you conduct this job
search.)*

STEP 3. Calculate Your Economic Needs
My estimated minimum annual salary requirement is:
*(Write the salary you have calculated based on your
budget.)*

Starting salaries for the positions I'm considering are:
*(List the name of each job you are considering and
the associated starting salary.)*

STEP 4. Explore Your Longer-Term Goals
My thoughts on longer-term goals right now are:
*(Jot down some of your longer-term goals as you
know them right now.)*

STEP 5. Enumerate Your Skill Base
The general skills I possess are: *(List the skills that underlie tasks you are able to complete.)*

The specific skills I possess are:
(List more technical or specific skills that you possess and indicate your level of expertise.)

General and specific skills that I want to promote to employers for the jobs I'm considering are:
(List general and specific skills for each type of job you are considering.)

STEP 6. Recognize Your Preferred Skills
Skills that I would like to use on the job include:
(List skills that you hope to use on the job, and indicate how often you'd like to use them.)

STEP 7. Assess Skills Needing Further Development
Some skills that I'll need to acquire for the jobs I'm considering include:
(Write down skills listed in job advertisements or job descriptions that you don't currently possess.)

I believe I can build these skills by:
(Describe how you plan to acquire these skills.)

evaluate job and career choices. Identifying these traits and then finding employment that allows you to draw on at least some of them can create a rewarding and fulfilling work experience. If potential employment doesn't allow you to use these preferred traits, it is important to decide whether you can find other ways to express them or whether you would be better off not considering this type of job. Interests and hobbies pursued outside of work hours can be one way to use personal traits you don't have an opportunity to draw on in your work. For example, if you consider yourself an outgoing person and the kinds of jobs you are examining allow little contact with other people, you may be able to achieve the level of interaction that is comfortable for you outside of your work setting. If such a compromise seems impractical or otherwise unsatisfactory, you probably should explore only jobs that provide the interaction you want and need on the job.

Many young adults who are not very confident about their attractiveness to employers will downplay their need for income. They will say, "Money is not all that important if I love my work." But if you begin to document exactly what you need for housing, transportation, insurance, clothing, food, and utilities, you will begin to understand that some jobs cannot meet your financial needs and it doesn't matter how wonderful the job is. If you have to worry each payday about bills and other financial obligations, you won't be very effective on the job. Begin now to be honest with yourself about your needs.

Exhibit 1.2

Personal Traits

Accurate	Curious	Good-natured
Active	Daring	Helpful
Adaptable	Decisive	Honest
Adventurous	Deliberate	Humorous
Affectionate	Detail-oriented	Idealistic
Aggressive	Determined	Imaginative
Ambitious	Discreet	Impersonal
Analytical	Dominant	Independent
Appreciative	Eager	Individualistic
Artistic	Easygoing	Industrious
Brave	Efficient	Informal
Businesslike	Emotional	Innovative
Calm	Empathetic	Intellectual
Capable	Energetic	Intelligent
Caring	Excitable	Introverted
Cautious	Expressive	Intuitive
Cheerful	Extroverted	Inventive
Clean	Fair-minded	Jovial
Competent	Farsighted	Just
Confident	Feeling	Kind
Conscientious	Firm	Liberal
Conservative	Flexible	Likable
Considerate	Formal	Logical
Cool	Friendly	Loyal
Cooperative	Future-oriented	Mature
Courageous	Generous	Methodical
Critical	Gentle	Meticulous

Mistrustful	Productive	Sociable
Modest	Progressive	Spontaneous
Motivated	Quick	Strong
Objective	Quiet	Strong-minded
Observant	Rational	Structured
Open-minded	Realistic	Subjective
Opportunistic	Receptive	Tactful
Optimistic	Reflective	Thorough
Organized	Relaxed	Thoughtful
Original	Reliable	Tolerant
Outgoing	Reserved	Trusting
Patient	Resourceful	Trustworthy
Peaceable	Responsible	Truthful
Personable	Reverent	Understanding
Persuasive	Sedentary	Unexcitable
Pleasant	Self-confident	Uninhibited
Poised	Self-controlled	Verbal
Polite	Self-disciplined	Versatile
Practical	Sensible	Wholesome
Precise	Sensitive	Wise
Principled	Serious	
Private	Sincere	

Inventorying Your Personal Traits. Begin the self-assessment process by creating an inventory of your personal traits. Using the list in Exhibit 1.2, decide which of these personal traits describe you.

Focusing on Selected Personal Traits. Of all the traits you identified from the list in Exhibit 1.2, select the ten you believe most accurately describe you. If you are having a difficult time deciding, think about which words people who know you well would use to describe you. Keep track of these ten traits.

Considering Your Personal Traits in the Job Search Process. As you begin exploring jobs and careers, watch for matches between your personal traits and the job descriptions you read. Some jobs will require many personal traits you know you possess, and others will not seem to match those traits.

● ●

An author's work, for example, requires self-discipline, motivation, curiosity, and observation. Authors usually work alone, with limited opportunities to interact with others. A corporate trainer, on the other hand, must interact regularly with staff or clients to carry out their teaching programs. Corporate trainers need strong inter-personal and verbal skills, imagination, and a good sense of humor. They must enjoy being up in front of groups and must become skilled at presenting information using a variety of methods.

•••••••••••••••••••••••••••••••••••••••

Your ability to respond to changing conditions, your decision-making abil-ity, productivity, creativity, and verbal skills all have a bearing on your suc-cess in and enjoyment of your work life. To better guarantee success, be sure to take the time needed to understand these traits in yourself.

STEP 2 Identifying Your Personal Values

Your personal values affect every aspect of your life, including employment, and they develop and change as you move through life. Values can be defined as principles that we hold in high regard, qualities that are important and desirable to us. Some values aren't ordinarily connected to work (love, beauty, color, light, relationships, family, or religion), and others are (autonomy, cooperation, effectiveness, achievement, knowledge, and security). Our val-ues determine, in part, the level of satisfaction we feel in a particular job.

Defining Acceptable Working Conditions. One facet of employment is the set of working conditions that must exist for someone to consider taking a job.

Each of us would probably create a unique list of acceptable working con-ditions, but items that might be included on many people's lists are the amount of money you would need to be paid, how far you are willing to drive or travel, the amount of freedom you want in determining your own schedule, whether you would be working with people or data or things, and the types of tasks you would be willing to do. Your conditions might include statements of working conditions you will *not* accept; for example, you might not be willing to work at night or on weekends or holidays.

If you were offered a job tomorrow, what conditions would have to exist for you to realistically consider accepting the position? Take some time and make a list of these conditions.

Realizing Associated Values. Your list of working conditions can be used to create an inventory of your values relating to jobs and careers you are explor-ing. For example, if one of your conditions stated that you wanted to earn at least $30,000 per year, the associated value would be financial gain. If

---

Exhibit 1.3

Work Values

Achievement	Development	Physical activity
Advancement	Effectiveness	Power
Adventure	Excitement	Precision
Attainment	Fast pace	Prestige
Authority	Financial gain	Privacy
Autonomy	Helping	Profit
Belonging	Humor	Recognition
Challenge	Improvisation	Risk
Change	Independence	Security
Communication	Influencing others	Self-expression
Community	Intellectual stimulation	Solitude
Competition	Interaction	Stability
Completion	Knowledge	Status
Contribution	Leading	Structure
Control	Mastery	Supervision
Cooperation	Mobility	Surroundings
Creativity	Moral fulfillment	Time freedom
Decision making	Organization	Variety

---

another condition was that you wanted to work with a friendly group of people, the value that went along with that might be belonging or interaction with people. Exhibit 1.3 provides a list of commonly held values that relate to the work environment; use it to create your own list of personal values.

Relating Your Values to the World of Work. As you read the job descriptions in this book and in other suggested resources, think about the values associated with each position.

• •

For example, the duties of a technical writer would include researching and investigating; writing and editing papers, articles, and reports; and designing the flow of information. Associated values are intellectual stimulation, communication, and creativity.

• •

If you were thinking about a career in this field, or any other field you're exploring, at least some of the associated values should match those you extracted from your list of working conditions. Take a second look at any values that don't match up. How important are they to you? What will happen if they are not satisfied on the job? Can you incorporate those personal values elsewhere? Your answers need to be brutally honest. As you continue your exploration, be sure to add to your list any additional values that occur to you.

STEP 3 Calculating Your Economic Needs

Each of us grew up in an environment that provided for certain basic needs, such as food and shelter, and, to varying degrees, other needs that we now consider basic, such as cable TV, reading materials, or an automobile. Needs such as privacy, space, and quiet, which at first glance may not appear to be monetary needs, may add to housing expenses and so should be considered as you examine your economic needs. For example, if you place a high value on a large, open living space for yourself, it would be difficult to satisfy that need without an associated high housing cost, especially in a densely popu-lated city environment.

As you prepare to move into the world of work and become responsible for meeting your own basic needs, it is important to consider the salary you will need to be able to afford a satisfying standard of living. The three-step process outlined here will help you plan a budget, which in turn will allow you to evaluate the various career choices and geographic locations you are considering. The steps include (1) developing a realistic budget, (2) exam-ining starting salaries, and (3) using a cost-of-living index.

Developing a Realistic Budget. Each of us has certain expectations for the kind of lifestyle we want to maintain. In order to begin the process of defining your economic needs, it will be helpful to determine what you expect to spend on routine monthly expenses. These expenses include housing, food, trans-portation, entertainment, utilities, loan repayments, and revolving charge accounts. A worksheet that details many of these expenses is shown in Exhibit 1.4. You may not currently spend for certain items, but you probably will have to once you begin supporting yourself. As you develop this bud-get, be generous in your estimates, but keep in mind any items that could

---

Exhibit 1.4

Estimated Monthly Expenses Worksheet

		Could Reduce Spending? (Yes/No)
Cable	$ _____	_____
Child care	_____	_____

		Could Reduce Spending? (Yes/No)
Clothing	$ _____	_____
Educational loan repayment	_____	_____
Entertainment	_____	_____
Food		
At home	_____	_____
Meals out	_____	_____
Gifts	_____	_____
Housing		
Rent/mortgage	_____	_____
Insurance	_____	_____
Property taxes	_____	_____
Medical insurance	_____	_____
Reading materials		
Newspapers	_____	_____
Magazines	_____	_____
Books	_____	_____
Revolving loans/charges	_____	_____
Savings	_____	_____
Telephone	_____	_____
Transportation		
Auto payment	_____	_____
Insurance	_____	_____
Parking	_____	_____
Gasoline	_____	_____
or		
Cab/train/bus fare	_____	_____
Utilities		
Electric	_____	_____
Gas	_____	_____
Water/sewer	_____	_____
Vacations	_____	_____
Miscellaneous expense 1	_____	_____
Expense: _____		
Miscellaneous expense 2	_____	_____
Expense: _____		
Miscellaneous expense 3	_____	_____
Expense: _____		

TOTAL MONTHLY EXPENSES: _____

YEARLY EXPENSES (Monthly expenses × 12): _____

INCREASE TO INCLUDE TAXES (Yearly expenses × 1.35): ____ =

MINIMUM ANNUAL SALARY REQUIREMENT: _____

be reduced or eliminated. If you are not sure about the cost of a certain item, talk with family or friends who would be able to give you a realistic estimate.

If this is new or difficult for you, start to keep a log of expenses right now. You may be surprised at how much you actually spend each month for food or stamps or magazines. Household expenses and personal grooming items can often loom very large in a budget, as can auto repairs or home maintenance.

Income taxes must also be taken into consideration when examining salary requirements. State and local taxes vary by location, so it is difficult to calculate exactly the effect of taxes on the amount of income you need to generate. To roughly estimate the gross income necessary to generate your minimum annual salary requirement, multiply the minimum salary you have calculated (see Exhibit 1.4 on page 10) by a factor of 1.35. The resulting figure will be an approximation of what your gross income would need to be, given your estimated expenses.

Examining Starting Salaries. Starting salaries for each of the career tracks are provided throughout this book. These salary figures can be used in conjunction with the cost-of-living index (discussed in the next section) to determine whether you would be able to meet your basic economic needs in a given geographic location.

Using a Cost-of-Living Index. If you are thinking about trying to get a job in a geographic region other than the one where you now live, understanding differences in the cost of living will help you come to a more informed decision about making a move. By using a cost-of-living index, you can compare salaries offered and the cost of living in different locations with what you know about the salaries offered and the cost of living in your present location.

Many variables are used to calculate the cost-of-living index. Often included are housing, groceries, utilities, transportation, health-care, clothing, and entertainment expenses. Right now you do not need to worry about the details associated with calculating a given index. The main purpose of this exercise is to help you understand that pay ranges for entry-level positions may not vary greatly, but the cost of living in different locations *can* vary tremendously.

· ·

If you lived in Cleveland, Ohio, for example, and you were interested in working as a human resources generalist, you would plan on earning $29,053 annually. But let's say you're also thinking about moving to New York,

Los Angeles, or Houston. You know you can live on $29,053 in Cleveland, but you want to be able to equal that salary in the other locations you're considering. How much will you have to earn in those locations to do this? Determining the cost of living for each city will show you.

There are many websites like Home Fair's (http://www .homefair.com/homefair/cmr/salcalc.html) that can assist you as you undertake this research. Use any search engine and enter the keywords *cost of living index*. Several choices will appear. Choose one site and look for options like cost-of-living analysis or cost-of-living comparator. Some sites will ask you to register and/or pay for the information, but most sites are free. Follow the instructions provided and you will be able to create a table of information like the one shown below.

Job: Human Resources Generalist		
City	Base Amount	Equivalent Salary
Cleveland, OH	$29,053	
New York, NY		$32,772
Los Angeles, CA		$35,795
Minneapolis, MN		$31,738

At the time this comparison was done, you would have needed to earn $32,772 in New York, $35,795 in Los Angeles, and $31,738 in Minneapolis to match the buying power of $29,053 in Cleveland.

If you would like to determine whether it's financially worthwhile to make any of these moves, one more piece of information is needed: the salaries of human resources generalists in these other cities. One example of a website that contains job descriptions and salary information is WageWeb (http://www.wageweb.com). This site focuses information and services on the following fields: human resources, administration, finance, information management, engineering, health care, sales/marketing, and manufacturing. WageWeb reports the following average actual lowest salary paid for the cities being considered. These figures reflect entry-level salaries.

City	Actual L:owest Salary	Equivalent Salary Needed	Change in Buying Power
New York, NY	$33,301	$32,772	+ $529
Los Angeles, CA	$36,465	$35,795	+ $670
Minneapolis, MN	$30,895	$31,738	− $843

If you moved to New York City and secured employment as a human resources generalist you would be able to maintain a lifestyle similar to the one you lead in Cleveland. In fact, you would be able to enhance your lifestyle (if renting) very modestly given the slight increase in buying power. The same would be true with a move to Los Angeles. Moving to Minneapolis from Cleveland, however, would modestly decrease your buying power. Remember, these figures change all the time, so be sure to undertake your own calculations. If you would like to see the formula used, you can visit a website like Deloitte & Touche (http://www.dtonline.com/tip/1997/tip0728.htm).

• •

You can work through a similar exercise for any type of job you are considering and for many locations when current salary information is available. It will be worth your time to undertake this analysis if you are seriously considering a relocation. By doing so you will be able to make an informed choice.

STEP 4 Exploring Your Longer-Term Goals

There is no question that when we first begin working, our goals are to use our skills and education in a job that will reward us with employment, income, and status relative to the preparation we brought with us to this position. If we are not being paid as much as we feel we should for our level of education, or if job demands don't provide the intellectual stimulation we had hoped for, we experience unhappiness and as a result often seek other employment.

Most jobs we consider "good" are those that fulfill our basic "lower-level" needs of security, food, clothing, shelter, income, and productive work. But even when our basic needs are met and our jobs are secure and productive, we as individuals are constantly changing. As we change, the demands and expectations we place on our jobs may change. Fortunately, some jobs grow and change with us, and this explains why some people are happy throughout many years in a job.

But more often people are bigger than the jobs they fill. We have more goals and needs than any job could fulfill. These are "higher-level" needs of self-esteem, companionship, affection, and an increasing desire to feel we are employing ourselves in the most effective way possible. Not all of these higher-level needs can be fulfilled through employment, but for as long as we are employed, we increasingly demand that our jobs play their part in moving us along the path to fulfillment.

Another obvious but important fact is that we change as we mature. Although our jobs also have the potential for change, they may not change as frequently or as markedly as we do. There are increasingly fewer one-job, one-employer careers; we must think about a work future that may involve voluntary or forced moves from employer to employer. Because of that very real possibility, we need to take advantage of the opportunities in each position we hold to acquire skills and competencies that will keep us viable and attractive as employees in a job market that is not only technology/computer dependent, but also is populated with more and more small, self-transforming organizations rather than the large, seemingly stable organizations of the past.

It may be difficult in the early stages of the job search to determine whether the path you are considering can meet these longer-term goals. Reading about career paths and individual career histories in your field can be very helpful in this regard. Meeting and talking with individuals further along in their careers can be enlightening as well. Older workers can provide valuable guidance on "self-managing" your career, which will become an increasingly valuable skill in the future. Some of these ideas may seem remote as you read this now, but you should be able to appreciate the need to ensure that you are growing, developing valuable new skills, and researching other employers who might be interested in your particular skills package.

....

If you are considering a position in book publishing, for example, you would gain a far better perspective on your

potential future if you could talk to an entry-level editorial assistant, a more experienced production or managing editor, and, finally, a senior editor with a significant work history in publishing. Each will have a different perspective, unique concerns, and an individual set of value priorities.

STEP 5 Enumerating Your Skill Base

In terms of the job search, skills can be thought of as capabilities that can be developed in school, at work, or by volunteering and then used in specific job settings. Many studies have documented the kinds of skills that employers seek in entry-level applicants. For example, some of the most desired skills for individuals interested in the teaching profession include the ability to interact effectively with students one on one, to manage a classroom, to adapt to varying situations as necessary, and to get involved in school activities. Business employers have also identified important qualities, including enthusiasm for the employer's product or service, a businesslike mind, the ability to follow written or verbal instructions, the ability to demonstrate self-control, the confidence to suggest new ideas, the ability to communicate with all members of a group, an awareness of cultural differences, and loyalty, to name just a few. You will find that many of these skills are also in the repertoire of qualities demanded in your college major.

In order to be successful in obtaining any given job, you must be able to demonstrate that you possess a certain mix of skills that will allow you to carry out the duties required by that job. This skill mix will vary a great deal from job to job; to determine the skills necessary for the jobs you are seeking, you can read job advertisements or more generic job descriptions, such as those found later in this book. If you want to be effective in the job search, you must directly show employers that you possess the skills needed to be successful in filling the position. These skills will initially be described on your resume and then discussed again during the interview process.

Skills are either general or specific. General skills are those that are developed throughout the college years by taking classes, being employed, and getting involved in other related activities such as volunteer work or campus organizations. General skills include the ability to read and write, to perform computations, to think critically, and to communicate effectively. Specific skills are also acquired on the job and in the classroom, but they allow you to complete tasks that require specialized knowledge. Computer programming, drafting, language translating, and copyediting are just a few examples of specific skills that may relate to a given job.

In order to develop a list of skills relevant to employers, you must first identify the general skills you possess, then list specific skills you have to offer, and, finally, examine which of these skills employers are seeking.

Identifying Your General Skills. Because you possess or will possess a college degree, employers will assume that you can read and write, perform certain basic computations, think critically, and communicate effectively. Employers will want to see that you have acquired these skills, and they will want to know which additional general skills you possess.

One way to begin identifying skills is to write an experiential diary. An experiential diary lists all the tasks you were responsible for completing for each job you've held and then outlines the skills required to do those tasks. You may list several skills for any given task. This diary allows you to distinguish between the tasks you performed and the underlying skills required to complete those tasks. Here's an example:

Tasks	Skills
Answering telephone	Effective use of language, clear diction, ability to direct inquiries, ability to solve problems
Waiting on tables	Poise under conditions of time and pressure, speed, accuracy, good memory, simultaneous completion of tasks, sales skills

For each job or experience you have participated in, develop a worksheet based on the example shown here. On a resume, you may want to describe these skills rather than simply listing tasks. Skills are easier for the employer to appreciate, especially when your experience is very different from the employment you are seeking. In addition to helping you identify general skills, this experiential diary will prepare you to speak more effectively in an interview about the qualifications you possess.

Identifying Your Specific Skills. It may be easier to identify your specific skills because you can definitely say whether you can speak other languages, program a computer, draft a map or diagram, or edit a document using appropriate symbols and terminology.

Using your experiential diary, identify the points in your history where you learned how to do something very specific, and decide whether you have a beginning, intermediate, or advanced knowledge of how to use that particular skill. Right now, be sure to list *every* specific skill you have, and don't consider whether you like using the skill. Write down a list of specific skills you have acquired and the level of competence you possess—beginning, intermediate, or advanced.

Relating Your Skills to Employers. You probably have thought about a couple of different jobs you might be interested in obtaining, and one way to begin relating the general and specific skills you possess to a potential employer's needs is to read actual advertisements for these types of positions (see Part Two for resources listing actual job openings).

··

For example, you might be interested in a career as a reporter. A typical job listing might read, "Requires 2–5 years' beat experience, precision, imagination, drive, and proven enterprise ability." If you then used any one of a number of general sources of information that describe the job of reporter, you would find additional information. Reporters also gather information, conduct background research, develop a network of reliable contacts, and use word-processing and tape recording equipment.

Begin building a comprehensive list of required skills with the first job description you read. Exploring advertisements for descriptions of several types of related positions will reveal an important core of skills that are necessary for obtaining the type of work you're interested in. In building this list, include both general and specific skills.

Following is a sample list of skills you would need to be successful as a reporter. These items were extracted from general resources and actual job listings.

Job: Reporter

General Skills	Specific Skills
Disseminate information	Write stories
Gather information	Take notes
Present differing viewpoints	Use tape recorder
Conduct research	Report "live" from the field
Work in hectic environment	Take photographs
Meet deadlines	Lay out pages
Work in noisy environment	Edit wire service copy
Work in dangerous settings	Present news in compelling format
Work varying hours including nights and weekends	Work in computerized newsroom
Be willing to travel	

Exhibit precision	Be familiar with word
Exhibit imagination	processing
Exhibit drive	
Display enterprise ability	
Collaborate on projects	

On separate sheets of paper, try to generate a comprehensive list of skills required for at least one job you are considering.

The list of general skills that you develop for a given career path will be valuable for any number of jobs you might apply for. Many of the specific skills also will be transferable to other types of positions. For example, evaluating performance is a required specific skill for some reporters, and it also would be required for photographers and some artists.

....

Now review the list of skills you developed and check off those skills that *you know you possess* and that are required for jobs you are considering. You should refer to these specific skills on the resume that you write for this type of job. See Chapter 2 for details on resume writing.

STEP 6   Recognizing Your Preferred Skills

In the previous section you developed a comprehensive list of skills that relate to particular career paths that are of interest to you. You can now relate these to skills that you prefer to use. We all use a wide range of skills (some researchers say individuals have a repertoire of about 500 skills), but we may not be particularly interested in using all of them in our work. There may be some skills that come to us more naturally or that we use successfully time and time again and that we want to continue to use; these are best described as our preferred skills. For this exercise use the list of skills that you developed for the previous section and decide which of them you are *most interested in using* in future work and how often you would like to use them. You might be interested in using some skills only occasionally, while others you would like to use more regularly. You probably also have skills that you hope you can use constantly.

As you examine job announcements, look for matches between this list of preferred skills and the qualifications described in the advertisements. These skills should be highlighted on your resume and discussed in job interviews.

STEP 7 Assessing Skills Needing Further Development

Previously you developed a list of general and specific skills required for given positions. You already possess some of these skills; those that remain to be developed are your underdeveloped skills.

If you are just beginning the job search, there may be gaps between the qualifications required for some of the jobs you're considering and skills you possess. These are your underdeveloped skills. The thought of having to admit to and talk about these underdeveloped skills, especially in a job interview, is a frightening one. One way to put a healthy perspective on this subject is to target and relate your exploration of underdeveloped skills to the types of positions you are seeking. Recognizing these shortcomings and planning to overcome them with either on-the-job training or additional formal education can be a positive way to address the concept of underdeveloped skills.

On your worksheet or in your journal, make a list of up to five general or specific skills required for the positions you're interested in that you *don't currently possess.* For each item list an idea you have for specific action you could take to acquire that skill. Do some brainstorming to come up with possible actions. If you have a hard time generating ideas, talk to people currently working in this type of position, professionals in your college career services office, trusted friends, family members, or members of related professional associations.

If, for example, you are interested in a job for which you don't have some specific required experience, you could locate training opportunities such as classes or workshops offered through a local college or university, community college, or club or association that would help you build the level of expertise you need for the job.

You may have noticed in this book that many excellent positions for your major demand computer skills. While basic word processing has been something you've done all through college, you may be surprised at the additional computer skills required by employers. Many positions for college graduates will ask for some familiarity with spreadsheet programming, and frequently some database-management software familiarity is a job demand as well. Desktop publishing software, graphics programs, and basic Web-page design also pop up frequently in job ads for college graduates. If your degree program hasn't introduced you to a wide variety of computer applications, what are your options? If you're still in college, take what computer courses you can before you graduate. If you've already graduated, look at evening programs, continuing education courses, or tutorial programs that may be available commercially. Developing a modest level of expertise will encourage you to be more confident in suggesting to potential employers that you can continue to add to your skill base on the job.

In Chapter 5 on interviewing, we will discuss in detail how to effectively address questions about underdeveloped skills. Generally speaking, though, employers want genuine answers to these types of questions. They want you to reveal "the real you," and they also want to see how you answer difficult questions. In taking the positive, targeted approach discussed above, you show the employer that you are willing to continue to learn and that you have a plan for strengthening your job qualifications.

USING YOUR SELF-ASSESSMENT

Exploring entry-level career options can be an exciting experience if you have good resources available and will take the time to use them. Can you effectively complete the following tasks?

1. Understand and relate your personality traits to career choices.

2. Define your personal values.

3. Determine your economic needs.

4. Explore longer-term goals.

5. Understand your skill base.

6. Recognize your preferred skills.

7. Express a willingness to improve on your underdeveloped skills.

If so, then you can more meaningfully participate in the job search process by writing a more effective resume, finding job titles that represent work you are interested in doing, locating job sites that will provide the opportunity for you to use your strengths and skills, networking in an informed way, participating in focused interviews, getting the most out of follow-up contacts, and evaluating job offers to find those that create a good match between you and the employer. The remaining chapters in Part One guide you through these next steps in the job search process. For many job seekers, this process can take anywhere from three months to a year to implement. The time you will need to put into your job search will depend on the type of job you want and the geographic location where you'd like to work. Think of your effort as a job in itself, requiring you to set aside time each week to complete the needed work. Carefully undertaken efforts may reduce the time you need for your job search.

CHAPTER TWO

THE RESUME AND COVER LETTER

*T*he task of writing a resume may seem overwhelming if you are unfamiliar with this type of document, but there are some easily understood techniques that can and should be used. This section was written to help you understand the purpose of the resume, the different types of resume formats available, and how to write the sections of information traditionally found on a resume. We will present examples and explanations that address questions frequently posed by people writing their first resume or updating an old resume.

Even within the formats and suggestions given, however, there are infinite variations. True, most resumes follow one of the outlines suggested, but you should feel free to adjust the resume to suit your needs and make it expressive of your life and experience.

WHY WRITE A RESUME?

The purpose of a resume is to convince an employer that you should be interviewed. Whether you're mailing, faxing, or E-mailing this document, you'll want to present enough information to show that you can make an immediate and valuable contribution to an organization. A resume is not an in-depth historical or legal document; later in the job search process you may be asked to document your entire work history on an application form and attest to its validity. The resume should, instead, highlight relevant information pertaining directly to the organization that will receive the document or to the type of position you are seeking.

We will discuss four types of resumes in this chapter: the chronological resume, functional resume, targeted resume, and the electronic resume. The reasons for using one type of resume over another and the typical format for each are addressed in the following sections.

THE CHRONOLOGICAL RESUME

The chronological resume is the most common of the various resume formats and therefore the format that employers are most used to receiving. This type of resume is easy to read and understand because it details the chronological progression of jobs you have held. (See Exhibit 2.1.) It begins with your most recent employment and works back in time. If you have a solid work history or have experience that provided growth and development in your duties and responsibilities, a chronological resume will highlight these achievements. The typical elements of a chronological resume include the heading, a career objective, educational background, employment experience, activities, and references.

The Heading

The heading consists of your name, address, telephone number, and other means of contact. This may include a fax number, E-mail address, and your home-page address. If you are using a shared E-mail account or a parent's business fax, be sure to let others who use these systems know that you may receive important professional correspondence via these systems. You wouldn't want to miss a vital E-mail or fax! Likewise, if your resume directs readers to a personal home page on the Web, be certain it's a *professional* personal home page designed to be viewed and appreciated by a prospective employer. This may mean making substantial changes in the home page you currently mount on the Web.

We suggest that you spell out your full name in your resume heading and type it in all capital letters in bold type. After all, you are the focus of the resume! If you have a current as well as a permanent address and you include both in the heading, be sure to indicate until what date your current address will be valid. The two-letter state abbreviation should be the only abbreviation that appears in your heading. Don't forget to include the zip code with your address and the area code with your telephone number.

The Objective

As you formulate the wording for this part of your resume, keep the following points in mind.

Exhibit 2.1

Chronological Resume

MICHAEL COLLINS WHITNEY

Student Apartment 108

Indiana University

Bloomington, IN 47401

(812) 555-9808

Fax (812) 555-8989

mcollins@aol.com

(until May 2004)

74 Winding Way

Lincolnshire, IL 60069

(847) 555-1823

OBJECTIVE

A career in telecommunications, initially as a technical specialist and ultimately as a technical writer.

EDUCATION

Bachelor of Arts in English

Indiana University at Bloomington

May 2004

Minor: Communications

Overall GPA 3.2 on a 4.0 scale

HONORS/AWARDS

Dean's List, Fall Semester 2003

Who's Who Among Universities and Colleges, 2001–04

The *Indiana Daily Student Reporting Award,* 2003

RELATED COURSES

Technical Writing

Management Information Systems

Telecommunications

Video Production

EXPERIENCE

Tutor, Academic Support Services, Indiana University.

Part-time, 2001–02

Taught students effective methods for studying English courses, such as composition, American and British literature, and speech.

Switchboard Operator, Indiana University, Summers, 2003–04
A full-time summer position as one of five central switchboard operators for a busy campus of 36,000. AT&T Plus 5000 system with sophisticated relay and switching capabilities.

Customer Relations, Quick Print Advertising, Bloomington, IN.
Part-time, 2003
A production job involving costing jobs, writing estimates, printing copies, and creating and placing small display ads in local papers.

ACTIVITIES
Television Studio Production Team, Indiana University,
2003–present
Computer Hackers Club (guest speaker on computer issues),
2002–03

REFERENCES
Both personal and professional references are available upon request.

The Objective Focuses the Resume. Without a doubt this is the most challenging part of the resume for most resume writers. Even for individuals who have quite firmly decided on a career path, it can be difficult to encapsulate all they want to say in one or two brief sentences. For job seekers who are unfocused or unclear about their intentions, trying to write this section can inhibit the entire resume writing process.

Recruiters tell us, time and time again, that the objective creates a frame of reference for them. It helps them see how you express your goals and career focus. In addition, the statement may indicate in what ways you can immediately benefit an organization. Given the importance of the objective, every point covered in the resume should relate to it. If information doesn't relate, it should be omitted. You'll file a number of resume variations in your computer. There's no excuse for not being able to tailor a resume to individual employers or specific positions.

Choose an Appropriate Length. Because of the brevity necessary for a resume, you should keep the objective as short as possible. Although objectives of only four or five words often don't show much direction, objectives that take three full lines could be viewed as too wordy and might possibly be ignored.

Consider Which Type of Objective Statement You Will Use. There are many ways to state an objective, but generally there are four forms this statement can take: (1) a very general statement; (2) a statement focused on a specific position; (3) a statement focused on a specific industry; or (4) a summary of your qualifications. In our contacts with employers, we often hear that many resumes don't exhibit any direction or career goals, so we suggest avoiding general statements when possible.

1. General Objective Statement. General objective statements look like the following:

- ❏ An entry-level educational programming coordinator position
- ❏ An entry-level marketing position

This type of objective would be useful if you know what type of job you want but you're not sure which industries interest you.

2. Position-Focused Objective. Following are examples of objectives focusing on a specific position:

- ❏ To obtain the position of Conference Coordinator at State College
- ❏ To obtain a position as Assistant Editor at *Time* magazine

When a student applies for an advertised job opening, this type of focus can be very effective. The employer knows that the applicant has taken the time to tailor the resume specifically for this position.

3. Industry-Focused Objective. Focusing on a particular industry in an objective could be stated as follows:

- ❏ To begin a career as a sales representative in the cruise line industry

4. Summary of Qualifications Statement. The summary of qualifications can be used instead of an objective or in conjunction with an objective. The purpose of this type of statement is to highlight relevant qualifications gained through a variety of experiences. This type of statement is often used by individuals with extensive and diversified work experience. An example of a qualifications statement follows:

· ·

A degree in English and four years of progressively increasing job responsibility within the hospitality industry have prepared me to begin a career as a manager trainee with an organization that values hard work and dedication.

· ·

Support Your Objective. A resume that contains any one of these types of objective statements should then go on to demonstrate why you are qualified to get the position. Listing academic degrees can be one way to indicate qualifications. Another demonstration would be in the way previous experiences, both volunteer and paid, are described. Without this kind of documentation in the body of the resume, the objective looks unsupported. Think of the resume as telling a connected story about you. All the elements should work together to form a coherent picture that ideally should relate to your statement of objective.

Education

This section of your resume should indicate the exact name of the degree you will receive or have received, spelled out completely with no abbreviations. The degree is generally listed after the objective, followed by the institution name and address, and then the month and year of graduation. This section could also include your academic minor, grade point average (GPA), and appearance on the Dean's List or President's List.

If you have enough space, you might want to include a section listing courses related to the field in which you are seeking work. The best use of a "related courses" section would be to list some course work that is not traditionally associated with the major. Perhaps you took several computer courses outside your degree that will be helpful and related to the job prospects you are entertaining. Several education section examples are shown here:

· ·

- ❑ Bachelor of Science Degree in English Education
  State College, Plymouth, NM, May 2000
  Minor: Art

- ❑ Bachelor of Arts Degree in English with a
  Writing Option, State College, San Francisco, CA,
  May 2000

❑ **Bachelor of Arts in Interdisciplinary Studies, a self-designed program concentrating in English and Graphic Design, State College, Columbus, OH, May 2000**

An example of a format for a related courses section follows:

RELATED COURSES	
Advanced Composition	Desktop Publishing
Creative Writing	Computer Graphics
Technical Writing	Software Systems Design

Experience

The experience section of your resume should be the most substantial part and should take up most of the space on the page. Employers want to see what kind of work history you have. They will look at your range of experiences, longevity in jobs, and specific tasks you are able to complete. This section may also be called "work experience," "related experience," "employment history," or "employment." No matter what you call this section, some important points to remember are the following:

1. **Describe your duties** as they relate to the position you are seeking.

2. **Emphasize major responsibilities** and indicate increases in responsibility. Include all relevant employment experiences: summer, part-time, internships, cooperative education, or self-employment.

3. **Emphasize skills**, especially those that transfer from one situation to another. The fact that you coordinated a student organization, chaired meetings, supervised others, and managed a budget leads one to suspect that you could coordinate other things as well.

4. **Use descriptive job titles** that provide information about what you did. A "Student Intern" should be more specifically stated as, for example, "Magazine Operations Intern." "Volunteer" is also too general; a title like "Peer Writing Tutor" would be more appropriate.

5. **Create word pictures** by using active verbs to start sentences. Describe *results* you have produced in the work you have done.

A limp description would say something like the following: "My duties included helping with production, proofreading, and editing. I used a word-processing package to alter text." An action statement would be stated as follows: "Coordinated and assisted in the creative marketing of brochures and seminar promotions, becoming proficient in Word."

Remember, an accomplishment is simply a result, a final measurable product that people can relate to. A duty is not a result, it is an obligation—every job holder has duties. For an effective resume, list as many results as you can. To make the most of the limited space you have and to give your description impact, carefully select appropriate and accurate descriptors from the list of action words in Exhibit 2.2.

Exhibit 2.2

Resume Action Verbs

Achieved	Demonstrated	Initiated
Acted	Designed	Innovated
Administered	Determined	Instituted
Advised	Developed	Instructed
Analyzed	Directed	Integrated
Assessed	Documented	Interpreted
Assisted	Drafted	Introduced
Attained	Edited	Learned
Balanced	Eliminated	Lectured
Budgeted	Ensured	Led
Calculated	Established	Maintained
Collected	Estimated	Managed
Communicated	Evaluated	Mapped
Compiled	Examined	Marketed
Completed	Explained	Met
Composed	Facilitated	Modified
Conceptualized	Finalized	Monitored
Condensed	Generated	Negotiated
Conducted	Handled	Observed
Consolidated	Headed	Obtained
Constructed	Helped	Operated
Controlled	Identified	Organized
Converted	Illustrated	Participated
Coordinated	Implemented	Performed
Corrected	Improved	Planned
Created	Increased	Predicted
Decreased	Influenced	Prepared
Defined	Informed	Presented

continued

continued

Processed	Reinforced	Solved
Produced	Reported	Staffed
Projected	Represented	Streamlined
Proposed	Researched	Studied
Provided	Resolved	Submitted
Qualified	Reviewed	Summarized
Quantified	Scheduled	Systematized
Questioned	Selected	Tabulated
Realized	Served	Tested
Received	Showed	Transacted
Recommended	Simplified	Updated
Recorded	Sketched	Verified
Reduced	Sold	

Here are some traits that employers tell us they like to see:

❑ Teamwork

❑ Energy and motivation

❑ Learning and using new skills

❑ Demonstrated versatility

❑ Critical thinking

❑ Understanding how profits are created

❑ Displaying organizational acumen

❑ Communicating directly and clearly, in both writing and speaking

❑ Risk taking

❑ Willingness to admit mistakes

❑ Manifesting high personal standards

SOLUTIONS TO FREQUENTLY ENCOUNTERED PROBLEMS

Repetitive Employment with the Same Employer

EMPLOYMENT: The Foot Locker, Portland, Oregon. Summer 2001, 2002, 2003. Initially employed in high school as salesclerk. Due to successful performance, asked to return next two summers at higher pay with added responsibility. Ranked as the #2 salesperson the first summer and #1 the next two summers. Assisted in arranging eye-catching retail displays; served as manager of other summer workers during owner's absence.

A Large Number of Jobs

EMPLOYMENT: Recent Hospitality Industry Experience: Affiliated with four upscale hotel/restaurant complexes (September 2000–February 2003), where I worked part- and full-time as a waiter, bartender, disc jockey, and bookkeeper to produce income for college.

Several Positions with the Same Employer

EMPLOYMENT: Coca-Cola Bottling Co., Burlington, VT, 2000–2003. In four years, I received three promotions, each with increased pay and responsibility.

Summer Sales Coordinator: Promoted to hire, train, and direct efforts of add-on staff of fifteen college-age route salespeople hired to meet summer peak demand for product.

Sales Administrator: Promoted to run home office sales desk, managing accounts and associated delivery schedules for professional sales force of ten people. Intensive phone work, daily interaction with all personnel, and strong knowledge of product line required.

Route Salesperson: Summer employment to travel and tourism industry sites that use Coke products. Met specific schedule demands, used good communication skills with wide variety of customers, and demonstrated strong selling skills. Named salesperson of the month for July and August of that year.

QUESTIONS RESUME WRITERS OFTEN ASK

How Far Back Should I Go in Terms of Listing Past Jobs?

Usually, listing three or four jobs should suffice. If you did something back in high school that has a bearing on your future aspirations for employment, by all means list the job. As you progress through your college career, high school jobs may be replaced on the resume by college employment.

Should I Differentiate Between Paid and Nonpaid Employment?

Most employers are not initially concerned about how much you were paid. They are anxious to know how much responsibility you held in your past employment. There is no need to specify that your work was volunteer if you had significant responsibilities.

How Should I Represent My Accomplishments or Work-Related Responsibilities?

Succinctly, but fully. In other words, give the employer enough information to arouse curiosity, but not so much detail that you leave nothing to the imagination. Besides, some jobs merit more lengthy explanations than others. Be sure to convey any information that can give an employer a better understanding of the depth of your involvement at work. Did you supervise others? How many? Did your efforts result in a more efficient operation? How much did you increase efficiency? Did you handle a budget? How much? Were you promoted in a short time? Did you work two jobs at once or fifteen hours per week after high school? Where appropriate, quantify.

Should the Work Section Always Follow the Education Section on the Resume?

Always lead with your strengths. If your education closely relates to the employment you now seek, put this section after the objective. Or, if you are weak on the academic side but have a surplus of good work experiences, consider reversing the order of your sections to lead with employment, followed by education.

How Should I Present My Activities, Honors, Awards, Professional Societies, and Affiliations?

This section of the resume can add valuable information for an employer to consider if used correctly. The rule of thumb for information in this section is to include only those activities that are in some way relevant to the objective stated on your resume. If you can draw a valid connection between your activities and your objective, include them; if not, leave them out.

Granted, this is hard to do. Playing center on the championship basketball team or serving as coordinator of the biggest homecoming parade ever held are roles that have meaning for you and represent personal accomplishments you'd like to share. But the resume is a brief document, and the information you provide on it should help the employer make a decision about your job eligibility. Including personal details can be confusing and could hurt your candidacy. Limiting your activity list to a few very significant experiences can be very effective.

If you are applying for a position as a safety officer, your certificate in Red Cross lifesaving skills or CPR would be related and valuable. You would want to include it. If, however, you are applying for a job as a junior account executive in an advertising agency, that information would be unrelated and superfluous. Leave it out.

Professional affiliations and honors should *all* be listed; especially important are those related to your job objective. Social clubs and activities need not be a part of your resume unless you hold a significant office or you are looking for a position related to your membership. Be aware that most prospective employers' principal concerns are related to your employability, not your social life. If you have any, publications can be included as an addendum to your resume.

The focus of the resume is your experience and education. It is not necessary to describe your involvement in activities. However, if your resume needs to be lengthened, this section provides the freedom either to expand on or mention only briefly the contributions you have made. If you have made significant contributions (e.g., an officer of an organization or a particularly long tenure with a group), you may choose to describe them in more detail. It is not always necessary to include the dates of your memberships with your activities the way you would include job dates.

There are a number of different ways in which to present additional information. You may give this section a number of different titles. Assess what you want to list, and then use an appropriate title. Do not use "extracurricular activities." This terminology is scholastic, not professional, and therefore not appropriate. The following are two examples:

❑ ACTIVITIES: Society for Technical Communication, Student Senate, Student Admissions Representative, Senior Class Officer

❑ ACTIVITIES:
  • Society for Technical Communication Member
  • Student Senator
  • Student Admissions Representative
  • Senior Class Officer

The position you are looking for will determine what you should or should not include. *Always* look for a correlation between the activity and the prospective job.

How Should I Handle References?

The use of references is considered a part of the interview process, and they should never be listed on a resume. You would always provide references to a potential employer if requested to, so it is not even necessary to include this section on the resume if room does not permit. If space is available, it is acceptable to include one of the following statements:

- ❑ REFERENCES: Furnished upon request.

- ❑ REFERENCES: Available upon request.

Individuals used as references must be protected from unnecessary contacts. By including names on your resume, you leave your references unprotected. Overuse and abuse of your references will lead to less-than-supportive comments. Protect your references by giving out their names only when you are being considered seriously as a candidate for a given position.

THE FUNCTIONAL RESUME

The functional resume departs from a chronological resume in that it organizes information by specific accomplishments in various settings: previous jobs, volunteer work, associations, etc. This type of resume permits you to stress the substance of your experiences rather than the position titles you have held. (See Exhibit 2.3.) You should consider using a functional resume if you have held a series of similar jobs that relied on the same skills or abilities.

Exhibit 2.3

Functional Resume

CAMILLE DAWSON

Student Apartment 12   12 Cornwall Street
Cleveland State University   Rocky River, OH 44116
Cleveland, OH 44115   (215) 555-6666
(216) 555-5555
Fax (216) 555-1122
camille@yahoo.com
(until May 2003)

OBJECTIVE
An entry-level research assistant position that allows me to use my problem-solving, computing, and communication skills.

CAPABILITIES
- Analytical problem solver
- Experienced software and hardware user
- Effective communicator

SELECTED ACCOMPLISHMENTS
PROBLEM SOLVING: Researched current and accurate sources of information for ongoing research projects. Developed methods and systems for processing survey data results for 23 different projects. Established processing priorities for several overlapping projects; answered questions and resolved problems for library patrons.

COMPUTING: Used SPSS and SAS software packages to process data; manipulated digitizers, plotters, and graphics software to create graphics for reports; utilized mainframe and personal computing hardware; helped implement library security system.

COMMUNICATING: Assisted in writing and editing project reports; conducted telephone and door-to-door surveys in the local community; coordinated writing, editing, and computer assignments with three other research assistants; presented survey findings to several audiences. Helped library patrons locate needed materials.

AWARDS
Awarded outstanding part-time employee of the year certificate
Graduated with honors in English
Nominated to National Honor Society

EMPLOYMENT HISTORY
Research Assistant, Center for Urban Studies, Cleveland State University, Cleveland, OH. Summers 2001–02
Library Worker, Cleveland State University Library, Cleveland, OH. 2001–03

EDUCATION
Bachelor of Arts in English
Cleveland State University, Cleveland, OH.
May 2003

REFERENCES
Provided upon request

The Objective

A functional resume begins with an objective that can be used to focus the contents of the resume.

Specific Accomplishments

Specific accomplishments are listed on this type of resume. Examples of the types of headings used to describe these capabilities might include research, computer skills, teaching, communication, production, management, marketing, or writing. The headings you choose will directly relate to your experience and the tasks that you carried out. Each accomplishment section contains statements related to your experience in that category, regardless of when or where it occurred. Organize the accomplishments and the related tasks you describe in their order of importance as related to the position you seek.

Experience or Employment History

Your actual work experience is condensed and placed after the specific accomplishments section. It simply lists dates of employment, position titles, and employer names.

Education

The education section of a functional resume is identical to that of the chronological resume, but it does not carry the same visual importance because it is placed near the bottom of the page.

References

Because actual reference names are never listed on a resume, this section is optional if space does not permit.

THE TARGETED RESUME

The targeted resume focuses on specific work-related capabilities you can bring to a given position within an organization. (See Exhibit 2.4.) It should be sent to an individual within the organization who makes hiring decisions about the position you are seeking.

The Objective

The objective on this type of resume should be targeted to a specific career or position. It should be supported by the capabilities, accomplishments, and achievements documented in the resume.

Exhibit 2.4

Targeted Resume

PETER THOMASON

Student Apartment 104B
University of Denver
Denver, CO 80201
(303) 555-5555
Fax (303) 555-2211
pthom@hotmail.com
(until May 2004)

12 West 80th Avenue
Denver, CO 80201
(303) 555-6666

JOB TARGET
Planning assistant with a state or regional planning agency

CAPABILITIES
- Provide technical and administrative support
- Work under broad direction of chief planner
- Review and revise reports
- Collect and analyze data
- Use a variety of software and hardware

ACHIEVEMENTS
- Edit prize-winning university literary review
- Research background material for campus author
- Ran successful house painting business
- Maintained an A average throughout college

WORK HISTORY

2003–present	*Research Assistant,* City of Denver Planning Board • Analyze data to report to city planner
2001–present	*Editor,* THE CLARION, campus newspaper • Responsible for editing entire newspaper
2001–02	*Tutor,* English Department • Tutored students in writing and literature
2000	*Laborer,* Facility Services, University of Denver • Member of grounds maintenance crew

continued

---

continued

EDUCATION

2004
Bachelor of Arts in English
University of Denver
Minor: Geography

Capabilities

Capabilities should be statements that illustrate tasks you believe you are capable of based on your accomplishments, achievements, and work history. Each should relate to your targeted career or position. You can stress your qualifications rather than your employment history. This approach may require research to obtain an understanding of the nature of the work involved and the capabilities necessary to carry out that work.

Accomplishments/Achievements

This section relates the various activities you have been involved in to the job market. These experiences may include previous jobs, extracurricular activities at school, internships, and part-time summer work.

Experience

Your work history should be listed in abbreviated form and may include position title, employer name, and employment dates.

Education

Because this type of resume is directed toward a specific job target and an individual's related experience, the education section is not prominently located at the top of the resume as is done on the chronological resume.

DIGITAL RESUMES

Today's employers have to manage an enormous number of resumes. One of the most frequent complaints the writers of this series hear from students is the failure of employers to even acknowledge the receipt of a resume and cover letter. Frequently, the reason for this poor response or nonresponse is the volume of applications received for every job. In an attempt to better manage the considerable labor investment involved in processing large numbers of resumes, many employers are requiring digital submission of resumes. There are two types of digital resumes: those that can be E-mailed or posted to a website called *electronic resumes,* and those that can be "read" by a computer, commonly called *scannable resumes.* Though the format may be a bit different than the traditional "paper" resume, the goal of both types of digital resumes is the same—to get you an interview! These resumes must be designed to be "technologically friendly." What that basically means to you is that they should be free of graphics and fancy formatting.

Electronic Resumes

Sometimes referred to as plain-text resumes, electronic resumes are designed to be E-mailed to an employer or posted to a commercial Internet database such as CareerMosaic.com, America's Job Bank (www.ajb.dni.us), or Monster.com.

Some technical considerations:

- Electronic resumes must be written in American Standard Code for Information Interchange (ASCII), which is simply a plain-text format. These characters are universally recognized so that every computer can accurately read and understand them. To create an ASCII file of your current resume, open your document, then save it as a text or ASCII file. This will eliminate all formatting. Edit as needed using your computer's text editor application.

- Use a standard-width typeface. Courier is a good choice because it is the font associated with ASCII in most systems.

- Use a font size of 11 to 14 points. A 12-point font is considered standard.

- Your margin should be left-justified.

- Do not exceed sixty-five characters per line, because the word-wrap function doesn't operate in ASCII.

- Do not use boldface, italics, underlining, bullets, and various font sizes. Instead, use asterisks, plus signs, and all capital letters when you want to emphasize something.

- Avoid graphics and shading.

- Use as many "keywords" as you possibly can. These are words or phrases usually relating to skills or experience that are either specifically used in the job announcement or are popular buzzwords in the industry.

- Minimize abbreviations. One exception is B.S. or B.A. for your degree.

- Your name should be the first line of text.
- Conduct a "test run" by E-mailing your resume to yourself and a friend before you send it to the employer. See how it transmits, and make any changes you need to. Continue to test it until it's exactly how you want it to look.
- Unless an employer specifically requests that you send the resume in the form of an attachment, don't. Employers can encounter problems opening a document as an attachment, and there are always viruses to consider.
- Don't forget your cover letter. Send it along with your resume as a single message.

Scannable Resumes

Some companies are relying on technology to narrow the candidate pool for available job openings. Electronic Applicant Tracking uses imaging to scan, sort, and store resumes in a database. Then, through OCR (Optical Character Recognition) software, the computer scans the resumes for keywords and phrases. To have the best chance at getting an interview, you want to increase the number of "hits"—matches of your skills, abilities, experience, and education to those the computer is scanning for—your resume will get. You can see how critical using the right keywords is for this type of resume.

Technical considerations include:

- Again, do not use boldface (newer systems may read this OK, but many older ones won't), italics, underlining, bullets, shading, graphics, and multiple font sizes. Instead, for emphasis, use asterisks, plus signs, and all capital letters. Minimize abbreviations.
- Use a popular typeface such as Courier, Helvetica, Ariel, or Palatino. Avoid decorative fonts.
- Font size should be between 11 and 14 points.
- Do not compress the spacing between letters.
- Use horizontal and vertical lines sparingly; the computer may misread them as the letters L or I.
- Left-justify the text.
- Do not use parentheses or brackets around telephone numbers, and be sure your phone number is on its own line of text.
- Your name should be the first line of text and on its own line. If your resume is longer than one page, be sure to put your name on the top of all pages.

- Use a traditional resume structure. The chronological format may work best.

- Use nouns that are skill-focused, such as *management, writer,* and *programming*. This is different from traditional paper resumes, which use action-oriented verbs.

- Laser printers produce the finest copies. Avoid dot-matrix printers.

- Use standard, light-colored paper with text on one side only. Since the higher the contrast the better, your best choice is black ink on white paper.

- Always send original copies. If you must fax, set the fax on fine mode, not standard.

- Do not staple or fold your resume. This can confuse the computer.

- Before you send your scannable resume, be certain the employer uses this technology. If you can't determine this, you may want to send two versions (scannable and traditional) to be sure your resume gets considered.

Exhibit 2.5

DIGITAL RESUME

SARAH MCDOUGLE — Put your name at the top on its own line.
117 Stetson Avenue
Small School, MA 02459 — Put your phone number on its own line.
859-425-5478
saramc@bwn.com — Use a standard-width typeface—like Courier.

KEYWORD SUMMARY
BS Computer Science, 2002, C++, Visual
Basic, Assemble, FORTRAN, TUTOR, — Keywords make your
HTML, CAD, PATRAN, Oracle, MS Office, resume easier to find in a
IBM 630-670, Windows NT, UNIX, database.
Programmer

EDUCATION — Capital letters emphasize
Bachelor of Science, Computer Science headings.
2002
Small State College, Small School,
Massachusetts

continued

continued

Minor: Graphic Design

G.P.A.: 3.0/4.0

Related Courses
Database Design, Compiler Design,
System Architecture, Operating Systems,
Data Structures

No line should exceed sixty-five characters.

COMPUTER SKILLS

Languages: C/C++, Visual Basic, Assembly,
FORTRAN, TUTOR, HTML

Software: CAD, PATRAN, Oracle, MS
Office

Systems: IBM 360/370, Windows NT,
UNIX

EXPERIENCE

Support Desk, Small State College, 2001–02

End each line by hitting the ENTER key.

* Maintained computer systems in
computer lab
* Installed application and performed
troubleshooting
* Instructed students on application and
systems

Programmer (intern), Large Company, 2001
* Wrote instructional programs using
TUTOR language
* Corrected errors in prewritten
programs using C++
* Altered existing programs to fit user
needs

Use a space between asterisk and text.

Data-Entry Clerk, XYZ Sales, Winter 2000
* Updated inventory and sales data

COMMUNICATION SKILLS
Served as a Vice President of Computer Science Society
Received As in technical writing and speech class

REFERENCES
Available upon request
++ Willing to relocate ++

Asterisks and plus signs replace bullets.

RESUME PRODUCTION AND OTHER TIPS

An ink-jet printer is the preferred option for printing your resume. Begin by printing just a few copies. You may find a small error or you may simply want to make some changes, and this is less frustrating and less expensive if you print in small batches.

Resume paper color should be carefully chosen. You should consider the types of employers who will receive your resume and the types of positions for which you are applying. Use white or ivory paper for traditional or conservative employers or for higher-level positions.

Black ink on sharply white paper can be harsh on the reader's eyes. Think about an ivory or cream paper that will provide less contrast and be easier to read. Pink, green, and blue tints should generally be avoided.

Many resume writers buy packages of matching envelopes and cover sheet stationery that, although not absolutely necessary, do convey a professional impression.

If you'll be producing many cover letters at home, be sure you have high quality printing equipment. Learn standard envelope formats for business and retain a copy of every cover letter you send out. You can use the copies to take notes of any telephone conversations that may occur.

If attending a job fair, either carry a briefcase or place your resume in a nicely covered legal-size pad holder.

THE COVER LETTER

The cover letter provides you with the opportunity to tailor your resume by telling the prospective employer how you can be a benefit to the organization. It will allow you to highlight aspects of your background that are not already discussed in your resume and that might be especially relevant to the organization you are contacting or to the position you are seeking. Every resume should have a cover letter enclosed when you send it out. Unlike the resume, which may be mass-produced, a cover letter is most effective when it is individually typed and focused on the particular requirements of the organization in question.

A good cover letter should supplement the resume and motivate the reader to review the resume. The format shown in Exhibit 2.6 is only a suggestion to help you decide what information to include in writing a cover letter.

Begin the cover letter with your street address twelve lines down from the top. Leave three to five lines between the date and the name of the person to whom you are addressing the cover letter. Make sure you leave one blank line between the salutation and the body of the letter and between paragraphs.

After typing "Sincerely," leave four blank lines and type your name. This should leave plenty of room for your signature. A sample cover letter is shown in Exhibit 2.7.

Exhibit 2.6

Cover Letter Format

Your Name
Your Street Address
Your Town, State, Zip
Phone Number
Fax Number
E-mail

Date

Name
Title
Organization
Address

Dear _____:

First Paragraph. In this paragraph state the reason for the letter, name the specific position or type of work you are applying for, and indicate from which resource (career services office, newspaper, contact, employment service) you learned of this opening. The first paragraph can also be used to inquire about future openings.

Second Paragraph. Indicate why you are interested in this position, the company, its products or services, and what you can do for the employer. If you are a recent graduate, explain how your academic background makes you a qualified candidate. Try not to repeat the same information found in the resume.

Third Paragraph. Refer the reader to the enclosed resume for more detailed information.

Fourth Paragraph. In this paragraph say what you will do to follow up on your letter. For example, state that you will call by a certain date to set up an interview or to find out if the company will be recruiting in your area. Finish by indicating your willingness to answer any questions they may have. Be sure you have provided your phone number.

Sincerely,

Type your name

Enclosure

The following guidelines will help you write good cover letters:

1. Be sure to type your letter; ensure there are no misspellings.

2. Avoid unusual typefaces, such as script.

3. Address the letter to an individual, using the person's name and title. To obtain this information, call the company. If answering a blind

---

Exhibit 2.7

Sample Cover Letter

Jennifer Smith
143 Randon Way
Shreveport, LA 71130
(318) 555-5555
Fax (318) 555-2112
jsmith@aol.com

November 29, 2002

Kimberly Crane
Director of Personnel
Acme Distributors
279 Main Street
Shreveport, LA 71130

Dear Ms. Crane:

In May of 2003 I will graduate from Louisiana State University with a bachelor of arts degree in English. I read of your sales opening in *The Times* on Sunday, November 28, 2002, and I am very interested in the possibilities it offers. I am writing to explore the opportunity for employment with your company.

continued

continued

The ad indicated that you were looking for enthusiastic individuals with exceptional communication skills. I believe that I possess those qualities. Through my job as a waitress at a busy diner, I have learned the importance of having high energy and maintaining a positive attitude toward customers. In addition to the various marketing classes in my academic program, I felt it important to enroll in some communication courses, such as human communication skills, interpersonal communication, and public speaking. These courses helped me to become comfortable in my interactions with other people, and they taught me how to communicate clearly. These characteristics will help me to represent Acme in a professional and enthusiastic manner.

As you will see by my enclosed resume, I was an admissions representative for three years of college. This position provided me with sales experience in that campus tours involved a certain degree of persuasive presentation of the college and its features to prospective students.

I would like to meet with you to discuss how my education experience would be consistent with your needs. I will contact your office next week to discuss the possibility of an interview. In the meantime, if you have any questions or require additional information, please contact me at home, (318) 555-5555.

Sincerely,

Jennifer Smith

Enclosure

newspaper advertisement, address the letter "To Whom It May Concern" or omit the salutation.

4. Be sure your cover letter directly indicates the position you are applying for and tells why you are qualified to fill it.

5. Send the original letter, not a photocopy, with your resume. Keep a copy for your records.

6. Make your cover letter no more than one page.

7. Include a phone number where you can be reached.

8. Avoid trite language and have someone read the letter over to react to its tone, content, and mechanics.

9. For your own information, record the date you send out each letter and resume.

CHAPTER THREE

RESEARCHING CAREERS

· ·

One common question a career counselor encounters is "What can I do with my degree?" English majors often struggle with this problem because, unlike their fellow students in more applied fields, such as accounting, computer science, or health and physical education, there is real confusion about just what kinds of jobs they can do with their degree and what kinds of organizations hire for those positions. An accounting major becomes an accountant. A computer science major can apply for a job as a data analyst. But what does an English major become?

· ·

WHAT DO THEY CALL THE JOB YOU WANT?

There is every reason to be unaware. One reason for confusion is perhaps a mistaken assumption that a college education provides job training. In most cases it does not. Of course, applied fields such as engineering, management, or education provide specific skills for the workplace, whereas most liberal arts degrees simply provide an education. A liberal arts education exposes you to numerous fields of study and teaches you quantitative reasoning, critical thinking, writing, and speaking, all of which can be successfully applied to a number of different job fields. But it still remains up to you to choose a job field and to learn how to articulate the benefits of your education in a way the employer will appreciate.

As indicated in Chapter 1 on self-assessment, your first task is to understand and value what parts of that education you enjoyed and were good at and would continue to enjoy in your life's work. Did your writing courses encourage you in your ability to express yourself in writing? Did you enjoy the research process, and did you find your work was well received? Did you enjoy any of your required quantitative subjects like algebra or calculus?

The answers to questions such as these provide clues to skills and interests you bring to the employment market over and above the credential of your degree. In fact, it is not an overstatement to suggest that most employers who demand a college degree immediately look beyond that degree to you as a person and your own individual expression of what you like to do and think you can do for them, regardless of your major.

Collecting Job Titles

The world of employment is a big place, and even seasoned veterans of the job hunt can be surprised about what jobs are to be found in what organizations. You need to become a bit of an explorer and adventurer and be willing to try a variety of techniques to begin a list of possible occupations that might use your talents and education. Once you have a list of possibilities that you are interested in and qualified for, you can move on to find out what kinds of organizations have these job titles.

••

Not every employer seeking to hire an editor may be equally desirable to you. Some employment environments may be more attractive to you than others. An English major considering technical writing as a job title could do that in a major corporation for either industrial or consumer goods, in a medical institution, a financial organization, or a small venture capital start-up company producing specialized computer software. Each of these environments presents a different "culture" with associated norms in the pace of work, the subject matter of interest, and the backgrounds of its employees. Although the job titles may be the same, not all locations may present the same "fit" for you.

If you majored in English and enjoyed the in-class presentations you made as part of your degree and developed some good writing skills, you might naturally think law is a possibility for you. You're considering graduate school and a J.D. degree. But English majors with these skills also become government managers, advertising executives, reporters, trainers, public relations practitioners, and bank officers. Each of these job titles can also be found in a number of different settings.

....

Take training, for example. Trainers write policy and procedural manuals and actively teach to assist all levels of employees in mastering various tasks and work-related systems. Trainers exist in all large corporations, banks, consumer goods manufacturers, medical diagnostic equipment firms, sales organizations, and any organization that has processes or materials that need to be presented to and learned by the staff.

In reading job descriptions or want ads for any of these positions, you would find your four-year degree a "must." However, the academic major might be less important than your own individual skills in critical thinking, analysis, report writing, public presentations, and interpersonal communication. Even more important than thinking or knowing you have certain skills is your ability to express those skills concretely and the examples you use to illustrate them to an employer.

The best beginning to a job search is to create a list of job titles you might want to pursue, learn more about the nature of the jobs behind those titles, and then discover what kinds of employers hire for those positions. In the following section we'll teach you how to build a job title directory to use in your job search.

Developing a Job Title Directory That Works for You

A job title directory is simply a complete list of all the job titles you are interested in, are intrigued by, or think you are qualified for. Combining the understanding gained through self-assessment with your own individual interests and the skills and talents you've acquired with your degree, you'll soon start to read and recognize a number of occupational titles that seem right for you. There are several resources you can use to develop your list, including computer searches, books, and want ads.

Computerized Interest Inventories. One way to begin your search is to identify a number of jobs that call for your degree and the particular skills and interests you identified as part of the self-assessment process. There are excellent interactive computer career guidance programs on the market to help you produce such selected lists of possible job titles. Most of these are available at high schools and colleges and at some larger town and city libraries. Two of the industry leaders are SIGI and DISCOVER. Both allow you to enter interests, values, educational background, and other information to produce lists of possible occupations and industries. Each of the resources listed here will produce different job title lists. Some job titles will appear again and again, while others will be unique to a particular source. Investigate them all!

Reference Books. Books on the market that may be available through your local library, bookstore, or career counseling office also suggest various occupations related to a number of majors. The following are only two of the many good books on the market: *Occupational Outlook Handbook (OOH)* and *Occupational Projections and Training Data*, both put out annually by the U.S. Department of Labor, Bureau of Labor Statistics. The *OOH* describes hundreds of job titles under several broad categories such as Executive, Administrative, and Managerial Occupations and also identifies those jobs by their *Dictionary of Occupational Titles (DOT)* code. (See the following discussion.)

· ·

For English majors, over fifty job titles are listed. Some are familiar ones, such as news editor and teacher, and others are interestingly different, such as art critic or fund-raiser.

The *Occupational Thesaurus* is another good resource, which essentially lists job title possibilities under general categories. So, if as an English major you discover advertising executive as a job title in the book *What Can I Do with a Major in . . . ?*, you can then go to the *Occupational Thesaurus,* which lists scores of jobs under that title. Under "Advertising," there is a list of more than twenty associated job titles, including manufacturer's representative and customer relations specialist. So if advertising was a suggested job title for you, this source adds some depth by suggesting a number of different occupations within that field.

· ·

Each job title deserves your consideration. Like the layers of an onion, the search for job titles can go on and on! As you spend time doing this activity, you are actually learning more about the value of your degree. What's important in your search at this point is not to become critical or selective, but rather to develop as long a list of possibilities as you can. Every source used will help you add new and potentially exciting jobs to your growing list.

Want Ads. It has been well publicized that newspaper want ads represent only about 10 to 15 percent of the current job market. Nevertheless, the Sunday want ads can be a great help to you in your search. Although they may not be the best place to look for a job, they can teach the job seeker much about the job market and provide a good education in job descriptions, duties and responsibilities, active industries, and some indication of the volume of job traffic. For our purposes they are a good source for job titles to add to your list.

Read the Sunday want ads in a major market newspaper for several Sundays in a row. Circle and then cut out any and all ads that interest you and seem to call for something close to your education and experience. Remember, because want ads are written for what an organization *hopes* to find, you don't have to meet absolutely every criterion. However, if certain requirements are stated as absolute minimums and you cannot meet them, it's best not to waste your time.

A recent examination of the *Boston Sunday Globe* (www.boston.com) reveals the following possible occupations for a liberal arts major with some computer skills and limited prior work experience. (This is only a partial list of what was available.)

- Admissions representative
- Salesperson
- Compliance director
- Assistant principal gifts writer
- Public relations officer
- Technical writer
- Personnel trainee
- GED examiner
- Direct mail researcher
- Associate publicist

After performing this exercise for a few Sundays, you'll find you have collected a new library of job titles.

The Sunday want ad exercise is important because these jobs are out in the marketplace. They truly exist, and people with your qualifications are being sought to apply. What's more, many of these advertisements describe the duties and responsibilities of the job advertised and give you a beginning sense of the challenges and opportunities such a position presents. Some will indicate salary, and that will be helpful as well. This information will better define the jobs for you and provide some good material for possible interviews in that field.

Exploring Job Descriptions

Once you've arrived at a solid list of possible job titles that interest you and for which you believe you are somewhat qualified, it's a good idea to do some research on each of these jobs. The preeminent source for such job information is the *Dictionary of Occupational Titles,* or *DOT* (www.wave .net/upg/immigration/dot_index.html). This directory lists every conceivable job and provides excellent up-to-date information on duties and responsibilities, interactions with associates, and day-to-day assignments and tasks. These descriptions provide a thorough job analysis, but they do not consider the possible employers or the environments in which a job may be performed. So, although a position as public relations officer may be well defined in terms of duties and responsibilities, it does not explain the differences in doing public relations work in a college or a hospital or a factory or a bank. You will need to look somewhere else for work settings.

Learning More About Possible Work Settings

After reading some job descriptions, you may choose to edit and revise your list of job titles once again, discarding those you feel are not suitable and keeping those that continue to hold your interest. Or you may wish to keep your list intact and see where these jobs may be located. For example, if you are interested in public relations and you appear to have those skills and the requisite education, you'll want to know what organizations do public relations. How can you find that out? How much income does someone in public relations make a year and what is the employment potential for the field of public relations?

To answer these and many other good questions about your list of job titles, we recommend you try any of the following resources: *Careers Encyclopedia,* a career information center site such as that provided by the American Marketing Association at www.amaboston.org/jobs.htm; *College to Career: The Guide to Job Opportunities*; and the *Occupational Outlook Handbook* (http://stats.bls.gov/ocohome.htm). Each of these resources, in a different way, will help to put the job titles you have selected into an employer context. *VGM's Handbook of Business and Management Careers* contains detailed career descriptions for more than fifty fields. Entries include complete information on duties and responsibilities for individual careers and detailed entry-level requirements. There is information on working conditions and promotional opportunities as well. Salary ranges and career outlook projections are also provided. Perhaps the most extensive discussion is found in the *Occupational Outlook Handbook,* which gives a thorough presentation of the nature of the work, the working conditions, employment statistics, training, other qualifications, and advancement possibilities as well as job outlook and earnings. Related occupations are also detailed, and a select bibliography is provided to help you find additional information.

Continuing with our public relations example, your search through these reference materials would teach you that the public relations jobs you find attractive are available in larger hospitals, financial institutions, most corporations (both consumer goods and industrial goods), media organizations, and colleges and universities.

Networking to Get the Complete Story

You now have not only a list of job titles but also, for each of these job titles, a description of the work involved and a general list of possible employment settings in which to work. You'll want to do some reading and keep talking to friends, colleagues, teachers, and others about the possibilities. Don't neglect to ask if the career office at your college maintains some kind of alumni network. Often such alumni networks will connect you with another graduate from the college who is working in the job title or industry you are seeking information about. These career networkers offer what assistance they can. For some it is a full day "shadowing" the alumnus as he or she goes about the job. Others offer partial-day visits, tours, informational interviews, resume reviews, job postings, or, if distance prevents a visit, telephone interviews. As fellow graduates, they'll be frank and informative about their own jobs and prospects in their field.

Take them up on their offer and continue to learn all you can about your own personal list of job titles, descriptions, and employment settings. You'll probably continue to edit and refine this list as you learn more about the realities of the job, the possible salary, advancement opportunities, and supply and demand statistics.

In the next section we'll describe how to find the specific organizations that represent these industries and employers so that you can begin to make contact.

WHERE ARE THESE JOBS, ANYWAY?

Having a list of job titles that you've designed around your own career interests and skills is an excellent beginning. It means you've really thought about who you are and what you are presenting to the employment market.

It has caused you to think seriously about the most appealing environments to work in, and you have identified some employer types that represent these environments.

The research and the thinking that you've done thus far will be used again and again. They will be helpful in writing your resume and cover letters, in talking about yourself on the telephone to prospective employers, and in answering interview questions.

Now is a good time to begin to narrow the field of job titles and employment sites down to some specific employers to initiate the employment contact.

Finding Out Which Employers Hire People Like You

This section will provide tips, techniques, and specific resources for developing an actual list of specific employers that can be used to make contacts. It is only an outline that you must be prepared to tailor to your own particular needs and according to what you bring to the job search. Once again, it is important to stress the need to communicate with others along the way exactly what you're looking for and what your goals are for the research you're doing. Librarians, employers, career counselors, friends, friends of friends, business contacts, and bookstore staff will all have helpful information on geographically specific and new resources to aid you in locating employers who'll hire you.

Identifying Information Resources

Your interview wardrobe and your new resume may have put a dent in your wallet, but the resources you'll need to pursue your job search are available for free (although you might choose to copy materials on a machine instead of taking notes by hand). The categories of information detailed here are not hard to find and are yours for the browsing.

Numerous resources described in this section will help you identify actual employers. Use all of them or any others that you identify as available in your geographic area. As you become experienced in this process, you'll quickly figure out which information sources are helpful and which are not. If you live in a rural area, a well-planned day trip to a major city that includes a college career office, a large college or city library, state and federal employment centers, a chamber of commerce office, and a well-stocked bookstore can produce valuable results.

There are many excellent resources available to help you identify actual job sites. They are categorized into employer directories (usually indexed by product lines and geographic location), geographically based directories (designed to highlight particular cities, regions, or states), career-specific directories (e.g., *Sports Market Place,* which lists tens of thousands of firms involved with sports), periodicals and newspapers, targeted job posting publications, and videos. This is by no means meant to be a complete list of resources, but rather a starting point for identifying useful resources.

Working from the more general references to highly specific resources, we will provide a basic list to help you begin your search. Many of these you'll find easily available. In some cases reference librarians and others will suggest even better materials for your particular situation. Start to create your own customized bibliography of job search references. Use copying services to save time and to allow you to carry away information about organizations' missions, locations, company officers, phone numbers, and addresses.

Employer Directories. There are many employer directories available to give you the kind of information you need for your job search. Some of our favorites are listed here, but be sure to ask the professionals you are working with to make additional suggestions.

- *America's Corporate Families*
  (www.chime-net.org/crc/interview/intev2.htm) identifies many major U.S. ultimate parent companies and displays corporate family linkage of subsidiaries and divisions. Businesses can be identified by their industrial code.

- *Million Dollar Directory: America's Leading Public and Private Companies* lists about 160,000 companies.

- *Moody's* (www.moodys.com) various manuals are intended as guides for investors, so they contain a history of each company. Each manual contains a classification of companies by industries and products.

- *Standard and Poor's Register of Corporations*
  (www.stockinfo.standardpoor.com) contains listings for 45,000 businesses, some of which are not listed in the *Million Dollar Directory.*

- *Job Seekers Guide to Private and Public Companies*
  (www.tomah.com/jobseeker) profiles 15,000 employers in four volumes, each covering a different geographic region. Company entries include contact information, business descriptions, and application procedures.

- *The Career Guide: Dun's Employment Opportunities Directory* includes more than 5,000 large organizations, including hospitals and local governments. Profiles include an overview and history of the employer as well as opportunities, benefits, and contact names. It contains geographic and industrial indexes and indexes by discipline or internship availability. This guide also includes a state-by-state list of professional personnel consultants and their specialties.

❑ *Professional's Job Finder/Government Job Finder/Non-Profits Job Finder* (www.einsys.einpgh.org) are specific directories of job services, salary surveys, and periodical listings in which advertisements for jobs in the professional, government, or not-for-profit sector are found.

❑ *Opportunities in Nonprofit Organizations* is a VGM career series edition that opens up the world of not-for-profit by helping you match your interest profile to the aims and objectives of scores of nonprofit employers in business, education, health and medicine, social welfare, science and technology, and many other fields. There is also a special section on fund-raising and development career paths.

❑ *The 100 Best Companies to Sell For* lists companies by industry and provides contact information and describes benefits and corporate culture.

❑ *The 100 Best Companies to Work For in America* rates organizations on several factors including opportunities, job security, and pay.

❑ *Companies That Care* lists organizations that the authors believe are family-friendly. One index organizes information by state.

❑ *Infotrac CD-ROM Business Index* (http://infotrac.galegroup.com) covers business journals and magazines as well as news magazines and can provide information on public and private companies.

❑ *ABI/Inform On Disc* (CD-ROM) indexes articles in more than 800 journals.

Geographically Based Directories. The Job Bank series published by Bob Adams, Inc. (www.aip.com) contains detailed entries on each area's major employers, including business activity, address, phone number, and hiring contact name. Many listings specify educational backgrounds being sought in potential employees. Each volume contains a solid discussion of each city's or state's major employment sectors. Organizations are also indexed by industry. Job Bank volumes are available for the following places: Atlanta, Boston, Chicago, Denver, Dallas–Ft. Worth, Florida, Houston, Ohio, St. Louis, San Francisco, Seattle, Los Angeles, New York, Detroit, Philadelphia, Minneapolis, the Northwest, and Washington, D.C.

National Job Bank lists employers in every state, along with contact names and commonly hired job categories. Included are many small companies often overlooked by other directories. Companies are also indexed by industry. This publication provides information on educational backgrounds sought and lists company benefits.

Career-Specific Directories. VGM publishes a number of excellent series detailing careers for college graduates. In the Professional Career series are guides to careers in the following fields, among others:

- Advertising

- Business

- Communications

- Computers

- Health Care

- High Tech

Each provides an excellent discussion of the industry, educational require-ments for jobs, salary ranges, duties, and projected outlooks for the field.

Another VGM series, Opportunities in . . . , has an equally wide range of titles relating to specific majors, such as the following:

- *Opportunities in Education*

- *Opportunities in Film*

- *Opportunities in Insurance*

- *Opportunities in Journalism*

- *Opportunities in Law*

- *Opportunities in Nursing*

- *Opportunities in Government*

- *Opportunities in Teaching*

- *Opportunities in Technical Writing*

Sports Market Place (Sportsguide) lists organizations by sport. It also describes trade/professional associations, college athletic organizations, multisport publications, media contacts, corporate sports sponsors, promo-tion/event/athletic management services, and trade shows.

Periodicals and Newspapers. Several sources are available to help you locate which journals or magazines carry job advertisements in your field. Other resources help you identify opportunities in other parts of the country.

- *Where the Jobs Are: A Comprehensive Directory of 1,200 Journals Listing Career Opportunities* links specific occupational titles to corresponding periodicals that carry job listings for your field.

- *Social & Behavioral Sciences Jobs Handbook* contains a periodicals matrix organized by academic discipline and highlights periodicals containing job listings.

- *National Business Employment Weekly* (www.nbew.com) compiles want ads from four regional editions of the *Wall Street Journal* (http:interactive.wsj.com). Most are business and management positions.

- *National Ad Search* (www.creditconnection.net/led/classads2.htm) reprints ads from seventy-five metropolitan newspapers across the country. Although the focus is on management positions, technical and professional postings are also included. *Caution:* Watch deadline dates carefully on listings because deadlines may have already passed by the time the ad is printed.

- *The Federal Jobs Digest* (www.jobsfed.com) and *Federal Career Opportunities* list government positions.

- *World Chamber of Commerce Directory* (www.search.cnet.com/single/0,7,150354,00.html) lists addresses for chambers worldwide, state boards of tourism, convention and visitors' bureaus, and economic development organizations.

This list is certainly not exhaustive; use it to begin your job search work.

Targeted Job Posting Publications. Although the resources that follow are national in scope, they are either targeted to one medium of contact (telephone), focused on specific types of jobs, or are less comprehensive than the sources previously listed.

- *Job Hotlines USA* (www.careers.org/topic/0102_job_hotlines_from_job_factory.html) pinpoints more than 1,000 hard-to-find telephone numbers for companies and government agencies that use prerecorded job messages and listings. Very few of the telephone numbers listed are toll-free, and sometimes recordings are long, so callers beware!

- *The Job Hunter* (www.jobhunter.com) is a national biweekly newspaper listing business, arts, media, government, human services, health, community-related, and student services job openings.

- *Current Jobs for Graduates* (www.graduatejobs.com) is a national employment listing for liberal arts professions, including editorial positions, management opportunities, museum work, teaching, and nonprofit work.

- *Environmental Opportunities* (www.ecojobs.com) serves environmental job interests nationwide by listing administrative, marketing, and human resources positions along with education-related jobs and positions directly related to a degree in an environmental field.

- *Y National Vacancy List* (www.ymcahrm.ns.ca/employed/jobleads.html) shows YMCA professional vacancies, including development, administration, programming, membership, and recreation postings.

- *ARTSearch* is a national employment service bulletin for the arts, including administration, managerial, marketing, and financial management jobs.

- *Community Jobs* is an employment newspaper for the nonprofit sector that provides a variety of listings, including project manager, canvas director, government relations specialist, community organizer, and program instructor.

- *College Placement Council Annual: A Guide to Employment Opportunities for College Graduates* is an annual guide containing solid job-hunting information and, more importantly, displaying ads from large corporations actively seeking recent college graduates in all majors. Company profiles provide brief descriptions and available employment opportunities. Contact names and addresses are given. Profiles are indexed by organization name, geographic location, and occupation.

Videos. You may be one of the many job seekers who like to get information via a medium other than paper. Many career libraries, public libraries, and career centers in libraries carry an assortment of videos that will help you learn new techniques and get information helpful in the job search.

Locating Information Resources

An essay by John Case that appeared in the *Boston Globe* alerts both new and seasoned job seekers that the job market is changing, and the old guarantees of lifelong employment no longer hold true. Some of our major corporations, which were once seen as the most prestigious of employment destinations, are now laying off thousands of employees. Middle management is especially hard hit in downsizing situations. On the other side of the coin, smaller, more entrepreneurial firms are adding employees and realizing enormous profit margins. The geography of the new job market is unfamiliar, and the terrain is much harder to map. New and smaller firms can mean different kinds of jobs and new job titles. The successful job seeker will keep an open mind about where he or she might find employment and what that employment might be called.

In order to become familiar with this new terrain, you will need to undertake some research, which can be done at any of the following locations:

- Public libraries

- Business organizations

- Employment agencies

- Bookstores

- Career libraries

Each one of these places offers a collection of resources that will help you get the information you need.

As you meet and talk with service professionals at all these sites, be sure to let them know what you're doing. Inform them of your job search, what you've already accomplished, and what you're looking for. The more people who know you're job seeking, the greater the possibility that someone will have information or know someone who can help you along your way.

Public Libraries. Large city libraries, college and university libraries, and even well-supported town library collections contain a variety of resources to help you conduct a job search. It is not uncommon for libraries to have separate "vocational choices" sections with books, tapes, and associated materials relating to job search and selection. Some are now even making resume creation software available for use by patrons.

Some of the publications we name throughout this book are expensive reference items that are rarely purchased by individuals. In addition, libraries carry a wide range of newspapers and telephone yellow pages as well as the usual array of books. If resources are not immediately available, many libraries have loan arrangements with other facilities and can make information available to you relatively quickly.

Take advantage of not only the reference collections, but also the skilled and informed staff. Let them know exactly what you are looking for, and they'll have their own suggestions. You'll be visiting the library frequently, and the reference staff will soon come to know who you are and what you're working on. They'll be part of your job search network!

Business Organizations. Chambers of Commerce, Offices of New Business Development, Councils on Business and Industry, Small Business Administration (SBA) offices, and professional associations can all provide geographically specific lists of companies and organizations that have hiring needs. They also have an array of other available materials, including visitors' guides and regional fact books that provide additional employment information.

These agencies serve to promote local and regional businesses and ensure their survival and success. Although these business organizations do not advertise job openings or seek employees for their members, they may be very aware of staffing needs among their member firms. In your visits to each of these locations, spend some time with the personnel, getting to know who they are and what they do. Let them know of your job search and your intentions regarding employment. You may be surprised and delighted at the information they may provide.

Employment Agencies. Employment agencies (including state and federal employment offices), professional "headhunters" or executive search firms, and some private career counselors can provide direct leads to job openings. Don't overlook these resources. If you are mounting a complete job search program and want to ensure that you are covering the potential market for employers, consider the employment agencies in your territory. Some of these organizations work contractually with several specific firms and may have access that is unavailable to you. Others may be particularly well-informed about supply and demand in particular industries or geographic locations.

In the case of professional (commercial) employment agencies, which include those executive recruitment firms labeled "headhunters," you should be cautious about entering into any binding contractual agreement. Before doing so, be sure to get the information you need to decide whether their services can be of use to you. Questions to ask include the following: Who pays the fee when employment is obtained? Are there any other fees or costs associated with this service? What is their placement rate? Can you see a list of previous clients and can you talk to any for references? Do they typically work with entry-level job seekers? Do they tend to focus on particular kinds of employment or industries?

A few cautions are in order, however, when you work with professional agencies. Remember, the professional employment agency is, in most cases, paid by the hiring organization. Naturally, their interest and attention is largely directed to the employer, not to the candidate. Of course, they want to provide good candidates to guarantee future contracts, but they are less interested in the job seeker than the employer.

For teacher candidates there are a number of good placement firms that charge the prospective teacher, not the employer. This situation has evolved over time as a result of supply and demand and financial structuring of most school systems, which cannot spend money on recruiting teachers. Usually these firms charge a nonrefundable administrative fee and, upon successful placement, require a fee based on a percentage of salary, which may range from 10 to 20 percent of annual compensation. Often, this can be repaid over a number of months. Check your contract carefully.

State and federal employment offices are no-fee services that maintain extensive "job boards" and can provide detailed specifications for each job advertised and help with application forms. Because government employment application forms are detailed, keep a master copy along with copies of all additional documentation (resumes, educational transcripts, military discharge papers, proof of citizenship, etc.). Successive applications may require separate filings. Visit these offices as frequently as you can because most deal with applicants on a "walk-in" basis and will not telephone prospective candidates or maintain files of job seekers. Check your telephone book for the address of the nearest state and federal offices.

The Web is also a great source of job listings for teachers, especially for entry-level positions. A good search tactic on the Web is to use a "metaengine" that combines several search engines in one. *Dogpile.com* is an example of a metasearch engine. Using search string descriptors such as "teacher recruitment," "teacher supply," or "K12 jobs," you will discover job boards with current postings. At the time of publication, three excellent sites were: www.teachersatwork.com, www.K12jobs.com/jobfinder, and www.edweek .org, which has listings by region.

One type of employment service that causes much confusion among job seekers is the outplacement firm. Their advertisements tend to suggest they will put you in touch with the "hidden job market." They use advertising phrases such as "We'll work with you until you get that job" or "Maximize your earnings and career opportunities." In fact, if you read the fine print on these ads, you will notice these firms must state they are "Not an employment agency." These firms are, in fact, corporate and private outplacement counseling agencies whose work involves resume editing, counseling to provide leads for jobs, interview skills training, and all the other aspects of hiring preparation. They do this for a fee, sometimes in the thousands of dollars range, which is paid by you, the client. Some of these firms have good reputations and provide excellent materials and techniques. Most, however, provide a service you as a college student or graduate can receive free from your alma mater or through a reciprocity agreement between your college and a college or university located closer to your current address.

Bookstores. Any well-stocked bookstore will carry some job search books that are worth buying. Some major stores will even have an extensive section devoted to materials, including excellent videos, related to the job search process. You will also find copies of local newspapers and business magazines. The one advantage that is provided by resources purchased at a bookstore is that you can read and work with the information in the comfort of your own home and do not have to conform to the hours of operation of a library, which can present real difficulties if you are working full time as you seek employment. A few minutes spent browsing in a bookstore might be a beneficial break from your job search activities and turn up valuable resources.

Career Libraries. Career libraries, which are found in career centers at colleges and universities and sometimes within large public libraries, contain a unique blend of the job search resources housed in other settings. In addition, career libraries often purchase a number of job listing publications, each of which targets a specific industry or type of job. You may find job listings specifically for entry-level positions for English majors. Ask about job posting newsletters or newspapers specifically focused on careers in the area that most interests you. Each center will be unique, but you are certain to discover some good sources of jobs.

Most college career libraries now hold growing collections of video material on specific industries and on aspects of your job search process, including dress and appearance, how to manage the luncheon or dinner interview, how to be effective at a job fair, and many other specific titles. Some larger corporations produce handsome video materials detailing the variety of career paths and opportunities available in their organizations.

Some career libraries also house computer-based career planning and information systems. These interactive computer programs help you to clarify your values and interests and will combine that with your education to provide possible job titles and industry locations. Some even contain extensive lists of graduate school programs.

One specific kind of service a career library will be able to direct you to is computerized job search services. These services, of which there are many, are run by private companies, individual colleges, or consortiums of colleges. They attempt to match qualified job candidates with potential employers. The candidate submits a resume (or an application) to the service. This information (which can be categorized into hundreds of separate "fields" of data) is entered into a computer database. Your information is then compared with the information from employers about what they desire in a prospective employee. If there is a "match" between what they want and what you have indicated you can offer, the job search service or the employer will contact you directly to continue the process.

Computerized job search services can complement an otherwise complete job search program. They are *not*, however, a substitute for the kinds of activities described in this book. They are essentially passive operations that are random in nature. If you have not listed skills, abilities, traits, experiences, or education *exactly* as an employer has listed its needs, there is simply no match.

Consult with the staff members at the career libraries you use. These professionals have been specifically trained to meet the unique needs you present. Often you can just drop in and receive help with general questions, or you may want to set up an appointment to speak one-on-one with a career counselor to gain special assistance.

Every career library is different in size and content, but each can provide valuable information for the job search. Some may even provide some limited counseling. If you have not visited the career library at your college or alma mater, call and ask if these collections are still available for your use. Be sure to ask about other services that you can use as well.

If you are not near your own college as you work on your job search, call the career office and inquire about reciprocal agreements with other colleges that are closer to where you live. Very often your own alma mater can arrange for you to use a limited menu of services at another school. This typically would include access to a career library and job posting information and might include limited counseling.

CHAPTER FOUR

NETWORKING

*N*etworking is the process of deliberately establishing relationships to get career-related information or to alert potential employers that you are available for work. Networking is critically important to today's job seeker for two reasons: it will help you get the information you need, and it can help you find out about *all* of the available jobs.

Getting the Information You Need

Networkers will review your resume and give you feedback on its effectiveness. They will talk about the job you are looking for and give you a candid appraisal of how they see your strengths and weaknesses. If they have a good sense of the industry or the employment sector for that job, you'll get their feelings on future trends in the industry as well. Some networkers will be very forthcoming about salaries, job-hunting techniques, and suggestions for your job search strategy. Many have been known to place calls right from the interview desk to friends and associates who might be interested in you. Each networker will make his or her own contribution, and each will be valuable.

Because organizations must evolve to adapt to current global market needs, the information provided by decision makers within various organizations will be critical to your success as a new job market entrant. For example, you might learn about the concept of virtual organizations from a networker. Virtual organizations coordinate economic activity to deliver value to customers using resources outside the traditional boundaries of the organization. This concept is being discussed and implemented by chief executive officers of many organizations, including Ford Motor, Dell, and IBM.

Networking can help you find out about this and other trends currently affecting the industries under your consideration.

Finding Out About All of the Available Jobs

Not every job that is available at this very moment is advertised for potential applicants to see. This is called the *hidden job market*. Only 15 to 20 percent of all jobs are formally advertised, which means that 80 to 85 percent of available jobs do not appear in published channels. Networking will help you become more knowledgeable about all the employment opportunities available during your job search period.

Although someone you might talk to today doesn't know of any openings within his or her organization, tomorrow or next week or next month an opening may occur. If you've taken the time to show an interest in and knowledge of their organization, if you've shown the company representative how you can help achieve organizational goals and that you can fit into the organization, you'll be one of the first candidates considered for the position.

Networking: A Proactive Approach

Networking is a proactive rather than a reactive approach. You, as a job seeker, are expected to initiate a certain level of activity on your own behalf; you cannot afford to simply respond to jobs listed in the newspaper. Being proactive means building a network of contacts that includes informed and interested decision makers who will provide you with up-to-date knowledge of the current job market and increase your chances of finding out about employment opportunities appropriate for your interests, experience, and level of education.

An old axiom of networking says "You are only two phone calls away from the information you need." In other words, by talking to enough people, you will quickly come across someone who can offer you help. Start with your professors. Each of them probably has a wide circle of contacts. In their work and travel they might have met someone who can help you or direct you to someone who can.

Control and the Networking Process

In deliberately establishing relationships, the process of networking begins with you in control—*you* are contacting specific individuals. As your network expands and you establish a set of professional relationships, your search for information or jobs will begin to move outside of your total control. A part of the networking process involves others assisting you by gathering information for you or recommending you as a possible job candidate. As additional people become a part of your networking system, you will have less knowledge about activities undertaken on your behalf; you will undoubt-edly be contacted by individuals whom you did not initially approach. If you want to function effectively in surprise situations, you must be prepared at all times to talk with strangers about the informational or employment needs that motivated you to become involved in the networking process.

PREPARING TO NETWORK

In deliberately establishing relationships, maximize your efforts by organiz-ing your approach. Five specific areas in which you can organize your efforts include reviewing your self-assessment, reviewing your research on job sites and organizations, deciding who it is you want to talk to, keeping track of all your efforts, and creating your self-promotion tools.

Review Your Self-Assessment

Your self-assessment is as important a tool in preparing to network as it has been in other aspects of your job search. You have carefully evaluated your personal traits, personal values, economic needs, longer-term goals, skill base, preferred skills, and underdeveloped skills. During the networking process you will be called upon to communicate what you know about yourself and relate it to the information or job you seek. Be sure to review the exercises that you completed in the self-assessment section of this book in prepara-tion for networking. We've explained that you need to assess what skills you have acquired from your major that are of general value to an employer and to be ready to express those in ways employers can appreciate as useful in their own organizations.

Review Research on Job Sites and Organizations

In addition, individuals assisting you will expect that you'll have at least some background information on the occupation or industry of interest to you. Refer to the appropriate sections of this book and other relevant publications to acquire the background information necessary for effective networking. They'll explain how to identify not only the job titles that might be of interest to you, but also what kinds of organizations employ people to do that job. You will develop some sense of working conditions and expectations about duties and responsibilities—all of which will be of help in your networking interviews.

Decide Who It Is You Want to Talk To

Networking cannot begin until you decide who it is that you want to talk to and, in general, what type of information you hope to gain from your contacts. Once you know this, it's time to begin developing a list of contacts. Five useful sources for locating contacts are described here.

College Alumni Network. Most colleges and universities have created a formal network of alumni and friends of the institution who are particularly interested in helping currently enrolled students and graduates of their alma mater gain employment-related information.

....

Because English is a classic degree program, you'll find an abundance of English graduates spanning the full spectrum of possible employment. Just the diversity of employment by such an alumni list should be encouraging and informative to the English graduate. Among such a diversified group, there are likely to be scores you would enjoy talking with and perhaps meet.

....

It is usually a simple process to make use of an alumni network. You need only visit the alumni or career office at your college or university and follow the procedure that has been established. Often, you will simply complete a form indicating your career goals and interests and you will be given the names of appropriate individuals to contact. In many cases staff members will coach you on how to make the best use of the limited time these alumni contacts may have available for you.

Alumni networkers may provide some combination of the following services: day-long shadowing experiences, telephone interviews, in-person interviews, information on relocating to given geographic areas, internship information, suggestions on graduate school study, and job vacancy notices.

....

What a valuable experience! Perhaps you are interested in public relations (PR) but don't think your writing skills are up to the expectations of most employers in this area. Spending a day with an alumnus in PR, asking lots of questions about the role of writing in his or her job, and observing firsthand how much and what kind of writing is going on will be a far better decision criterion for you than any reading on the subject could possibly provide.

In addition to your own observations, the alumnus will have his or her own perspective on the importance of writing to a public relations career and which settings emphasize writing and which may not. The PR professional will give you realistic and honest feedback on your job search concerns.

....

Present and Former Supervisors. If you believe you are on good terms with present or former job supervisors, they may be an excellent resource for providing information or directing you to appropriate resources that would have information related to your current interests and needs. Additionally, these supervisors probably belong to professional organizations that they might be willing to utilize to get information for you.

....

If, for example, you were interested in working as a research associate and you were currently working on the wait staff of a local restaurant, talk with your supervisor or the owner. He or she may belong to the local chamber of commerce, whose director would have information on local employers who conduct research as part of their operations. You would probably be able to obtain the names and telephone numbers of these people, which would allow you to begin the networking process.

....

Employers in Your Area. Although you may be interested in working in a geographic location different from the one where you currently reside, don't overlook the value of the knowledge and contacts those around you are able to provide. Use the local telephone directory and newspaper to identify the types of organizations you are thinking of working for or professionals who have the kinds of jobs you are interested in. Recently, a call made to a local hospital's financial administrator for information on working in health-care financial administration yielded more pertinent information on training seminars, regional professional organizations, and potential employment sites than a national organization was willing to provide.

Employers in Geographic Areas Where You Hope to Work. If you are thinking about relocating, identifying prospective employers or informational contacts in this new location will be critical to your success. Many resources are available to help you locate contact names. These include the yellow pages directory, the local newspapers, local or state business publications, and local chambers of commerce.

Professional Associations and Organizations. Professional associations and organizations can provide valuable information in several areas: career paths that you may not have considered, qualifications relating to those career choices, publications that list current job openings, and workshops or seminars that will enhance your professional knowledge and skills. They can also be excellent sources for background information on given industries: their health, current problems, and future challenges.

There are several excellent resources available to help you locate professional associations and organizations that would have information to meet your needs. Two especially useful publications are the *Encyclopedia of Associations* and *National Trade and Professional Associations of the United States.*

Keep Track of All Your Efforts

It can be difficult, almost impossible, to remember all the details related to each contact you make during the networking process, so you will want to develop a record-keeping system that works for you. Formalize this process by using a notebook or index cards to organize the information you gather. Begin by creating a list of the people or organizations you want to contact. Record the contact's name, address, telephone number, and what information you hope to gain. Each entry might look something like this:

Contact Name	Address/E-Mail	Phone/Fax	Purpose
Mr. Tim Keefe	Wrigley Bldg.	(P) (312) 555-8906	Resume
Dir. of Mines	Suite 72	(F) (312) 555-9806	screen
	tkeefe@mail.com		

Once you have created this initial list, it will be helpful to keep more detailed information as you begin to actually make the contacts. Using the Network Contact Record form in Exhibit 4.1 will help you keep good information on all your network contacts. They'll appreciate your recall of details of your meetings and conversations, and the information will help you to focus your networking efforts.

Exhibit 4.1

Network Contact Record

Name: Be certain your spelling is absolutely correct.

Title: Pick up a business card to be certain of the correct title.

Employing organization: Note any parent company or subsidiaries.

Business mailing address: This is often different from the street address.

Business E-mail address:

Business telephone number: Include area code and alternative numbers.

Business fax number:

Source for this contact: Who referred you, and what is their relationship to the contact?

Date of call or letter: Use plenty of space here to record multiple phone calls or visits, other employees you may have met, names of secretaries/receptionists, etc.

Content of discussion: Keep enough notes here to remind you of the substance of your visits and telephone conversations in case some time elapses between contacts.

Follow-up necessary to continue working with this contact: Your contact may request that you send him or her some materials or direct you to contact an associate. Note any such instructions or assignments in this space.

Name of additional networker: Here you would record the
Address: names and phone numbers of
E-Mail: additional contacts met at this
Phone: employer's site. Often you will
Fax: be introduced to many people,
Name of additional networker: some of whom may indicate
Address: a willingness to help in your
E-mail: job search.
Phone:
Fax:

Name of additional networker:	
Address:	
E-mail:	
Phone:	
Fax:	
Date thank-you note written:	May help to date your next contact.
Follow-up action taken:	Phone calls, visits, additional notes.
Other miscellaneous notes:	Record any other additional interaction you think may be important to remember in working with this networking client. You will want this form in front of you when telephoning or just before and after a visit.

Create Your Self-Promotion Tools

There are two types of promotional tools that are used in the networking process. The first is a resume and cover letter, and the second is a one-minute "infomercial," which may be given over the telephone or in person.

Techniques for writing an effective resume and cover letter are discussed in Chapter 2. Once you have reviewed that material and prepared these important documents, you will have created one of your self-promotion tools.

The one-minute infomercial will demand that you begin tying your interests, abilities, and skills to the people or organizations you want to network with. Think about your goal for making the contact to help you understand what you should say about yourself. You should be able to express yourself easily and convincingly. If, for example, you are contacting an alumnus of your institution to obtain the names of possible employment sites in a distant city, be prepared to discuss why you are interested in moving to that location, the types of jobs you are interested in, and the skills and abilities you possess that will make you a qualified candidate.

To create a meaningful one-minute infomercial, write it out, practice it if it will be a spoken presentation, rewrite it, and practice it again if necessary until expressing yourself comes easily and is convincing.

Here's a simplified example of an infomercial for use over the telephone:

•••

Hello, Mr. Jones? My name is Joan Standish. I am a recent graduate of Polytechnic University, and I wish to enter the public relations field. I was an English major and feel confident I have many of the skills I understand are valued in PR, such as writing, speaking, preparing, and delivering effective presentations. What's more, I work well under pressure. I have read that can be a real advantage in your business!

Mr. Jones, I'm calling you because I still need more information about the PR field. I'm hoping you'll have the time to sit down with me for about half an hour and discuss your perspective on PR careers with me. There are so many possible places to practice public relations, and I am seeking some advice on which of those settings might be the best bet for my particular combination of skills and experience.

Would you be willing to do that for me? I would greatly appreciate it. I am available most mornings, if that's convenient for you.

It very well may happen that your employer contact wishes you to communicate by E-mail. The infomercial quoted above could easily be rewritten for an E-mail message. You should "cut and paste" your resume right into the E-mail text itself.

Other effective self-promotion tools include portfolios for those in the arts, writing professions, or teaching. Portfolios show examples of work, photographs of projects or classroom activities, or certificates and credentials that are job related. There may not be an opportunity to use the portfolio during an interview, and it is not something that should be left with the organization. It is designed to be explained and displayed by the creator. However, during some networking meetings, there may be an opportunity to illustrate a point or strengthen a qualification by exhibiting the portfolio.

BEGINNING THE NETWORKING PROCESS

Set the Tone for Your Contacts

It can be useful to establish "tone words" for any communications you embark upon. Before making your first telephone call or writing your first letter, decide what you want your contact to think of you. If you are networking to try to obtain a job, your tone words might include words like *genuine, informed,* and *self-knowledgeable.* When trying to acquire information, your tone words may have a slightly different focus, such as *courteous, organized, focused,* and *well-spoken.* Use the tone words you establish for your contacts to guide you through the networking process.

Honestly Express Your Intentions

When contacting individuals, it is important to be honest about your reasons for making the contact. Establish your purpose in your own mind and be able and ready to articulate it concisely. Determine an initial agenda, whether it be informational questioning or self-promotion, present it to your contact, and be ready to respond immediately. If you don't adequately prepare before initiating your contacts, you may find yourself at a disadvantage if you're asked to immediately begin your informational interview or self-promotion during the first phone conversation or visit.

Start Networking Within Your Circle of Confidence

Once you have organized your approach—by utilizing specific researching methods, creating a system for keeping track of the people you will contact, and developing effective self-promotion tools—you are ready to begin networking. The best way to begin networking is by talking with a group of people you trust and feel comfortable with. This group is usually made up of your family, friends, and career counselors. No matter who is in this inner circle, they will have a special interest in seeing you succeed in your job search. In addition, because they will be easy to talk to, you should try taking some risks in terms of practicing your information-seeking approach. Gain confidence in talking about the strengths you bring to an organization and the underdeveloped skills you feel hinder your candidacy. Be sure to review the section on self-assessment for tips on approaching each of these areas. Ask for critical but constructive feedback from the people in your circle of confidence on the letters you write and the one-minute infomercial you have developed. Evaluate whether you want to make the changes they suggest, then practice the changes on others within this circle.

Stretch the Boundaries of Your Networking Circle of Confidence

Once you have refined the promotional tools you will use to accomplish your networking goals, you will want to make additional contacts. Because you will not know most of these people, it will be a less comfortable activity to undertake. The practice that you gained with your inner circle of trusted friends should have prepared you to now move outside of that comfort zone.

It is said that any information a person needs is only two phone calls away, but the information cannot be gained until you (1) make a reasonable guess about who might have the information you need and (2) pick up the telephone to make the call. Using your network list that includes alumni, instructors, supervisors, employers, and associations, you can begin preparing your list of questions that will allow you to get the information you need. Review the question list that follows and then develop a list of your own.

Questions You Might Want to Ask

1. In the position you now hold, what do you do on a typical day?

2. What are the most interesting aspects of your job?

3. What part of your work do you consider dull or repetitious?

4. What were the jobs you had that led to your present position?

5. How long does it usually take to move from one step to the next in this career path?

6. What is the top position to which you can aspire in this career path?

7. What is the next step in *your* career path?

8. Are there positions in this field that are similar to your position?

9. What are the required qualifications and training for entry-level positions in this field?

10. Are there specific courses a student should take to be qualified to work in this field?

11. What are the entry-level jobs in this field?

12. What types of training are provided to persons entering this field?

13. What are the salary ranges your organization typically offers to entry-level candidates for positions in this field?

14. What special advice would you give a person entering this field?

15. Do you see this field as a growing one?

16. How do you see the content of the entry-level jobs in this field changing over the next two years?

17. What can I do to prepare myself for these changes?

18. What is the best way to obtain a position that will start me on a career in this field?

19. Do you have any information on job specifications and descriptions that I may have?

20. What related occupational fields would you suggest I explore?

21. How could I improve my resume for a career in this field?

22. Who else would you suggest I talk to, both in your organization and in other organizations?

Questions You Might Have to Answer

In order to communicate effectively, you must anticipate questions that will be asked of you by the networkers you contact. Review the list below and see if you can easily answer each of these questions. If you cannot, it may be time to revisit the self-assessment process.

1. Where did you get my name, or how did you find out about this organization?

2. What are your career goals?

3. What kind of job are you interested in?

4. What do you know about this organization and this industry?

5. How do you know you're prepared to undertake an entry-level position in this industry?

6. What course work have you done that is related to your career interests?

7. What are your short-term career goals?

8. What are your long-term career goals?

9. Do you plan to obtain additional formal education?

10. What contributions have you made to previous employers?

11. Which of your previous jobs have you enjoyed the most, and why?

12. What are you particularly good at doing?

13. What shortcomings have you had to face in previous employment?

14. What are your three greatest strengths?

15. How comfortable do you feel with your communication style?

General Networking Tips

Make Every Contact Count. Setting the tone for each interaction is critical. Approaches that will help you communicate in an effective way include politeness, being appreciative of time provided to you, and being prepared and thorough. Remember, *everyone* within an organization has a circle of influence, so be prepared to interact effectively with each person you encounter in the networking process, including secretarial and support staff. Many information or job seekers have thwarted their own efforts by being rude to some individuals they encountered as they networked because they made the incorrect assumption that certain persons were unimportant.

Sometimes your contacts may be surprised at their ability to help you. After meeting and talking with you, they might think they have not offered much in the way of help. A day or two later, however, they may make a contact that would be useful to you and refer you to it.

With Each Contact, Widen Your Circle of Networkers. Always leave an informational interview with the names of at least two more people who can help you get the information or job that you are seeking. Don't be shy about asking for additional contacts; networking is all about increasing the number of people you can interact with to achieve your goals.

Make Your Own Decisions. As you talk with different people and get answers to the questions you pose, you may hear conflicting information or get conflicting suggestions. Your job is to listen to these "experts" and decide what information and which suggestions will help you achieve *your* goals. Only implement those suggestions that you believe will work for you.

SHUTTING DOWN YOUR NETWORK

As you achieve the goals that motivated your networking activity—getting the information you need or the job you want—the time will come to inactivate all or parts of your network. As you do so, be sure to tell your primary supporters about your change in status. Call or write to each one of them and give them as many details about your new status as you feel is necessary to maintain a positive relationship.

Because a network takes on a life of its own, activity undertaken on your behalf will continue even after you cease your efforts. As you get calls or are contacted in some fashion, be sure to inform these networkers about your change in status, and thank them for assistance they have provided.

Information on the latest employment trends indicates that workers will change jobs or careers several times in their lifetime. Networking, then, will be a critical aspect in the span of your professional life. If you carefully and thoughtfully conduct your networking activities during your job search, you will have a solid foundation of experience when you need to network the next time around.

CHAPTER FIVE

INTERVIEWING

*C*ertainly, there can be no one part of the job search process more fraught with anxiety and worry than the interview. Yet seasoned job seekers welcome the interview and will often say "Just get me an interview and I'm on my way!" They understand that the interview is crucial to the hiring process and equally crucial for them, as job candidates, to have the opportunity of a personal dialogue to add to what the employer may already have learned from a resume, cover letter, and telephone conversations.

Believe it or not, the interview is to be welcomed, and even enjoyed! It is a perfect opportunity for you, the candidate, to sit down with an employer and express yourself and display who you are and what you want. Of course, it takes thought and planning and a little strategy; after all, it *is* a job interview! But it can be a positive, if not pleasant, experience and one you can look back on and feel confident about your performance and effort.

For many new job seekers, a job, any job, seems a wonderful thing. But seasoned interview veterans know that the job interview is an important step for both sides—the employer and the candidate—to see what each has to offer and whether there is going to be a "fit" of personalities, work styles, and attitudes. And it is this concept of balance in the interview, that both sides have important parts to play, that holds the key to success in mastering this aspect of the job search strategy.

Try to think of the interview as a conversation between two interested and equal partners. You both have important, even vital, information to deliver and to learn. Of course, there's no denying the employer has some leverage, especially in the initial interview for recruitment or any interview scheduled by the candidate and not the recruiter. That should not prevent the interviewee from seeking to play an equal part in what should be a fair exchange of information. Too often the untutored candidate allows the interview to become one-sided. The employer asks all the questions and the candidate simply responds. The ideal would be for two mutually interested parties to sit down and discuss possibilities for each. This is a *conversation of significance,* and it requires pre-interview preparation, thought about the tone of the interview, and planning of the nature and details of the information to be exchanged.

PREPARING FOR THE INTERVIEW

Most initial interviews are about thirty minutes long. Given the brevity, the information that is exchanged ought to be important. The candidate should be delivering material that the employer cannot discover on the resume and, in turn, the candidate should be learning things about the employer that he or she could not otherwise find out. After all, if you have only thirty minutes, why waste time on information that is already published? The information exchanged is more than just factual, and both sides will learn much from what they see of each other, as well. How the candidate looks, speaks, and acts is important to the employer. The employer's attention to the interview and awareness of the candidate's resume, the setting, and the quality of information presented are important to the candidate.

Just as the employer has every right to be disappointed when a prospect is late for the interview, looks unkempt, and seems ill-prepared to answer fairly standard questions, the candidate may be disappointed with an interviewer who isn't ready for the meeting, hasn't learned the basic resume facts, and is constantly interrupted for telephone calls. In either situation there's good reason to feel let down.

There are many elements to a successful interview, and some of them are not easy to describe or prepare for. Sometimes there is just a chemistry between interviewer and interviewee that brings out the best in both, and a good exchange takes place. But there is much the candidate can do to pave the way for success in terms of his or her resume, personal appearance, goals, and interview strategy—each of which we will discuss. However, none of this preparation is as important as the time and thought the candidate gives to personal self-assessment.

Self-Assessment

Neither a stunning resume nor an expensive, well-tailored suit can compensate for candidates who do not know what they want, where they are going, or why they are interviewing with a particular employer. Self-assessment, the process by which we begin to know and acknowledge our own particular blend of education, experiences, needs, and goals, is not something that can be sorted out the weekend before a major interview. Of all the elements of interview preparation, this one requires the longest lead time and cannot be faked.

Because the time allotted for most interviews is brief, it is all the more important for job candidates to understand and express succinctly why they are there and what they have to offer. This is not a time for undue modesty (or for braggadocio either); it is a time for a compelling, reasoned statement of why you feel that you and this employer might make a good match. It means you have to have thought about your skills, interests, and attributes; related those to your life experiences and your own history of challenges and opportunities; and determined what that indicates about your strengths, preferences, values, and areas needing further development.

A common complaint of employers is that many candidates didn't take advantage of the interview time, didn't seem to know why they were there or what they wanted. When candidates are asked to talk about themselves and their work-related skills and attributes, employers don't want to be faced with shyness or embarrassed laughter; they need to know about you so they can make a fair determination of you and your competition. If you lose the opportunity to make a case for your employability, you can be certain the person ahead of you has or the person after you will, and it will be on the strength of those impressions that the employer will hire.

If you need some assistance with self-assessment issues, refer to Chapter 1. Included are suggested exercises that can be done as needed, such as making up an experiential diary and extracting obvious strengths and weaknesses from past experiences. These simple assignments will help you look at past activities as collections of tasks with accompanying skills and responsibilities. Don't overlook your high school or college career office. Many offer personal counseling on self-assessment issues and may provide testing instruments such as the Myers-Briggs Type Indicator (MBTI), the Harrington-O'Shea Career Decision Making System (CDM), the Strong Interest Inventory (SII), or any of a wide selection of assessment tools that can help you clarify some of these issues prior to the interview stage of your job search.

The Resume

Resume preparation has been discussed in detail, and some basic examples of various types were provided. In this section we want to concentrate on how best to use your resume in the interview. In most cases the employer will have seen the resume prior to the interview, and, in fact, it may well have been the quality of that resume that secured the interview opportunity.

An interview is a conversation, however, and not an exercise in reading. So, if the employer hasn't seen your resume and you have brought it along to the interview, wait until asked or until the end of the interview to offer it. Otherwise, you may find yourself staring at the back of your resume and simply answering "yes" and "no" to a series of questions drawn from that document.

Sometimes an interviewer is not prepared and does not know or recall the contents of the resume and may use the resume to a greater or lesser degree as a "prompt" during the interview. It is for you to judge what that may indicate about the individual doing the interview or the employer. If your interviewer seems surprised by the scheduled meeting, relies on the resume to an inordinate degree, and seems otherwise unfamiliar with your background, this lack of preparation for the hiring process could well be a symptom of general management disorganization or may simply be the result of poor planning on the part of one individual. It is your responsibility as a potential employee to be aware of these signals and make your decisions accordingly.

· ·

In any event, it is perfectly acceptable for you to get the conversation back to a more interpersonal style by saying something like, "Mr. Smith, you might be interested in some recent writing experience I gained through an internship that is not detailed on my resume. May I tell you about it?" This can return the interview to two people talking to each other, not one reading and the other responding.

· ·

By all means, bring at least one copy of your resume to the interview. Occasionally, at the close of an interview, an interviewer will express an interest in circulating a resume to several departments, and you could then offer the copy you brought. Sometimes an interview appointment provides an opportunity to meet others in the organization who may express an interest in you and your background, and it may be helpful to follow up with a copy of your resume. Our best advice, however, is to keep it out of sight until needed or requested.

Appearance

Although many of the absolute rules that once dominated the advice offered to job candidates about appearance have now been moderated significantly, conservative is still the watchword unless you are interviewing in a fashion-related industry. For men, conservative translates into a well-cut dark suit with appropriate tie, hosiery, and dress shirt. A wise strategy for the male job seeker looking for a good but not expensive suit would be to try the men's department of a major department store. They usually carry a good range of sizes, fabrics, and prices; offer professional sales help; provide free tailoring; and have associated departments for putting together a professional look.

For women, there is more latitude. Business suits are still popular, but they have become more feminine in color and styling with a variety of jacket and skirt lengths. In addition to suits, better-quality dresses are now worn in many environments and, with the correct accessories, can be most appropriate. Company literature, professional magazines, the business section of major newspapers, and television interviews can all give clues about what is being worn in different employer environments.

Both men and women need to pay attention to issues such as hair, jewelry, and makeup; these are often what separates the candidate in appearance from the professional workforce. It seems particularly difficult for the young job seeker to give up certain hairstyles, eyeglass fashions, and jewelry habits, yet those can be important to the employer, who is concerned with your ability to successfully make the transition into the organization. Candidates often find the best strategy is to dress conservatively until they find employment. Once employed and familiar with the norms within your organization, you can begin to determine a look that you enjoy, works for you, and fits your organization.

Choose clothes that suit your body type, fit well, and flatter you. Feel good about the way you look! The interview day is not the best for a new hairdo, a new pair of shoes, or any other change that will distract you or cause you to be self-conscious. Arrive a bit early to avoid being rushed, and ask the receptionist to direct you to a restroom for any last-minute adjustments of hair and clothes.

Employer Information

Whether your interview is for graduate school admission, an overseas corporate position, or a reporter position with a local newspaper, it is important to know something about the employer or the organization. Keeping in mind that the interview is relatively brief and that you will hopefully have other interviews with other organizations, it is important to keep your research in proportion. If secondary interviews are called for, you will have additional time to do further research. For the first interview, it is helpful to know the organization's mission, goals, size, scope of operations, etc. Your research may uncover recent areas of challenge or particular successes that may help to fuel the interview. Use the "Where Are These Jobs, Anyway?" section of Chapter 3, the Internet, your library, and your career or guidance office to help you locate this information in the most efficient way possible. Don't be shy in asking advice of these counseling and guidance professionals on how best to spend your preparation time. With some practice, you'll soon learn how much information is enough and which kinds of information are most useful to you.

INTERVIEW CONTENT

We've already discussed how it can help to think of the interview as an important conversation—one that, as with any conversation, you want to find pleasant and interesting and to leave you with a good feeling. But because this conversation is especially important, the information that's exchanged is critical to its success. What do you want them to know about you? What do you need to know about them? What interview technique do you need to particularly pay attention to? How do you want to manage the close of the interview? What steps will follow in the hiring process?

Except for the professional interviewer, most of us find interviewing stressful and anxiety-provoking. Developing a strategy before you begin interviewing will help you relieve some stress and anxiety. One particular strategy that has worked for many and may work for you is interviewing by objective. Before you interview, write down three to five goals you would like to achieve for that interview. They may be technique goals: smile a little more, have a firmer handshake, be sure to ask about the next stage in the interview process before leaving. They may be content-oriented goals: find out about the company's current challenges and opportunities, be sure to speak of your recent research writing experiences or foreign travel, etc. Whatever your goals, jot down a few of them as goals for each interview.

Most people find that, in trying to achieve these few goals, their interviewing technique becomes more organized and focused. After the interview, the most common question friends and family ask is "How did it go?" With this technique, you have an indication of whether you met *your* goals for the meeting, not just some vague idea of how it went. Chances are, if you accomplished what you wanted to, it improved the quality of the entire interview. As you continue to interview, you will want to revise your goals to continue improving your interview skills.

Now, add to the concept of the significant conversation the idea of a beginning, a middle, and a closing and you will have two thoughts that will give your interview a distinctive character. Be sure to make your introduction warm and cordial. Say your full name (and if it's a difficult-to-pronounce name, help the interviewer to pronounce it) and make certain you know your interviewer's name and how to pronounce it. Most interviews begin with some "soft talk" about the weather, chat about the candidate's trip to the interview site, national events, etc. This is done as a courtesy to relax both you and the interviewer, to get you talking, and to generally try to defuse the atmosphere of excessive tension. Try to be yourself, engage in the conversation, and don't try to second-guess the interviewer. This is simply what it appears to be—casual conversation.

Once you and the interviewer move on to exchange more serious information in the middle part of the interview, the two most important concerns become your ability to handle challenging questions and your success at asking meaningful ones. Interviewer questions will probably fall into one of three categories: personal assessment and career direction, academic background, and knowledge of the employer. The following are some examples of questions in each category:

Personal Assessment and Career Direction

1. How would you describe yourself?
2. What motivates you to put forth your best effort?
3. In what kind of work environment are you most comfortable?
4. What do you consider to be your greatest strengths and weaknesses?
5. How well do you work under pressure?
6. What qualifications do you have that make you think you will be successful in this career?
7. Will you relocate? What do you feel would be the most difficult aspect of relocating?
8. Are you willing to travel?
9. Why should I hire you?

Academic Assessment

1. Why did you select your college or university?
2. What changes would you make at your alma mater?
3. What led you to choose your major?
4. What subjects did you like best and least? Why?
5. If you could, how would you plan your academic study differently? Why?
6. Describe your most rewarding college experience.
7. How has your college experience prepared you for this career?
8. Do you think that your grades are a good indication of your ability to succeed with this organization?
9. Do you have plans for continued study?

Knowledge of the Employer

1. If you were hiring a graduate of your school for this position, what qualities would you look for?

2. What do you think it takes to be successful in an organization like ours?

3. In what ways do you think you can make a contribution to our organization?

4. Why did you choose to seek a position with this organization?

The interviewer wants a response to each question but is also gauging your enthusiasm, preparedness, and willingness to communicate. In each response you should provide some information about yourself that can be related to the employer's needs. A common mistake is to give too much information. Answer each question completely, but be careful not to run on too long with extensive details or examples.

Questions About Underdeveloped Skills

Most employers interview people who have met some minimum criteria of education and experience. They interview candidates to see who they are, to learn what kind of personality they exhibit, and to get some sense of how this person might fit into the existing organization. It may be that you are asked about skills the employer hopes to find and that you have not documented. Maybe it's grant-writing experience, knowledge of the European political system, or a knowledge of the film world.

To questions about skills and experiences you don't have, answer honestly and forthrightly and try to offer some additional information about skills you do have. For example, perhaps the employer is disappointed you have no grant-writing experience. An honest answer may be as follows:

> No, unfortunately, I was never in a position to acquire those skills. I do understand something of the complexities of the grant-writing process and feel confident that my attention to detail, careful reading skills, and strong writing would make grants a wonderful challenge in a new job. I think I could get up on the learning curve quickly.

The employer hears an honest admission of lack of experience but is reassured by some specific skill details that do relate to grant writing and a confident manner that suggests enthusiasm and interest in a challenge.

For many students, questions about their possible contribution to an employer's organization can prove challenging. Because your education has probably not included specific training for a job, you need to review your academic record and select capabilities you have developed in your major that an employer can appreciate. For example, perhaps you read well and can analyze and condense what you've read into smaller, more focused pieces. That could be valuable. Or maybe you did some serious research and you know you have valuable investigative skills. Your public speaking might be highly developed and you might use visual aids appropriately and effectively. Or maybe your skill at correspondence, memos, and messages is effective. Whatever it is, you must take it out of the academic context and put it into a new, employer-friendly context so your interviewer can best judge how you could help the organization.

Exhibiting knowledge of the organization will, without a doubt, show the interviewer that you are interested enough in the available position to have done some legwork in preparation for the interview. Remember, it is not necessary to know every detail of the organization's history, but rather to have a general knowledge about why it is in business and how the industry is faring.

Sometime during the interview, generally after the midway point, you'll be asked if you have any questions for the interviewer. Your questions will tell the employer much about your attitude and your desire to understand the organization's expectations so you can compare it to your own strengths. The following are some selected questions you might want to ask:

1. What are the main responsibilities of the position?

2. What are the opportunities and challenges associated with this position?

3. Could you outline some possible career paths beginning with this position?

4. How regularly do performance evaluations occur?

5. What is the communication style of the organization? (meetings, memos, etc.)

6. What would a typical day in this position be like for me?

7. What kinds of opportunities might exist for me to improve my professional skills within the organization?

8. What have been some of the interesting challenges and opportunities your organization has recently faced?

Most interviews draw to a natural closing point, so be careful not to prolong the discussion. At a signal from the interviewer, wind up your presentation, express your appreciation for the opportunity, and be sure to ask what the next stage in the process will be. When can you expect to hear from them?

Will they be conducting second-tier interviews? If you're interested and haven't heard, would they mind a phone call? Be sure to collect a business card with the name and phone number of your interviewer. On your way out, you might have an opportunity to pick up organizational literature you haven't seen before.

With the right preparation—a thorough self-assessment, professional clothing, and employer information—you'll be able to set and achieve the goals you have established for the interview process.

CHAPTER SIX

NETWORKING OR INTERVIEWING FOLLOW-UP

Quite often there is a considerable time lag between interviewing for a position and being hired, or, in the case of the networker, between your phone call or letter to a possible contact and the opportunity of a meeting. This can be frustrating. "Why aren't they contacting me?" "I thought I'd get another interview, but no one has telephoned." "Am I out of the running?" You don't know what is happening.

CONSIDER THE DIFFERING PERSPECTIVES

Of course, there is another perspective—that of the networker or hiring organization. Organizations are complex, with multiple tasks that need to be accomplished each day. Hiring is but one discrete activity that does not occur as frequently as other job assignments. The hiring process might have to take second place to other, more immediate organizational needs. Although it may be very important to you and it is certainly ultimately significant to the employer, other issues such as fiscal management, planning and product development, employer vacation periods, or financial constraints may prevent an organization or individual within that organization from acting on your employment or your request for information as quickly as you or they would prefer.

USE YOUR COMMUNICATION SKILLS

Good communication is essential here to resolve any anxieties, and the responsibility is on you, the job or information seeker. Too many job seekers and networkers offer as an excuse that they don't want to "bother" the organization by writing letters or calling. Let us assure you here and now, once and for all, that if you are troubling an organization by over-communicating, someone will indicate that situation to you quite clearly. If not, you can only assume you are a worthwhile prospect and the employer appreciates being reminded of your availability and interest in them. Let's look at follow-up practices in both the job interview process and the networking situation separately.

FOLLOWING UP ON THE EMPLOYMENT INTERVIEW

A brief thank-you note following an interview is an excellent and polite way to begin a series of follow-up communications with a potential employer with whom you have interviewed and want to remain in touch. It should be just that—a thank you for a good meeting. If you failed to mention some fact or experience during your interview that you think might add to your candidacy, you may use this note to do that. However, this should be essentially a note whose overall tone is appreciative and, if appropriate, indicative of a continuing interest in pursuing any opportunity that may exist with that organization. It is one of the few pieces of business correspondence that may be handwritten, but always use plain, good quality, standard-size paper.

If, however, at this point you are no longer interested in the employer, the thank-you note is an appropriate time to indicate that. You are under no obligation to identify any reason for not continuing to pursue employment with that organization, but if you are so inclined to indicate your professional reasons (pursuing other employers more akin to your interests, looking for greater income production than this employer can provide, a different geographic location than is available, etc.), you certainly may. It should not be written with an eye to negotiation for it will not be interpreted as such.

As part of your interview closing, you should have taken the initiative to establish lines of communication for continuing information about your candidacy. If you asked permission to telephone, wait a week following your thank-you note, then telephone your contact simply to inquire how things are progressing on your employment status. The feedback you receive here should be taken at face value. If your interviewer simply has no information, he or she will tell you so and indicate whether you should call again and when. Don't be discouraged if this should continue over some period of time.

If during this time something occurs that you think improves or changes your candidacy (some new qualification or experience you may have had), including any offers from other organizations, by all means telephone or write to inform the employer about this. In the case of an offer from a competing but less desirable or equally desirable organization, telephone your contact, explain what has happened, express your real interest in the organization, and inquire whether some determination on your employment might be made before you must respond to this other offer. If the organization is truly interested in you, they may be moved to make a decision about your candidacy. Equally possible is the scenario in which they are not yet ready to make a decision and so advise you to take the offer that has been presented. Again, you have no ethical alternative but to deal with the information presented in a straightforward manner.

When accepting other employment, be sure to contact any employers still actively considering you and inform them of your new job. Thank them graciously for their consideration. There are many other job seekers out there just like you who will benefit from having their candidacy improved when others bow out of the race. Who knows, you might at some future time have occasion to interact professionally with one of the organizations with whom you sought employment. How embarrassing to have someone remember you as the candidate who failed to notify them of taking a job elsewhere!

In all of your follow-up communications, keep good notes of who you spoke with, when you called, and any instructions that were given about return communications. This will prevent any misunderstandings and provide you with good records of what has transpired.

FOLLOWING UP ON THE NETWORK CONTACT

Far more common than the forgotten follow-up after an interview is the situation where a good network contact is allowed to lapse. Good communications are the essence of a network, and follow-up is not so much a matter of courtesy here as it is a necessity. In networking for job information and contacts, you are the active network link. Without you, and without continual contact from you, there is no network. You and your need for employment is often the only shared element between members of the network. Because network contacts were made regardless of the availability of any particular employment, it is incumbent upon the job seeker, if not simple common sense, that unless you stay in regular communication with the network, you will not be available for consideration should some job become available in the future.

This brings up the issue of responsibility, which is likewise very clear. The job seeker initiates network contacts and is responsible for maintaining those contacts; therefore, the entire responsibility for the network belongs with him or her. This becomes patently obvious if the network is left unattended. It very shortly falls out of existence because it cannot survive without careful attention by the networker.

A variety of ways are open to you to keep the lines of communication open and to attempt to interest the network in you as a possible employee. You are limited only by your own enthusiasm for members of the network and your creativity. However, you as a networker are well advised to keep good records of whom you have met and contacted in each organization. Be sure to send thank-you notes to anyone who has spent any time with you, be it an E-mail message containing information or advice, a quick tour of a department, or a sit-down informational interview. All of these communications should, in addition to their ostensible reason, add some information about you and your particular combination of strengths and attributes.

You can contact your network at any time to convey continued interest, to comment on some recent article you came across concerning an organization, to add information about your training or changes in your qualifications, to ask advice or seek guidance in your job search, or to request referrals to other possible network opportunities. Sometimes just a simple note to network members reminding them of your job search, indicating that you have been using their advice, and noting that you are still actively pursuing leads and hope to continue to interact with them is enough to keep communications alive.

The Internet has opened up the world of networking. You may be able to find networkers who graduated from your high school or from the college you're attending, who live in a geographic region where you hope to work, or who are employed in a given industry. The Internet makes it easy to reach out to many people, but don't let this perceived ease lull you into complacency. Internet networking demands the same level of preparation as the more traditional forms of networking do.

Because networks have been abused in the past, it's important that your conduct be above reproach. Networks are exploratory options, they are not backdoor access to employers. The network works best for someone who is exploring a new industry or making a transition into a new area of employment and who needs to find information or to alert people to his or her search activity. Always be candid and direct with contacts in expressing the purpose of your E-mail, call, or letter and your interest in their help or information about their organization. In follow-up contacts keep the tone professional and direct. Your honesty will be appreciated, and people will respond as best they can if your qualifications appear to meet their forthcoming needs. The network does not owe you anything, and that tone should be clear to each person you meet.

FEEDBACK FROM FOLLOW-UPS

A network contact may prove to be miscalculated. Perhaps you were referred to someone and it became clear that your goals and his or her particular needs did not make a good match. Or the network contact may simply not be in a position to provide you with the information you are seeking. Or in some unfortunate situations, the contact may become annoyed by being contacted for this purpose. In such a situation, many job seekers simply say "Thank you" and move on.

If the contact is simply not the right contact, but the individual you are speaking with is not annoyed by the call, it might be a better tactic to express regret that the contact was misplaced and then tell the contact what you are seeking and ask for his or her advice or possible suggestions as to a next step. The more people who are aware you are seeking employment, the better your chances of connecting, and that is the purpose of a network. Most people in a profession have excellent knowledge of their field and varying amounts of expertise on areas near to or tangent to their own. Use their expertise and seek some guidance before you dissolve the contact. You may be pleasantly surprised.

Occasionally, networkers will express the feeling that they have done as much as they can or provided all the information that is available to them. This may be a cue that they would like to be released from your network. Be alert to such attempts to terminate, graciously thank the individual by letter, and move on in your network development. A network is always changing, adding, and losing members, and you want the network to be composed only of those who are actively interested in supporting you.

A FINAL POINT ON NETWORKING FOR ENGLISH MAJORS

In any of the fields an English major might consider as a potential career path, it's important to remember that networkers and interviewers will be critically evaluating all of your written and oral communications. As an English major, this should be gratifying, but at the same time it should serve to emphasize the importance of the quality of your communications with people in a position to help you in your job search.

In your telephone communications, interview presentation, and follow-up correspondence, your warmth, style, and personality as evidenced in your written and spoken use of English will be part of the portfolio of impressions you create in those you meet along the way.

••

CHAPTER SEVEN

JOB OFFER CONSIDERATIONS

For many recent college graduates, the thrill of their first job and, for some, the most substantial regular income they have ever earned seems an excess of good fortune coming at once. To question that first income or to be critical in any way of the conditions of employment at the time of the initial offer seems like looking a gift horse in the mouth. It doesn't seem to occur to many new hires even to attempt to negotiate any aspect of their first job. And, as many employers who deal with entry-level jobs for recent college graduates will readily confirm, the reality is that there simply isn't much movement in salary available to these new college recruits. The entry-level hire generally does not have an employment track record on a professional level to provide any leverage for negotiation. Real negotiations on salary, benefits, retirement provisions, etc., come to those with significant employment records at higher income levels.

Of course, the job offer is more than just money. It can be composed of geographic assignment, duties and responsibilities, training, benefits, health and medical insurance, educational assistance, car allowance or company vehicle, and a host of other items. All of this is generally detailed in the formal letter that presents the final job offer. In most cases this is a follow-up to a personal phone call from the employer representative who has been principally responsible for your hiring process.

That initial telephone offer is certainly binding as a verbal agreement, but most firms follow up with a detailed letter outlining the most significant parts of your employment contract. You may certainly choose to respond immediately at the time of the telephone offer (which would be considered a binding oral contract), but you will also be required to formally answer the letter of offer with a letter of acceptance, restating the salient elements of the employer's description of your position, salary, and benefits. This ensures that both parties are clear on the terms and conditions of employment and remuneration and any other outstanding aspects of the job offer.

IS THIS THE JOB YOU WANT?

Most new employees will write this letter of acceptance back, glad to be in the position to accept employment. If you've worked hard to get the offer and the job market is tight, other offers may not be in sight, so you will say, "Yes, I accept!" What is important here is that the job offer you accept be one that does fit your particular needs, values, and interests as you've outlined them in your self-assessment process. Moreover, it should be a job that will not only use your skills and education, but also challenge you to develop new skills and talents.

Jobs are sometimes accepted too hastily, for the wrong reasons, and without proper scrutiny by the applicant. For example, an individual might readily accept a sales job only to find the continual rejection by potential clients unendurable. An office worker might realize within weeks the constraints of a desk job and yearn for more activity. Employment is an important part of our lives. It is, for most of our adult lives, our most continuous productive activity. We want to make good choices based on the right criteria.

If you have a low tolerance for risk, a job based on commission will certainly be very anxiety-provoking. If being near your family is important, issues of relocation could present a decision crisis for you. If you're an adventurous person, a job with frequent travel would provide needed excitement and be very desirable. The importance of income, the need to continue your education, your personal health situation—all of these have an impact on whether the job you are considering will ultimately meet your needs. Unless you've spent some time understanding and thinking about these issues, it will be difficult to evaluate offers you do receive.

More importantly, if you make a decision that you cannot tolerate and feel you must leave that job, you will then have both unemployment and self-esteem issues to contend with. These will combine to make the next job search tough going, indeed. So make your acceptance a carefully considered decision.

NEGOTIATING YOUR OFFER

It may be that there is some aspect of your job offer that is not particularly attractive to you. Perhaps there is no relocation allotment to help you move your possessions, and this presents some financial hardship for you. It may be that the medical and health insurance is less than you had hoped. Your initial assignment may be different than you expected, either in its location or in the duties and responsibilities that comprise it. Or it may simply be that the salary is less than you anticipated. Other considerations may be your official starting date of employment, vacation time, evening hours, dates of training programs or schools, etc.

If you are considering not accepting the job because of some item or items in the job offer "package" that do not meet your needs, you should know that most employers emphatically wish that you would bring that issue to their attention. It may be that the employer can alter it to make the offer more agreeable for you. In some cases it cannot be changed. In any event the employer would generally like to have the opportunity to try to remedy a difficulty rather than risk losing a good potential employee over an issue that might have been resolved. After all, they have spent time and funds in securing your services, and they certainly deserve an opportunity to resolve any possible differences.

Honesty is the best approach in discussing any objections or uneasiness you might have over the employer's offer. Having received your formal offer in writing, contact your employer representative and indicate your particular dissatisfaction in a straightforward manner. For example, you might explain that, while very interested in being employed by this organization, the salary (or any other benefit) is less than you have determined you require. State the terms you do need, and listen to the response. You may be asked to put this in writing, or you may be asked to hold off until the firm can decide on a response. If you are dealing with a senior representative of the organization, one who has been involved in hiring for some time, you may get an immediate response or a solid indication of possible outcomes.

Perhaps the issue is one of relocation. Your initial assignment is in the Midwest, and because you had indicated a strong West Coast preference, you are surprised at the actual assignment. You might simply indicate that, while you understand the need for the company to assign you based on its needs, you are disappointed and had hoped to be placed on the West Coast. You could inquire if that were still possible and, if not, would it be reasonable to expect a West Coast relocation in the future.

If your request is presented in a reasonable way, most employers will not see this as jeopardizing your offer. If they can agree to your proposal, they will. If not, they will simply tell you so, and you may choose to continue your candidacy with them or remove yourself from consideration as a possible employee. The choice will be up to you.

Some firms will adjust benefits within their parameters to meet the candidate's need if at all possible. If a candidate requires a relocation cost allowance, he or she may be asked to forgo tuition benefits for the first year to accomplish this adjustment. An increase in life insurance may be adjusted by some other benefit trade-off; perhaps a family dental plan is not needed. In these decisions you are called upon, sometimes under time pressure, to know how you value these issues and how important each is to you.

Many employers find they are more comfortable negotiating for candidates who have unique qualifications or who bring especially needed expertise to the organization. Employers hiring large numbers of entry-level college graduates may be far more reluctant to accommodate any changes in offer conditions. They are well supplied with candidates with similar education and experience, so that if rejected by one candidate, they can draw new candidates from an ample labor pool.

COMPARING OFFERS

The conditions of the economy, the job seekers' academic major and particular geographic job market, and their own needs and demands for certain employment conditions may not provide more than one job offer at a time. Some job seekers may feel that no reasonable offer should go unaccepted for the simple fear there won't be another.

In a tough job market, or if the job you seek is not widely available, or when your job search goes on too long and becomes difficult to sustain financially and emotionally, it may be necessary to accept an offer. The alternative is continued unemployment. Even here, when you feel you don't have a choice, you can at least understand that in accepting this particular offer, there may be limitations and conditions you don't appreciate. At the time of acceptance, there were no other alternatives, but the new employee can begin to use that position to gain the experience and talent to move toward a more attractive position.

Sometimes, however, more than one offer is received at one time, and the candidate has the luxury of choice. If the job seeker knows what he or she wants and has done the necessary self-assessment honestly and thoroughly, it may be clear that one of the offers conforms more closely to those expressed wants and needs.

However, if, as so often happens, the offers are similar in terms of conditions and salary, the question then becomes which organization might provide the necessary climate, opportunities, and advantages for your professional development and growth. This is the time when solid employer research and astute questioning during the interviews really pays off. How much did you learn about the employer through your own research and skillful questioning? When the interviewer asked during the interview "Do you have any questions?" did you ask the kinds of questions that would help resolve a choice between one organization and another? Just as an employer must decide among numerous applicants, so must the applicant learn to assess the potential employer. Both are partners in the job search.

RENEGING ON AN OFFER

An especially disturbing occurrence for employers and career counseling professionals is when a job seeker formally (either verbally or by written contract) accepts employment with one organization and later reneges on the agreement and goes with another employer.

There are all kinds of rationalizations offered for this unethical behavior. None of them satisfies. The sad irony is that what the job seeker is willing to do to the employer—make a promise and then break it—he or she would be outraged to have done to them—have the job offer pulled. It is a very bad way to begin a career. It suggests the individual has not taken the time to do the necessary self-assessment and self-awareness exercises to think and judge critically. The new offer taken may, in fact, be no better or worse than the one refused. Job candidates should be aware that there have been incidents of legal action following job candidates reneging on an offer. This adds a very sour note to what should be a harmonious beginning of a lifelong adventure.

CHAPTER EIGHT

THE GRADUATE SCHOOL CHOICE

*T*he reasons for continuing one's education in graduate school can be as varied and unique as the individuals electing this course of action. Many continue their studies at an advanced level because they simply find it difficult to end the educational process. They love what they are learning and want to learn more and continue their academic exploration.

· ·

Studying a particular subject, such as Victorian women writers, in great depth and thinking, studying, and writing critically on what others have discovered can provide excitement, challenge, and serious work. Some English majors have loved this aspect of their academic work and want to continue that activity.

Others go on to graduate school for purely practical reasons; they have examined employment prospects in their field of study, and all indications are that a graduate degree is requisite. If you have earned a B.A. in English and have not pursued a teaching degree, opportunities directly related to English will be difficult to come by in a tight job market. Yet you love the study of English and feel strongly that you want to make that part of your livelihood. A review of jobs directly related to English will suggest at least a master's degree is required to become competitive. Alumni who are working in editing, writing, or publishing can be a good source of what degree level the fields are hiring. Ask your college career office for some alumni names and give them a telephone call. Prepare some questions on specific job prospects in their field at each degree level. A thorough examination of the marketplace and talking to employers and professors will give you a sense of the scope of employment for a bachelor's degree, master's degree, or doctorate.

College teaching requires an advanced degree. Technical writing will demand specialization in an additional field (computers, engineering, medicine, etc.). Editing and publishing may well put a premium on the advanced degree because the market is oversupplied and the employer can afford to make this demand.

CONSIDER YOUR MOTIVES

The answer to the question of "Why graduate school?" is a personal one for each applicant. Nevertheless, it is important to consider your motives carefully. Graduate school involves additional time out of the employment market, a high degree of critical evaluation, significant autonomy as you pursue your studies, and considerable financial expenditure. For some students in doctoral programs, there may be additional life choice issues, such as relationships, marriage, and parenthood, that may present real challenges while in a program of study. You would be well-advised to consider the following questions as you think about your decision to continue your studies.

Are You Postponing Some Tough Decisions by Going to School?

Graduate school is not a place to go to avoid life's problems. There is intense competition for graduate school slots and for the fellowships, scholarships, and financial aid available. This competition means extensive interviewing, resume submission, and essay writing that rivals corporate recruitment. Likewise, the graduate school process is a mentored one in which faculty stay aware of and involved in the academic progress of their students and continually challenge the quality of their work. Many graduate students are called upon to participate in teaching and professional writing and research as well.

In other words, this is no place to hide from the spotlight. Graduate students work very hard and much is demanded of them individually. If you elect to go to graduate school to avoid the stresses and strains of the "real world," you will find no safe place in higher academics. Vivid accounts, both fictional and nonfictional, have depicted quite accurately the personal and professional demands of graduate school work.

The selection of graduate studies as a career option should be a positive choice—something you *want* to do. It shouldn't be selected as an escape from other, less attractive or more challenging options, nor should it be selected as the option of last resort (i.e., "I can't do anything else; I'd better just stay in school."). If you're in some doubt about the strength of your reasoning about continuing in school, discuss the issues with a career counselor. Together you can clarify your reasoning, and you'll get some sound feedback on what you're about to undertake.

On the other hand, staying on in graduate school because of a particularly poor employment market and a lack of jobs at entry-level positions has proven to be an effective "stalling" strategy. If you can afford it, pursuing a graduate degree immediately after your undergraduate education gives you a year or two to "wait out" a difficult economic climate while at the same time acquiring a potentially valuable credential.

Have You Done Some "Hands-On" Reality Testing?

There are experiential options available to give some reality to your decision-making process about graduate school. Internships or work in the field can give you a good idea about employment demands, conditions, and atmosphere.

Perhaps, as an English major, you're considering a graduate program in technical writing. A technical writing internship or summer job that puts you in contact with technical writers may help to define for you exactly what a technical writer does. Even with the experience of only one employer, you have a stronger concept of the pace of the job, interaction with colleagues, subject matter, and opportunities for personal development. Talking to people and asking questions is invaluable as an exercise to help you better understand the objective of your graduate study.

For English majors especially, the opportunity to do this kind of reality testing in invaluable. It demonstrates far more authoritatively than any other method what your real-world skills are, how they can be put to use, and what aspects of your academic preparation you rely on. It has been well documented that English majors do well in their occupations once they identify them. Internships and co-op experiences speed that process up and prevent the frustrating and expensive process of investigation many graduates begin only after graduation.

·····················

Do You Need an Advanced Degree to Work in Your Field?

Certainly there are fields such as law, psychiatry, medicine, and college teaching that demand advanced degrees. Is the field of employment you're considering one that also puts a premium on an advanced degree? You may be surprised. Read job ads on the Internet and in a number of major Sunday newspapers for positions you would enjoy. How many of those require an advanced degree?

Retailing, for example, has always put a premium on what people can do, rather than how much education they have had. Successful people in retailing come from all academic preparations. A Ph.D. in English may bring only prestige to the individual employed as a magazine researcher. It may not bring a more senior position or better pay. In fact, it may disqualify you for some jobs because an employer might believe you will be unhappy to be overqualified for a particular position. Or your motives in applying for the work may be misconstrued, and the employer might think you will only be working at this level until something better comes along. None of this may be true for you, but it comes about because you are working outside of the usual territory for that degree level.

When economic times are especially difficult, we tend to see stories featured about individuals with advanced degrees doing what is considered unsuitable work, such as the Ph.D. in English driving a cab or the Ph.D. in chemistry waiting tables. Actually, this is not particularly surprising when you consider that as your degree level advances, the job market narrows appreciably. At any one time, regardless of economic circumstances, there are only so many jobs for your particular level of expertise. If you cannot find employment for your advanced degree level, chances are you will be considered suspect for many other kinds of employment and may be forced into temporary work far removed from your original intention.

Before making an important decision such as graduate study, learn your options and carefully consider what you want to do with your advanced degree. Ask yourself whether it is reasonable to think you can achieve your goals. Will there be jobs when you graduate? Where will they be? What will they pay? How competitive will the market be at that time, based on current predictions?

If you're uncertain about the degree requirements for the fields you're interested in, you should check a publication such as the U.S. Department of Labor's *Occupational Outlook Handbook*. Each entry has a section on training and other qualifications that will indicate clearly what the minimum educational requirement is for employment, what degree is the standard, and what employment may be possible without the required credential.

For example, for physicists and astronomers a doctoral degree in physics or a closely related field is essential. Certainly this is the degree of choice in academic institutions. However, the *Occupational Outlook Handbook* also indicates what kinds of employment may be available to individuals holding a master's or even a bachelor's degree in physics.

Have You Compared Your Expectations of What Graduate School Will Do for You with What It Has Done for Alumni of the Program You're Considering?

Most colleges and universities perform some kind of postgraduate survey of their students to ascertain where they are employed, what additional education they have received, and what levels of salary they are enjoying. Ask to see this information either from the university you are considering applying to or from your own alma mater, especially if it has a similar graduate program. Such surveys often reveal surprises about occupational decisions, salaries, and work satisfaction. This information may affect your decision.

The value of self-assessment (the process of examining and making decisions about your own hierarchy of values and goals) is especially important in this process of analyzing the desirability of possible career paths involving graduate education. Sometimes a job requiring advanced education seems to hold real promise but is disappointing in salary potential or number of opportunities available. Certainly it is better to research this information before embarking on a program of graduate studies. It may not change your mind about your decision, but by becoming better informed about your choice, you become better prepared for your future.

Have You Talked with People in Your Field to Explore What You Might Be Doing After Graduate School?

In pursuing your undergraduate degree, you will have come into contact with many individuals trained in the field you are considering. You might also have the opportunity to attend professional conferences, workshops, seminars, and job fairs where you can expand your network of contacts. Talk to them all! Find out about their individual career paths, discuss your own plans and hopes, get their feedback on the reality of your expectations, and heed their advice about your prospects. Each will have a unique tale to tell, and each will bring a different perspective on the current marketplace for the credentials you are seeking. Talking to enough people will make you an expert on what's out there.

Are You Excited by the Idea of Studying the Particular Field You Have in Mind?

This question may be the most important one of all. If you are going to spend several years in advanced study, perhaps engendering some debt or postponing some lifestyle decisions for an advanced degree, you simply ought to enjoy what you're doing. Examine your work in the discipline so far. Has it been fun? Have you found yourself exploring various paths of thought? Do you read in your area for fun? Do you enjoy talking about it, thinking about it, and sharing it with others? Advanced degrees often are the beginning of a lifetime's involvement with a particular subject. Choose carefully a field that will hold your interest and your enthusiasm.

It is fairly obvious by now that we think you should give some careful thought to your decision and take some action. If nothing else, do the following:

- Talk and question (remember to listen!)
- Reality test
- Soul-search by yourself or with a person you trust

FINDING THE RIGHT PROGRAM FOR YOU: SOME CONSIDERATIONS

There are several important factors in coming to a sound decision about the right graduate program for you. You'll want to begin by locating institutions that offer appropriate programs, examining each of these programs and their requirements, undertaking the application process by reviewing catalogs and obtaining application materials, visiting campuses if possible, arranging for letters of recommendation, writing your application statement, and finally following up on your applications.

Locate Institutions with Appropriate Programs

Once you decide on a particular advanced degree, it's important to develop a list of schools offering such a degree program. Perhaps the best source of graduate program information is Peterson's. Their website (www.petersons .com) and their printed *Guides to Graduate Study* allow you to search for information by institution name, location, or academic area. The website also allows you to do a keyword search. Use their website and guides to build your list. In addition, you may want to consult the College Board's *Index of Majors and Graduate Degrees,* which will help you find graduate programs offering the degree you seek. It is indexed by academic major and then categorized by state.

Now, this may be a considerable list. You may want to narrow the choices down further by a number of criteria: tuition, availability of financial aid, public versus private institutions, United States versus international institutions, size of student body, size of faculty, application fee, and geographic location. This is only a partial list; you will have your own important considerations. Perhaps you are an avid scuba diver and you find it unrealistic to think you could pursue graduate study for a number of years without being able to ocean dive from time to time. Good! That's a decision and it's honest. Now, how far from the ocean is too far, and what schools meet your other needs? In any case, and according to your own criteria, begin to build a reasonable list of graduate schools that you are willing to spend time investigating.

Examine the Degree Programs and Their Requirements

Once you've determined the criteria by which you want to develop a list of graduate schools, you can begin to examine the degree program requirements, faculty composition, and institutional research orientation. Again, using resources such as Peterson's website or guides can reveal an amazingly rich level of material by which to judge your possible selections.

In addition to degree programs and degree requirements, entries will include information about application fees, entrance test requirements, tuition, percentage of applicants accepted, numbers of applicants receiving financial aid, gender breakdown of students, numbers of full- and part-time faculty, and often gender breakdown of faculty as well. Numbers graduating in each program and research orientations of departments are also included in some entries. There is information on graduate housing, student services, and library, research, and computer facilities. A contact person, phone number, and address are also standard pieces of information in these listings.

It can be helpful to draw up a chart and enter relevant information about each school you are considering in order to have a ready reference on points of information that are important to you.

Undertake the Application Process

Program Information. Once you've decided on a selection of schools, obtain program information and applications. Nearly every school has a website that contains most of the detailed information you need to narrow your choices. In addition, applications can be printed from the site. If, however, you don't want to print out lots of information, you can request that a copy of the catalog and application materials be sent to you.

When you have your information in hand, give it all a careful reading and make notes of issues you might want to discuss via E-mail, on the telephone, or in a personal interview.

> If you are interested in graduate work in English, for example, in addition to graduate courses in literature, are there additional courses in poetry, prose, literary criticism, Shakespeare, European theatre, Milton, and others?

What is the ratio of faculty to the required number of courses for your degree? How often will you encounter the same faculty member as an instructor?

If, for example, your program offers a practicum or off-campus experience, who arranges this? Does the graduate school select a site and place you there, or is it your responsibility? What are the professional affiliations of the faculty? Does the program merit any outside professional endorsement or accreditation?

Critically evaluate the catalogs of each of the programs you are considering. List any questions you have and ask current or former teachers and colleagues for their impressions as well.

The Application. Preview each application thoroughly to determine what you need to provide in the way of letters of recommendation, transcripts from undergraduate schools or any previous graduate work, and personal essays that may be required. Make a notation for each application of what you need to complete that document.

Additionally, you'll want to determine entrance testing requirements for each institution and immediately arrange to register for appropriate tests.

Information can be obtained from associated websites, including www.ets.org (GRE, GMAT, TOEFL, PRAXIS, SLS, Higher Education Assessment), www.lsat.org (LSAT), and www.tpcweb.com/mat (MAT). Your college career office should also be able to provide you with advice and additional information.

Visit the Campus if Possible

If time and finances allow, a visit, interview, and tour can help make your decision easier. You can develop a sense of the student body, meet some of the faculty, and hear up-to-date information on resources and the curriculum. You will have a brief opportunity to "try out" the surroundings to see if they fit your needs. After all, it will be home for a while. If a visit is not possible but you have questions, don't hesitate to call and speak with the dean of the graduate school. Most are more than happy to talk to candidates and want them to have the answers they seek. Graduate school admission is a very personal and individual process.

Arrange for Letters of Recommendation

This is also the time to begin to assemble a group of individuals who will support your candidacy as a graduate student by writing letters of recommendation or completing recommendation forms. Some schools will ask you to provide letters of recommendation to be included with your application or sent directly to the school by the recommender. Other graduate programs will provide a recommendation form that must be completed by the recommender. These graduate school forms vary greatly in the amount of space provided for a written recommendation. So that you can use letters as you need to, ask your recommenders to address their letters "To Whom It May Concern," unless one of your recommenders has a particular connection to one of your graduate schools or knows an official at the school.

Choose recommenders who can speak authoritatively about the criteria important to selection officials at your graduate school. In other words, choose recommenders who can write about your grasp of the literature in your field of study, your ability to write and speak effectively, your class performance, and your demonstrated interest in the field outside of class. Other characteristics that graduate schools are interested in assessing include your emotional maturity, leadership ability, breadth of general knowledge, intellectual ability, motivation, perseverance, and ability to engage in independent inquiry.

When requesting recommendations, it's especially helpful to put the request in writing. Explain your graduate school intentions and express some of your thoughts about graduate school and your appreciation for their support. Don't be shy about "prompting" your recommenders with some suggestions of what you would appreciate being included in their comments. Most recommenders will find this direction helpful and will want to produce a statement of support that you can both stand behind. Consequently, if your interaction with one recommender was especially focused on research projects, he or she might be best able to speak of those skills and your critical thinking ability. Another recommender may have good comments to make about your public presentation skills.

Give your recommenders plenty of lead time in which to complete your recommendation, and set a date by which they should respond. If they fail to meet your deadline, be prepared to make a polite call or visit to inquire if they need more information or if there is anything you can do to move the process along.

Whether or not you are providing a graduate school form or asking for an original letter to be mailed, be sure to provide an envelope and postage if the recommender must mail the form or letter directly to the graduate school.

Each recommendation you request should provide a different piece of information about you for the selection committee. It might be pleasant for letters of recommendation to say that you are a fine, upstanding individual, but a selection committee for graduate school will require specific information. Each recommender has had a unique relationship with you, and their letters should reflect that. Think of each letter as helping to build a more complete portrait of you as a potential graduate student.

Write Your Application Statement

• •

Many graduate applications require a personal statement. For an English major, this should be an exciting and challenging assignment and one you should be able to complete successfully. Certainly, any required essays on a graduate application for English will weigh heavily in the decision process of the graduate school admissions committee.

• •

An excellent source to help in thinking about writing this essay is *How to Write a Winning Personal Statement for Graduate and Professional School* by Richard J. Stelzer. It has been written from the perspective of what graduate school selection committees are looking for when they read these essays. It provides helpful tips to keep your essay targeted on the kinds of issues and criteria that are important to selection committees and that provide them with the kind of information they can best utilize in making their decision.

Follow Up on Your Applications

After you have finished each application and mailed it along with your transcript requests and letters of recommendation, be sure to follow up on the progress of your file. For example, call the graduate school administrative staff to see whether your transcripts have arrived. If the school required your recommenders to fill out a specific recommendation form that had to be mailed directly to the school, you will want to ensure that they have all arrived in good time for the processing of your application. It is your responsibility to make certain that all required information is received by the institution.

RESEARCHING FINANCIAL AID SOURCES, SCHOLARSHIPS, AND FELLOWSHIPS

Financial aid information is available from each graduate school. You may be eligible for federal, state, and/or institutional support. There are lengthy forms to complete, and some of these will vary by school, type of school (public versus private), and state. Be sure to note the deadline dates on each form.

There are many excellent resources available to help you explore all of your financial aid options. Visit your college career office or local public library to find out about the range of materials available. Two excellent resources are Peterson's website (www.petersons.com) and its book *Grants for Graduate Students*. Another good reference is the Foundation Center's *Foundation Grants to Individuals*. These types of resources generally contain information that can be accessed by indexes including field of study, specific eligibility requirements, administering agency, and geographic focus.

EVALUATING ACCEPTANCES

If you apply to and are accepted at more than one school, it is time to return to your initial research and self-assessment to evaluate your options and select the program that will best help you achieve the goals you set for pursuing graduate study. You'll want to choose a program that will allow you to complete your studies in a timely and cost-effective way. This may be a good time to get additional feedback from professors and career professionals who are familiar with your interests and plans. Ultimately, the decision is yours, so be sure you get answers to all the questions you can think of.

SOME NOTES ABOUT REJECTION

Each graduate school is searching for applicants who appear to have the qualifications necessary to succeed in its program. Applications are evaluated on a combination of undergraduate grade point average, strength of letters of recommendation, standardized test scores, and personal statements written for the application.

A carelessly completed application is one reason many applicants are denied admission to a graduate program. To avoid this type of needless rejection, be sure to carefully and completely answer all appropriate questions on the application form, focus your personal statement given the instructions provided, and submit your materials well in advance of the deadline. Remember that your test scores and recommendations are considered a part of your application, so they must also be received by the deadline.

If you are rejected by a school that especially interests you, you may want to contact the dean of graduate studies to discuss the strengths and weaknesses of your application. Information provided by the dean will be useful in reapplying to the program later on or applying to other, similar programs.

PART TWO

THE CAREER PATHS

CHAPTER NINE

INTRODUCTION TO THE ENGLISH CAREER PATHS

There is perhaps no major less subject to academic fads and fancies than English. It has always been not only a mainstay of the college curriculum, but also the foundation of our work in many other academic areas. Of all the liberal arts degrees, it opens the most doors and makes the graduate versatile and highly employable in any number of entry-level positions. The importance of English skills in all academic disciplines has been heightened by initiatives such as "writing across the curriculum" and other similar programs designed to emphasize to faculty in all subject areas the importance of writing skills and the need to introduce writing exercises into all fields of study.

APPLYING YOUR SKILLS TO THE WORLD OF WORK

Employment is all about English. Spoken English and written English underscore every aspect of employment for every level of worker. Conferences, one-on-one meetings, memoranda, short and long reports, agenda, instructions, training materials, and a host of other communications mark every decision in the workplace. Video production; user's manuals; procedures, specifications, and similar technical materials; and promotional materials all benefit from the attention of someone who is proficient in English usage. Business and industry leaders consistently call for applicants with a solid command of written and spoken English. It is what they need most and what they see least in interviewing sessions.

Thirty years ago, an English degree from a four-year school was all a graduate needed to launch a successful career. The vanguard of that generation are now at the senior levels of their careers and are anticipating retirement. A review of the biographies of many leaders and innovators from past generations across a number of occupational areas shows this to be true. What is equally true is that the English graduate today, armed with the additional skills of computer literacy and an aggressive and disciplined approach to the job search, can find an equally wide array of employment opportunities as the graduate of thirty years ago.

English is full of possibilities for a career based on solid skill with the written and spoken word, both now and throughout history. English can be marketing when expressed through the medium of copywriting. English can be computer science through technical writing. English can be newspaper reporting or book publishing through the techniques of editing and proofreading. English can be historical through the interpretation and archiving of ancient English and near-English texts. English can be international commerce as well, because English is increasingly the language of global business. English can be art through creative writing in fiction, poetry, and prose. What other degree offers so much?

Although today's English graduates do well in their chosen careers, as has been frequently documented, these new graduates have also been found to have difficulties in making the transition from college to the workplace. These same studies show that English majors and other liberal arts majors eventually do quite well in their employment settings, however. It is arriving at them that takes some doing.

The root of this problem may be confusion over what has been learned in college and its transferability to the workplace. English as a major is not job training; it is an education in the history and grandeur of the English language and what has been created from it. The content of this academic major, in and of itself, is only immediately transferable to those occupations closest to the subject itself, areas such as editing, writing, publishing, and teaching English.

Let's look again at your English education to see what is there for the employer. Of course, you have developed writing skills; these are very important to any employer. Look deeper. Behind writing is skill in research—understanding how to use informational resources and seek out the data you need. This investigative skill is an important function in all employment and is equally valuable. You also learned critical thinking: you needed to decide what pieces of information to include and not to include to have the most impact. Style, too, became a consideration as you learned to present your written material from a particular point of view. Style causes the reader to retain the importance of the writing and to return to it again and again.

Reading, too, loomed large in the educational process for an English major. But how can that reading help in the employment picture? There is reading for pleasure and reading for content. Each morning, the president of the United States reads a digest of important news culled for him from many, many sources. These original sources were read by others who selected critical pieces for the president to read. Or, after reading, they were edited down to more concise expressions of the original for speed and convenience. All of this is within the capabilities of the English major. The president isn't the only one who needs to have material read, selected, and digested.

But there is, of course, more to reading than this. English majors develop an appreciation of literary styles throughout history—the Old English of *Beowulf,* the Middle English of Chaucer, or the contemporary prose of Joyce Carol Oates, whose sometimes Gothic novels share much with the Shelleys or the Brontë sisters. The sweep of human history has been conveyed in both fiction and nonfiction, and the English major whose own vocabulary has been enriched through that study can use that vocabulary in the workplace.

Freewriting, keeping a journal, desktop publishing skills, college newspaper work, or a writing internship can all contribute finely honed communication skills that allow you to say what you want, directly, clearly, and concisely. There is no employer who does not need those abilities. But be ready to express these wonderful skills in a context the employer understands and finds desirable. To talk about your research skills in the context of the tradition of romance novelists would not make much sense to a newspaper editor. For example, research that editor could appreciate would be background work for an article on AIDS. Perhaps you could research the lineage of published books, films, and short stories that have used AIDS as a metaphor for loss. This might make a great story idea or background piece.

You need to isolate each of your skills and find a new context in which to explain their importance. That context may be in one of the career paths outlined here:

1. Writing, editing, and publishing

2. Teaching

3. Advertising and public relations

4. Business administration and management

5. Technical writing

Or it might be something entirely different, like screenwriting. Whatever you choose, you should be able to make a case for your English degree.

A SPECIAL NOTE: COMPUTERS AND THE ENGLISH MAJOR

Sadly missing from some English programs today and yet crucially needed in all of the career paths presented in this book are education and training in the use of computer technology. More than simply a new technique for inscribing the English language, computer technology is determining language forms itself. Recently, we have even seen the development of what might be termed the "evanescent novel," fiction on a diskette that erases itself as the reader scrolls through it on a computer screen. It remains then only as a story in the reader's mind to be retold and retold. It is simultaneously a return to the days of the oral tradition and a rejection of the infinite capacity of the computer to provide memory for us. It is both an interesting use of and an ironic comment on the juxtaposition of art and technology.

On a more prosaic note, the computer is omnipresent where language is written. A quick perusal of jobs for which English majors might be qualified reveals frequent and sometimes extensive demands for computer literacy, software familiarity, and experience with special applications. Throughout the following discussion of career paths, we cite many advertisements for jobs that seek English graduates but also demand a high level of computer facility.

The introduction of computers into the college English curriculum has certainly begun, but in some programs in only a very tentative way. And yet, computers are omnipresent in the world of professional writers. Fiction and nonfiction writers, poets, and word artists of all kinds use this technology. Specialized research studies in graduate school areas such as comparative literature have been greatly enhanced by computer search skills.

Research, a staple of the English student's academic program, is now commonly done electronically via CD-ROM technology, which is increasingly taking the place of printed reference materials because of its durability, ease in cataloging, and cost.

The older generation of liberal arts scholar did not employ the computer as students, and some of them have not yet learned the technology. In some ways, the computer is seen by this old guard as undermining much of what they profess. As a result, it does not appear in every curriculum.

The message here is crystal clear. If you are still in school as you read this, any computer skills you can acquire will be to your distinct advantage in the job search process. If you have already graduated, do what you can through community programs, self-study or part-time, and continuing education to learn some of the software packages you'll see mentioned in this book. If you are employed, take advantage of your situation and learn all you can about the technology that's available. It's a natural and essential adjunct to your English degree.

CHAPTER TEN

PATH 1: WRITING, EDITING, AND PUBLISHING

As an English major, creativity and visualization should come relatively easily to you. So let's do an exercise using both of these skills. Place yourself in the middle of Times Square in New York City. Look around you. What do you see? Listen to the people going by—what do you hear? On the Ginza in Tokyo, the Place de la Concorde in Paris, or the Spanish Steps in Rome, along with the other visual and auditory reminders of a shrinking world, you will see and hear English in constant use. English is preeminent in the United States, Great Britain, and Australia and is increasingly dominant around the world as the language of technology, business, and industry.

Let's return to Times Square. We go into a major bookstore and immediately are impressed with the breadth and scope of publications available. Books, manuals, newspapers, magazines all written, edited, and published using English skills. But even the largest general bookstore contains only the tip of the iceberg of publishing output. There is much more published in the fields of education and industry, which rival the consumer sector for employment possibilities. We are an information society, and much of that information is written.

We step into a corporate office tower, and at the reception desk we find the corporation newspaper or journal, an in-house publication written, edited, and produced for its employees. Many mid- to large-sized organizations need a number of in-house communication organs to share information about standards, employees and their activities (both professional and personal), new developments, and prospects for growth. These publications serve as a vital communications link in large organizations and also help to build the esprit de corps essential to an organization's success. The professionalism of these corporate publications, the technical resources available to produce them, and the corporate time and attention lavished on them rival the commercial publishing industry in quality.

We find ourselves outside the showroom of a major computer retailer. The Internet today holds perhaps more writing, editing, and publishing opportunities than all other fields combined. There are countless Web magazines, journals, articles, and texts that require people like you to produce. And if you're thinking that working in the computer industry means you'll need superior computer skills, you're mostly correct! Not only does working in this industry require superb computer skills, but it'll keep you on the cutting edge for the future. Many of these "cyber employers" are going to expect you to apply for your job on the Web, E-mail your resume to them, and have a home page of your own (a professional one) that they can visit to learn more about you. So get ready.

Next door at a major music and video retailer, we find on the counter a free magazine filled with articles, interviews, and behind-the-scenes views of the music industry. Designed to excite customers about the products and services of these retailers, it is, nevertheless, a substantial piece of publishing with all the editorial content, graphics, and readability of a weekly news magazine. The magazine is published only after careful story planning, assignment of writers, research checks for accuracy and legality, and the solicitation of advertising sponsors. Working on such a publication would be an excellent training ground for anyone contemplating a move to *Newsweek*, *Time*, or any other well-known magazine venture.

Continuing down the street, we stop in front of a large appliance store and watch on a bank of TVs the many duplications of a network news reader's countenance as he or she reports the day's events. We should remember the support staff working behind the scenes at such a news-gathering organization: reading and selecting pieces from the news wires, editing the field reports of stringers and reporters, and putting together written texts, all under intense time pressure. We discover here in broadcast news an entirely different industry hiring employees interested in careers in writing, editing, and publishing.

The television picture blinks, and the scene changes. A reporter is now interviewing a newly published author, and we realize once again that working within an organization is not your only career option. You might have your own story to tell from either facts or fantasy. The world of freelance writing is alive and well, and although only the strong survive the entrepreneurial demands of freelancing, those that do, do so very well, thank you! Many pursue freelance writing on their own while regularly employed in the hopes that publication will launch them into a career of pure writing; however, some find it difficult to balance writing with a regular job.

We hear a barker farther down the street and turn to see someone working at a kiosk filled with newspapers, magazines, and journals. We think of all the writers, editors, and publishers that have come together to produce all this material who depend on the same set of writing, critical thinking, and creative skills we polished as English majors. As we look over the selection of materials, we see some of these newspapers and magazines are in English but are published overseas. The *Japan Times* and the journal *Kyoto* are among these publications, and we realize that publishing in English is not something done only in the United States.

DEFINITION OF THE CAREER PATH

Our walk around Times Square has opened up unlimited prospects for us to consider in the fields of writing, editing, and publishing. Each of these arenas—newspapers and magazines, arts and entertainment, book publishing, freelance writing, and radio and television—offers employment prospects. Within these varied employment fields are countless employers of all sizes with staffs numbering from two or three to thousands. The size and scope of the employer will have much to do with the range of skills you are able to employ in your particular job and will, in turn, affect how you are judged as a job candidate.

Let's examine television and radio, for example. In a small station, you may find yourself writing copy for the announcers, researching and editing copy, helping an advertiser write an effective commercial, editing news stories as they come off the wire, and writing intros and segues for different parts of the broadcast. In a larger organization, your first job may simply be checking copy for accuracy or legal implications. Although your salary and benefits might be better than if you worked in a small station, and perhaps your advancement possibilities are equally excellent, your initial assignments may be very limited in scope.

Regardless of the size of your organization, it is a safe bet that one skill you will be called on to use in any size organization will be computer skills. A glance at the following job listings graphically shows the omnipresence of employers' demands that anyone working with English skills and written communication be computer literate. The software may be different from what you've known, but the elements are the same, and the employer will expect you to be conversant with word processing and perhaps desktop publishing capabilities. If you're still in school and have neglected these particular skills, take advantage of your remaining time and acquire the necessary familiarity to meet most computer requirements.

Assistant Editor Needed. The *Tribune*, a triweekly in the North Carolina foothills, seeks an assistant editor responsible for covering the geographic beat and working with young staff on reporting and writing. The right person will have a great attitude and some professional experience. Ability to write, shoot photos, design pages, and edit required. Only people who love the job and want to lead a paper to greatness should apply. Interested candidates should send a cover letter, clips, and references via snail mail to . . .

Copyeditor Needed. Several years' experience as a reporter or editor preferred, plus Quark/design skills. Entry-level considered. Our copyeditors share duties that include editing local and wire copy, writing headlines, and designing/laying out pages. Please send resume, clips, and letter to . . .

Even though all the career paths we will discuss in this section rely heavily on English skills, they don't all focus on the same skills, nor do they value the same areas of expertise within the general area of English. Some place their emphasis on the technical aspects of writing English: syntax, subject and tense agreement, point of view, vocabulary, spelling, and the parts of speech and their correct use in writing. Others are less concerned with technical details and more focused on style, imagery, metaphor, and other aspects of writing that can further the tone of a piece and keep the writing true to itself and accomplish the author's intention. Other practitioners emphasize their critical skills in reducing or expanding a piece of writing to fit some external demands of time or space. They are masters of condensing or extending the author's message without compromising the integrity of the piece. Still others focus on the facts and details of what has been written. Is it accurate? Did it happen just that way? Were those people all there? Did he or she actually say just that? Has it been reported anywhere else? Can we say this? Attention must be paid to countless other details about a piece of writing to prevent a later controversy or contradiction that might take the focus away from the author's overall message and mire it in a swamp of detail.

Still others are concerned with the challenging task of taking densely written material or complicated prose and making it clear to the average reader. And others look at a piece of writing to help to select art, illustrations, book cover designs, and typefaces that are most suited to the author's intention and style. Now take all these different realizations of editing, writing, and publishing and multiply them by the various industries in which they can occur: news organizations, broadcasting, the entertainment industry, theatre, text and trade book publishing, corporate in-house communications, etc., and you begin to see the possibilities.

The field of writing, editing, and publishing jobs is vast, and although five different career professionals might all share an English degree in common, it's a safe bet they are each using their education in a different way and emphasizing different facets of their academic preparation as they go about their jobs.

To illustrate the possibilities in the areas of writing, editing, and publishing, we will examine four possible career paths. You can use these as an entree to the myriad possibilities for English majors. They are representative, but hardly indicative, of the exhaustive list of combinations possible. Use your career office to create a network of graduates in these fields. Ask if you can visit alumni at their place of work and, even better, spend a day "shadowing" them as they go about their jobs. Pay attention to the pace of their day, the nature of their duties and assignments, and the work climate. Try the job on. Then go back and do your research about who hires people to do these jobs, how much they pay, and what the outlook for employment will be.

Add to this your own values and interests, your objective evaluation of your past experiences, and your skills in your academic major, and you will have developed a solid base from which to begin your exploration and eventual entry into one of these fields. Your commitment to one over another is not a matter of great risk, however. Whereas in medicine it's rather difficult for an orthopedic surgeon to easily change to internal medicine, that is not the case in the fields of editing, publishing, and writing. There are many crossover skills and many correspondences and overlaps within individual jobs. Your experience in a different field may, in fact, enhance your desirability to a new employer as you'll bring fresh perspective, insight, and critical judgment to your job while still using many of the same techniques and skills you have honed in your previous work.

Reporting

This job probably attracts more applicants than any other in the journalism field. The reporter's job is challenging, changing, and fast-paced and means you are always ahead of the general public in knowing what's going on. Reporters must feel a deep commitment to communicating news and informing people of the state of the world. Though there is desk work, it would be erroneous to assume that reporting is a "desk job." Reporters may work in either corporate communications or more traditional news organizations. Consider the following job advertisement found recently in the *Boston Globe*:

Writer. Reporting to the Institute's Manager of Communications, and working closely with the Coordinator of Targeted Initiatives (including Leading for Life), provides administrative support for the Institute's communication and advocacy programs. Supports the activities of the Leading for Life campaign, an educational effort targeting African-American and Latino leaders, and Marketing HIV Prevention, an initiative targeting youth. Assists in planning meetings and press conferences; drafts and copyedits press releases and meeting materials; researches and secures illustrations for publications. Maintains databases. Provides staff support at Institute events and press conferences. Performs related job duties as required. This is a grant-funded position.

Required education: college degree in English, communications, relevant discipline, or equivalent work experience; 3-plus years' related office experience, including editorial or media-relations experience; accuracy and attention to detail; excellent written communications skills; strong organizational skills and ability to use own initiative, prioritize multiple responsibilities, and meet deadlines in a fast-paced environment; ability to alternate between working independently and working in a team environment to bring projects to completion; proficiency with Microsoft Word and Filemaker Pro on Macintosh required; Quark XPress desirable. Note: Finalists may be required to furnish writing samples.

The following is a recent ad for what we tend to think of as a traditional reporting job.

Education Reporter. The *Herald-Palladium* in St. Joseph, MI, is looking for a reporter to cover the education beat. The position also offers opportunities for reporting unrelated to education. We're looking for someone with great writing skills and lots of enthusiasm. St. Joseph is a beautiful resort community located on the sandy shores of Lake Michigan, just 90 miles from Chicago. Send resume, writing samples to . . .

Working Conditions. Most reporting, whether in a corporate or news organization setting, is done under deadlines of time and of space. Consequently, there is usually a high degree of stress in fulfilling these outwardly imposed constraints. When several reporters are working together, each on his or her own schedule, this sense of anxiety, noise, and general confusion is apt to multiply. Additionally, one seldom has the luxury of working on one article, story, or project at a time. More likely, you will be juggling several different assignments, each at varying stages. One may be in fact checking and another may simply be a story outline. When one may require research, another needs a human touch. Reporting involves myriad assignments, myriad deadlines, all subject to change and acceleration or postponement. Significant telephone work and much time on the road characterize a reporter's working day.

Training and Qualifications. Certainly, writing skills and the ability to work under pressure are paramount in most hiring officials' minds when looking for a promising reporter. But others may look for many other indications of possible success in this line of work: intelligence, quickness, desire to succeed, and dedication. Aggressiveness and willingness to ask the difficult questions are important, too. Reporters often don't get an opportunity to revisit a situation, so the correct information must be gathered in one meeting. That takes thinking ahead, planning, and thoroughness.

Earnings. In a corporate setting, reporters are often found in the public relations department. The *Wall Street Journal's* career website reported an average salary of $32,600 for public relations professionals with one to five years' experience.

Many reporters working for news organizations belong to the Newspaper Guild, an arm of the AFL-CIO. The Guild reports salary information for reporters on their website (www.newsguild.org). Starting minimum weekly pay ranged from $245 at the Utica, New York, *Observer-Dispatch* to $1,332 at the *New York Times*.

Editing

Decisions, decisions, and more decisions characterize the editorial role. Making them, being comfortable with them, and sticking to them are important to an editor's success. Editors decide what stays and what goes, what's important and what's not. In newspaper work, many editors come up from the reporting ranks, whereas in publishing, editors are often groomed to work with one particular type of material or a unique cluster of authors. Editors provide guidance, in the newsroom or in consultation with a reporter, and their job is to oversee the operation and birth of a printed product and to understand what is appropriate and what is not. Assistant and associate editors also double-check facts and statistics used in the text for accuracy. Position titles include editorial assistant, assistant editor, associate editor, editor, copyeditor, and senior editor.

Working Conditions. Editing is a more focused occupation and one that suffers from distraction. To edit well is to take on the writer's persona, to carefully concentrate on the intention of the work, and to make what changes might be necessary in a seamless, unobtrusive manner. To edit well is to be anonymous. Although you might have seen editors effusively thanked by their authors in interviews and in book dedications, it is difficult for readers of the finished work to know what transformations the editor is responsible for when they read the final product.

Training and Qualifications. The ability to see the overall picture, be it a novel, short story, or newspaper edition, and the ability to make quick decisions about choice, tone, quality, inclusion or exclusion of detail, etc., are both important in editorial work. Very often, the editor represents the publisher and must balance his or her artistic judgment against institutional goals and considerations. The newspaper editor assigns work and maintains a flowchart of story assignments and completion dates. The book editor works closely with the author to help fully realize publication and will be involved in every aspect, including technical printing details. Superior communications skills, both oral and written, strong interpersonal skills, experience, and judgment are the hallmarks of the discerning editor.

Earnings. *Publisher's Weekly: The International News Magazine of Book Publishing*, publishes a salary survey that reports the average salary for an editorial secretary/assistant and a copyeditor. Be sure to check the latest survey available. The Newspaper Guild reported at the time of printing that copydesk weekly salaries ranged from $510 up to $1,222, depending on the size and location of the newspaper.

Researching

There are many different kinds of research work, e.g., historical research, literary research, and scientific research, but the focus of this particular research is work that integrates training in English/writing and the critical judgment and investigative skills developed through analytical and research-oriented paper writing in college. Research provides the framework for much prose production and is often essential in the outline of a particular project. There is very little written, including fiction, that does not require research support.

Open a copy of any popular weekly news magazine or daily paper and scan the stories of interest. Now read them more carefully. Note how many refer to statistics, events, dates, and all kinds of facts that had to be verified and documented by someone. Sometimes this research is done simply for the integrity of the story. It may be a lifestyle piece for Thanksgiving that needs to be certain exactly what the Pilgrims ate that first Thanksgiving Day (it wasn't turkey!). It may be a piece on Mexican illegal immigration into Texas that needs data on illegal aliens crossing into Texas in the past ten years. The number of different Barbie doll editions, the year the Edsel automobile came on the market, and the exact age of the Pope are all possible research topics.

Working Conditions. Far more creative than many would give credit for, researching is the investigative art utilized in the world of words. Developing leads, exhausting false trails, and running a fact or thematic possibility to ground can be exciting when you realize your provision of materials through research can ultimately affect the production of a piece of text. Most researchers tend to be experienced in certain specific areas, but their skills are highly transferable, and some are able to freelance for a variety of information users.

Both fiction and nonfiction writers buy research services. For example, a novelist might set a wedding scene in Fiji that is critical to the book but not very long. Nonfiction writers may need background on real events or people in history. And prose writers are not the researcher's only clients; advertising agencies, television reporters, newspapers, historical societies and museums, and private individuals also have needs for research work.

Training and Qualifications. A high level of general knowledge, curiosity, persistence, perseverance, and attention to detail are salient qualifications of a researcher. Caring about written text, facts, and accuracy is crucial. Very often, researchers have little to go on as they begin their quest for information, so they must be resourceful and efficient in their work.

Perhaps you've been assigned to do research for a film set in the 1960s. There is continuing interest in some of the cultural, social, and political effects of the '60s. President John F. Kennedy, Marilyn Monroe, the Beatles, and Vietnam are still very much with us as touchstones of a different time. You've been asked to help evoke this era by researching food trends. You discover in your research an emphasis on packaged foods. Americans had just discovered biscuits in a can, cake mixes, gelatin desserts, casseroles made with canned soup, and a host of other culinary delights (which thankfully have not all survived into the present). You've read newspapers and cookbooks and talked to homemakers who used these products. Your research leads you to contact some of the manufacturers who are still operating, and you discover a treasure trove of recipes, photographs, and even films of kitchens, table settings, and menus—more than you had expected it would be possible to dig up.

Perhaps some of what you discover even links some of the material that is being developed. You locate a film, with sound, of a teen party that effectively shows off clothing, party food, behavior, and musical selections that proves invaluable to the art director for the film.

Earnings. Because the researcher can work in so many different settings and have many different job titles, salaries will vary widely. To provide some sense for salary potential, some of the well-known researching job titles are included here. Entry-level salaries for market research analysts start at $27,900; magazine editors, who also undertake research, start between $27,000 and $30,000; entry-level government social science researchers (GS-5) with college degrees and no prior work experience start at $20,600; environmentalists who undertake research can start at up to $27,000.

Creative Writing

When we think of creative writing, we think immediately of the novelist, but creative writing is far more than that. It includes lyricists, songwriters, and poets. It is the work of those who write from their own inspiration (many would substitute perspiration) and who feel strongly the need to express in writing their own view of the world, be it in song, verse, or prose. There certainly exist employers who hire creative writers, but the overwhelming majority are self-employed *as writers,* although they may do many other kinds of work to support their writing efforts.

Working Conditions. The eternal juggling act of balancing the need for income with the desire to write exerts tremendous pressure on young creative writers. Many must use early-morning or late-night hours to do what they consider their "real" work of expressing themselves through words. Until able to support themselves by their writing, many work at jobs and schedules that, although perhaps not the best use of their talents, will allow them the freedom and time to write. Their writing is solitary work, often done under less than ideal conditions.

For example, Dr. Perri Klass, a young, active Boston obstetrician, wife, and mother of small children, somehow maintains the production of a fluid stream of newspaper articles, magazine pieces (she is an active knitter and designer), and books. Do a Web search under "Perri Klass" and you are certain to turn up reviews of her books, schedules of her speaking engagements, and audio clips from her national lecture tours.

Even acknowledging that some people have more energy than others, this kind of production speaks of a determined schedule of sitting down and doing the writing. The increments of time may not be as luxurious as a full-time writer can afford, but they are dedicated, honored moments set aside to *write.*

There is an excellent array of published materials to help the creative writer break into this field. These books include the current year's *Writer's Market, Poets Market, Humor & Cartoon Markets, Song Writer's Market,* and *Novel & Short Story Writer's Market.* Many college career offices and public libraries contain recent editions of these volumes. Each provides specific information on how to target your efforts and how to contact potential publishers. They also contain articles and interviews with top professional writers.

Training and Qualifications. Because so much of this work is independent and solitary, the qualifications here are simply the desire and compulsion to write and express oneself. However, close behind these primary qualifications are the ability to tolerate risk in a profession with no "safety nets," the poise and equanimity to stick with a job for the income to support your writing, and a saleable skill to keep you employed until you have your first "break" with a publication.

Most of all, the independent writer needs self-discipline. We have said that many work at home during "fringe time"—late at night or early in the morning. Many have written about the struggle to maintain these difficult schedules. Over and over again, the successful writer will be the self-disciplined writer who learns to stick to a schedule and accomplish something each day. Writers must see their writing as something that they do regardless of how they feel that day, of what problems or concerns have arisen, or of fine weather that may tempt them out of doors. They must stick to a schedule, whether of time or number of pages. In this way, they produce, and without that self-discipline they will have no product to present to the reading public.

Earnings. The greeting-card writer working for a large corporation goes to work each day and receives a salary for his or her efforts to match a verbal sentiment for any possible occasion with the artistic renderings of visual artists. Their scope may not be wide, but the challenge is all the greater for those limitations. But these creative writers and the conditions of their employment are decidedly in the minority.

Unlike any other of the career paths discussed in this book, the earnings of the self-employed creative writer tend to be accretive. Success builds on success, and usually published work begets published work.

There are writers who sell their work literally by the word (some mass-market magazines for targeted groups), and others receive a flat fee for a work. The artist or sculptor may set a price for a creation, but most writers will tell you that until they achieve some fame, the pricing for their efforts is established by the buyer. Many magazines and journals issue lists indicating what they pay for unsolicited work. One excellent source providing current pricing information for hundreds of creative writing opportunities is the latest edition of *Writer's Market.*

CAREER OUTLOOK

There are several projected industry trends that will affect employment prospects in writing, editing, and publishing. The U.S. Department of Commerce, in its *U.S. Industry and Trade Outlook,* indicates that if there are gains in print advertising expenditures, in disposable personal income, and in national economic activity, shipments of the U.S. printing and publishing industry should increase. There are approximately 70,000 firms in this industry employing 1.5 million people, making this sector of the economy one of the largest manufacturing employers. Any growth in this sector will increase the number of available jobs.

Competition for these jobs will be keen because many candidates perceive them to be among the most attractive. In order to gain an employer's attention as you apply for positions, you must very clearly indicate in your cover letters and resume what relevant skills you have to offer and how you can help accomplish the goals of the employing organization.

The creative writer should take heart at these indications. Book publishing is seeing some new growth. And we have an ever-increasing number of magazine editions for every taste and a burgeoning entertainment industry that is always looking for creative and original material. The career path of the creative writer is seldom secure and never guaranteed, but as long as media and vehicles for publishing continue to exist and thrive, there will be opportunities.

Technology is changing the face of the publishing industry. Although most industry experts say they do not believe the book will ever disappear, some individuals say that interactive media will replace books as the number of people comfortable with using various kinds of hardware and software increases. Available products, ways of doing business, and new job titles in the writing field, such as electronic publishing specialist, will continue to alter the face of editing and publishing as the industry embraces ever-changing technologies.

Desktop publishing has allowed many writers and editors with graphics ability to develop burgeoning businesses producing pamphlets, brochures, informational pieces, booklets, and electronic (digital) layouts for any number of small publishing ventures. This kind of activity will continue to increase and reduce the obstacles to small-scale publishing.

One of the most amazing technical changes for writers, scholars, reporters, and editors has been the availability of data due to the computer's ability to

store and retrieve data in response to various modes of inquiry. This proliferation of data means work for researchers, especially researchers skilled in
the new technology. Not only must they know how to find data, but they
will need to be able to create their own databases for their own professional
files and future reference.

Although print newspapers are suffering nationally as a medium, the possibilities for daily newspapers appearing on your television screen via telephone lines is already available as a technology. Television itself promises to
become more interactive and specialized. We have twenty-four-hour news
programs, which use substantial editorial and writing staffs, and we are seeing increasing numbers of programs devoted to news, features, health, business, international affairs, and senior citizen issues. The newsroom may now
be part of the television station, but the demand for skilled writing, reporting, and editing help is projected to grow in this industry.

STRATEGY FOR FINDING THE JOBS

Decide What Interests You and Focus on It

The preceding section is dramatic evidence that the opportunities in writing, editing, and publishing are both vast and diverse. Although traditional
areas of employment such as editing and publishing may be oversubscribed,
we have outlined many, many other clusters of potential jobs. Where to begin?
Begin with your strengths, energies, and enthusiasm. Simply put, select one
of the possible employment areas that interests and motivates you most (e.g.,
specialized publications, broadcasting, newspapers) and focus your initial
efforts on that sector.

Create a Specialized List of Employers

You have already developed a list of job titles. Now, using the suggested
employer contacts we have provided, begin to develop a full list of potential
employers in the field you are targeting. Don't stop with the material provided in this text. Use your local library, chamber of commerce, and college
career center for additional employers. Perhaps your college can put you in
touch with alumni who are already employed in the field you are interested
in and who are willing to help you with employment information.

Use All Your Experience

Perhaps, as you work through your list, you'll discover you need more technical background than you now have for a particular writing or publishing

field. Or it may be that the economy has had a negative impact on one of these areas, and hiring for new positions is frozen. If, after some investigation and interviewing, you decide to move on to a different employment sector where possibilities seem greater, your efforts are not wasted. The research skills you've employed, the contacts you've made, and the relationships you've established with helping professionals will serve only to enhance and speed your activity in a new direction.

POSSIBLE EMPLOYERS

As you begin to develop a list of employers that offer jobs in writing, editing, and publishing, you'll see there are many possibilities. You might, for example, be interested in working in news writing because, after all, we all have some level of awareness about what's going on in the world. If you read a daily newspaper, you probably glance at the headlines before you leave home for the day. You may flip on the TV to see what's happened overnight. News readers fill you in on the latest. Or you may have a very hectic schedule, and you catch up on the news by sitting down in a quiet moment and picking up one of the news magazines. No matter how you get your news, someone is writing it, editing it, and presenting it via one medium or another.

We will begin to explore possible employers by examining some of the media used in writing, editing, and publishing. These include newspapers; general circulation magazines; trade, technical, and professional publications; agricultural newspapers and magazines; targeted population publications; college and university newspapers and magazines; radio stations; TV stations; cable systems; book publishers; academic presses; and government.

Newspapers

Profile. There are tens of thousands of newspapers of various types (daily, weekly, monthly, etc.) available in the United States, and these newspapers employ hundreds of thousands of workers. Each one of these print and/or Internet newspapers is available because a group of people, some of whom have skills similar to those you possess, has worked together to get the written word out.

While the principal role of the daily newspaper has been to provide stories and background on local, regional, state, and national events, situations, and concerns as they occur, newspapers have become increasingly diversified. Many now have extensive indexes directing the public to sections on lifestyle, science and health, business, home and family, and entertainment. There are regular columnists writing on any number of subjects; in fact, some newspapers have returned to the tradition that launched the career of Charles Dickens, the daily serialization of novels. All of this has been designed to entice a larger and broader-based audience and to enculturate a younger generation to the rewards of daily newspaper reading.

The newspaper industry continually reexamines the way it delivers information to consumers and the way it services its advertisers. Because of the sheer number of newspapers being published, they continue to be a large employer of people interested in writing, editing, and publishing.

Help in Locating These Employers. If you would like to identify the newspapers currently in business, there are several resources that will be helpful: the *National Directory of Weekly Newspapers, Newspapers Career Directory,* or *Gale Directory of Publications and Broadcast Media.*

Some excellent resources for gaining additional information about the newspaper industry include the Newspaper Association of America, Vienna, Virginia (www.naa.org); National Newspaper Association, Arlington, Virginia (www.oweb.com/nna/); and Editor and Publisher Company, New York (http://emedia1.mediainfo.com/emedia/). Each website has links that will be extremely useful in your job search.

General Circulation Magazines

Profile. In the United States there are approximately 2,500 magazines in general circulation. These publications cover a range of interests from alternative, underground, and New Age to business, soccer, and youth. There are fashion magazines for infants and for men and for women over forty. There are craft magazines for every conceivable hobby and an equally broad array of specialized sport enthusiast publications. A new and growing segment is a range of magazine publications for young people age twenty to twenty-five with editorial content, advertisements, and graphics that speak distinctly to this target market.

A visit to a vendor with a large display of magazines would indicate graphically that there is still a considerable market for freelance article writers on every subject represented by this display of weekly and monthly publications. Each publication offers staff positions in the areas of publishing, editing, researching, graphics, and thematic planning.

Help in Locating These Employers. For more information about this industry, see current copies of *Folio: The Magazine for Magazine Management* or the *Gale Directory of Publications and Broadcast Media.*

Trade, Technical, and Professional Newspapers and Magazines

Profile. If you have ever examined the *Encyclopedia of Associations,* a four-volume set, you realize how many American nonprofit membership organizations there are. Tens of thousands of organizations are listed in this encyclopedia. You will see entries for nearly any type of organization you can imagine, from the National Institute of Benefits Administrators to the Psychic Rescue Squad, the Strategy Gaming Society, and the Swedish Chamber of Commerce of the U.S.A. Each of these organizations serves a specific purpose and accomplishes for their members what those members individually would not be able to do. One of the principal missions of this type of organization is education of its members, and nearly every association publishes *at least* one informational piece of material. This is often a directory of members or an annual report, or it may be a brochure outlining the organization's members, goals, and mission. Staff sizes range from one person to several hundred people, and larger organizations employ individuals specifically to write, edit, or publish.

A visit to a succession of business employers, from the largest and most sophisticated of corporations to the smallest of warehouse operations, would dramatically demonstrate the size and pervasiveness of the trade publication sector. On coffee tables in each of these organizations you would find on display beautiful publications that rival any in the commercial marketplace, the subjects ranging from industrial boilers to commercial food products. All contain photography, graphics, color work, editorial comment, and freelance articles. Contrary to popular belief, this is not all highly technical information, either. There are humorous articles, philosophical pieces, critical commentary, and futuristic writing. Many English majors who have found a home in the trade publishing industry make a strong case for the quality and creativity of these publications.

Help in Locating These Employers. Currently, there are about 8,000 publications that are classified as trade, technical, and professional newspapers and magazines, and you'll find them being published in nearly every state. The *Gale Directory of Publications and Broadcast Media* is an excellent resource for locating publications either by subject area or by geographic location. The *Encyclopedia of Associations* also lists the publications each professional organization makes available. Many professional organizations and associations maintain websites. These sites are often designated by an acronym that uses the first letter of each word in the organization's name. For example, the Public Relations Society of America can be found at www.PRSA.org. Given the huge number of associations and the publications they make available, this is an employment possibility that should not be overlooked.

Agricultural Newspapers and Magazines

Profile. The United States is fortunate to have a variety of soil types, climates, and resources that will support a great diversity of agricultural production. In this country alone there are about 500 publications that relate to agriculture: research, production livestock, etc. Some of the larger publications relating to this industry include *Progressive Farmer, Western Horseman, Successful Farming, FFA New Horizons,* and *Agribusiness: An International Journal.*

Agricultural publications represent the history and diversity of farming and the changes that industry has undergone as it moves from a labor-intensive to a technologically intensive business. Nevertheless, it remains one of the most challenging and frustrating areas of commercial endeavor, due in large part to the impact of the weather. The publications that support agriculture are indicative of those concerns, with articles and columns ranging from country cooking to the most sophisticated farming technology advice. There are interviews, biographies, historical articles, and pictorials. Be sure to obtain some copies and review them. You may be surprised at the content and delighted to find you could make a contribution.

Help in Locating These Employers. If you have a special interest in agriculture in addition to writing, editing, and publishing, it is easy to identify these publications using the agriculture, forestry, mining, and fishing section of the *Directory of Directories,* the *Gale Directory of Publications and Broadcast Media,* or *Business Rankings Annual.* Then check the Internet for publications' websites.

A few of the larger professional associations that could provide information and that also produce publications themselves include the American Society for Horticultural Science, Alexandria, Virginia (www.ashs.org); American Farm Bureau (www.fb.com); and Horticulture Research International (www.hri.ac.uk).

Targeted-Population Newspapers and Magazines

Profile. One exciting change in publishing has come about with this country's growing awareness and appreciation of our multicultural heritage. We are valuing and learning about this cultural pluralism in schools, festivals, on college campuses, and in cities and towns around the country. These communities of ethnic, cultural, racial, and gender-oriented populations are increasingly producing written materials to communicate with each other and with the general public.

These publications resist easy classification and may be found under a number of different headings in some directories. These newspapers and magazines reach out to such populations as African-Americans, foreign language speakers, members of fraternal organizations, lesbians and gay men, Hispanics, Jews, members of religious groups, and women. There are almost 800 publications that serve these various groups. Titles of just a few of these newspapers and magazines include *Columbia Black News, Afro-American Times, Philippine News, China Daily News, The Tulanian, M.S.U. Alumni Magazine, Hispanic USA Magazine, Nuevo Amanecer, The Jewish Herald, The Christian Reader, The California Southern Baptist, The Lutheran, Gender and Society, Gay Community News, Feminist Bookstore News,* and *The Woman CPA.*

Help in Locating These Employers. Each one of these newspapers and magazines requires a staff of qualified people to bring it to publication. If you are particularly interested in working with one of these targeted publications, develop a list of potential employers by reviewing resources such as the *National Directory of Weekly Newspapers, Burrelle's Media Directory, Gale Directory of Publications and Broadcast Media,* or the *Directory of Directories.* Many of these potential employers maintain a website that lists employment opportunities, so be sure to look on the Internet.

College and University Newspapers and Magazines
Profile. Nearly every college and university produces a student newspaper and at least one alumni newsletter or magazine. In the United States there are almost 1,000 such publications. At smaller institutions, a faculty member advises students working on the newspaper, and alumni publications are written by staff in that office. At larger schools, however, there are specific positions involving writing, editing, and publishing.

Working with a publication dedicated to an audience such as college alumni means you are writing for an educated, sophisticated audience. Indiana University's alumni magazine is a glossy magazine that runs almost seventy-five pages. Along with the usual class notes and advertisements for college logo products, there are stimulating articles on art, athletics, psychological issues, and alumni profiles. Production values are competitive with most commercial publications.

Help in Locating These Employers. Two sources that will help you to identify potential employers are *The Chronicle of Higher Education* (www.chronicle .com), which lists actual job openings, and the *Gale Directory,* which lists the schools that are publishing these types of newspapers and magazines.

Two associations that are worth contacting are College Media Advisors and the Council for Advancement and Support of Education, Washington, D.C.

Radio Stations

Profile. Radio, which includes both AM and FM stations, is the most pervasive of all media. Nearly every household and vehicle on the street, and even many people walking or running, use a radio to get news, hear favorite music choices, or find out about emergency situations. There are over 9,000 radio stations in the United States employing people who write and edit for the listening public.

Radio provides wonderful opportunities to write for the spoken word. Commercials, intros, bridges, commentaries, news, and weather provide excellent opportunities to practice the writer's craft. Some of this, depending on the size of the station, is done under pressure of time and may lack editorial control. Smaller stations can prove to be valuable entries into writing careers in the public media.

Help in Locating These Employers. If you would like to find out which radio stations are based in a given geographic location, check the *Broadcasting and Cable Market Place* or the *Gale Directory of Publications and Broadcast Media*.

Some of the professional societies that can provide additional information about working in radio include the National Association of Broadcasters (www.nab.org), Radio-Television News Directors Association (www.rtnda.org), and the International Radio and Television Society (www.irts.org).

Television Stations

Profile. Although many jobs in broadcast television are available at commercial stations, the biggest of which are ABC, NBC, and CBS, there are also a number of independent, cable, corporate, and government television stations throughout the United States. There are about 1,300 television stations operating, each of which provides job opportunities for people interested in writing and editing.

Local stations and affiliates provide a "feeder" system of professionals to the major stations, and there is considerable movement between employers in this industry. Moves are usually indicative of increased responsibility, salary, and professional development, so frequent job movement does not have the stigma that it might in some other industries. In fact, it is often positive.

Help in Locating These Employers. Some sources that can be used to identify television stations include the *Broadcasting and Cable Market Place,* National Association of Broadcasters (www.nab.org), International Television Association membership directory, *Audio Video Market Place, Video Register & Teleconferencing Resources Directory, New York Production Guide,* and *Gale Directory of Publications and Broadcast Media*.

Cable Systems

Profile. The cable television industry now counts almost 1,000 systems in use. The proliferation of competing cable companies, each offering its own package of systems and fees, has prompted intense public and government scrutiny. These firms, originally behind the scenes, now frequently find themselves in public forums and needing to produce more and more informational material for a market demanding quality and pricing standards. As this industry grows, the opportunities in writing, editing, and publishing will increase proportionately.

Help in Locating These Employers. Both the *Broadcasting and Cable Market Place* and the *Gale Directory of Publications and Broadcast Media* will help you identify potential employers. If you would like more information on working in cable television, contact the Cable Telecommunications Association, Fairfax, Virginia (www.catanet.org).

Book Publishers

Profile. This category of employer includes publishers of books for the general reader (both adults and children), textbooks, and paperbacks. There are hundreds of publishers listed in the *Writer's Market*, an excellent reference for those interested in writing, editing, and publishing.

For many English majors, book publishing remains a glamour industry, at least in image. The competition and attractiveness of the profession suggest that only the most aggressive and talented candidates will meet the increasingly demanding criteria for quality employees in an industry that is becoming leaner.

Help in Locating These Employers. Some excellent resources for identifying publishing houses include VGM's *Opportunities in Book Publishing Careers,* the current edition of *Writer's Market, Literary Marketplace,* and the news magazine of book publishing, *Publishers Weekly.*

Several associations can provide additional information on the book publishing industry. These include the Association of American Publishers (www.publishers.org), Association of Electronic Publishers (http://welcome.to/AEP/), and the Small Publishers Association of North America (www.SPANnet.org).

University Presses

Profile. University presses are the publishing division primarily of the large research universities. The tradition of university presses, which started at

Oxford University in 1478, continues today. These presses serve scholars by disseminating information critical to scholarship and spreading ideas necessary to the academic community. There are about 100 member presses in the Association of American University Presses.

University presses have transformed themselves from their beginnings as a simple expedient of large academic institutions needing in-house production for scholarly material to contenders as major publishing houses bringing high-quality publications to commercial success with the general public through aggressive marketing and distribution.

Help in Locating These Employers. If you are interested in finding out more about this type of publisher, examine the *Gale Directory of Publications and Broadcast Media* or contact the Association of American University Presses, New York (http://aaupnet.org).

Federal Government

Profile. There are several federal agencies that specifically hire English majors because of the specialized background these degree holders bring with them. These agencies include the Federal Trade Commission, Department of Labor, National Archives and Records Administration, Research and Special Programs Administration, and the Department of Commerce's General Services Administration and Government Printing Office.

Help in Locating These Employers. A good place to start looking for actual job listings is on the U.S. government's website (http://www.usajobs. opm.gov/index.htm). This site explains the federal employment process. It lets you look at current job openings, get general information on federal agencies, and submit an on-line application.

If you select the option "Current Job Openings" and then "Agency Job Search," you can enter the agency name in the keyword search box, complete other appropriate search items, and then submit your search. It may take more than one search to narrow the job listings to one federal agency. Once you narrow your search, a list of job openings will appear on your screen. Select any of the entries, and a detailed job description is provided, including information on who to contact for more information and how to apply for the specific position.

POSSIBLE JOB TITLES

There are a multitude of job titles associated with working in writing, editing, and publishing. Use the *Dictionary of Occupational Titles,* published by the U.S. Department of Labor, to get a generic description for the particular job titles that interest you the most.

Assignment Editor	Journalist
Assistant Editor	Lyricist
Associate Editor	Managing Editor
Associate News Director	News Director
Author	News Editor
Book Editor	News Writer
Bureau Chief	Newspaper Editor
Bureau Reporter	Playwright
City Editor	Poet
Columnist	Program Proposals
Continuity Writer	Coordinator
Copyeditor	Publications Editor
Copywriter	Reporter
Correspondent	Researcher
Critic	Scriptwriter
Desk Assistant	Senior Editor
Dictionary Editor	Speechwriter
Editorial Assistant	Story Editor
Editorial Writer	Stringer
Electronic Publishing	Syndicated Columnist
Specialist	Technical Editor
External Publications Editor	Technical Publications
Freelance Reporter	Writer
Ghostwriter	Wire Editor
Indexer	Writer
Internal Publications Editor	

RELATED OCCUPATIONS

The excellent communication skills that have led to your interest in working in writing, editing, and publishing are also valued in many other settings. Some positions directly relating to the media we have discussed include radio or television announcer, account director, account coordinator, assistant planner, creative director, media supervisor, production assistant, researcher, communications officer, public relations manager, technical writer, fundraiser, lobbyist, traffic manager, marketing manager, or teacher.

In exploring the personality traits that many writers possess, we find three words that can be used to describe them are *artistic, enterprising,* and *social.* These traits are also shared with many people who work as furniture designers, narrators, contestant coordinators, auctioneers, magicians, dance instructors, music teachers, and intelligence specialists.

PROFESSIONAL ASSOCIATIONS FOR WRITERS, EDITORS, AND PUBLISHERS

Review each of the associations listed below to see if any of them are of interest to you. If your budget allows, consider joining a group that serves a particular interest or need you have. The benefits these associations provide, such as job listings in a journal or newsletter, are available only to members of the group.

American Book Producers Association
160 Fifth Ave., Ste. 625
New York, NY 10010
Members/Purpose: Book-producing companies that develop the concepts
    for books. Purpose is to increase the book industry's awareness of
    members' capabilities and the state of the book producers' art.
Journal/Publication: Directory of members; newsletter.
Job Listings: Database of book producers open to members.

American Medical Publishers' Association
c/o Jill Rudansky
14 Fort Hill Rd.
Huntington, NY 11743
Website: www.am-pa.com
E-mail: jillrudansky-ampa@msn.com
Members/Purpose: U.S. medical publishing companies. Objectives are to
    exchange information among members; to improve the creation,
    distribution, and sale of medical books and journals; to facilitate
    communication with medical organizations, schools, and the medical
    community.
Training: Provides ongoing educational programs.
Journal/Publication: Newsletter; *AMPA Bulletin*; directory.

American Newspaper Publishers Association
The Newspaper Center
11600 Sunrise Valley Dr.
Reston, VA 22091
Website: www.adweb.com/adassoc12.html

Members/Purpose: Daily and nondaily newspapers in the Western Hemisphere, Europe, and the Pacific region. Serves as a clearinghouse for member newspapers on all phases of the newspaper business.

Training: Operates technical services and research facility in Reston, Virginia.

Journal/Publication: *Presstime.*

American Society of Journalists and Authors

1501 Broadway, Ste. 302

New York, NY 10036

Website: www.asja.org

E-mail: execdin@asja.org

Members/Purpose: Freelance writers of nonfiction magazine articles and books.

Journal/Publication: Membership directory; newsletter.

American Society of Magazine Editors

919 Third Ave.

New York, NY 10022

Website: asme.magazine.org

E-mail: asme@magazine.org

Members/Purpose: Professional organization of senior magazine editors.

American Society of Newspaper Editors

11690B Sunrise Valley Dr.

Reston, VA 20191-1409

Website: www.asne.org

E-mail: asne@asne.org

Members/Purpose: Directing editors who determine editorial and news policy on daily newspapers.

Journal/Publication: Bulletin; proceedings; *Editors' Exchange.*

Association of American Publishers

71 Fifth Ave.

New York, NY 10003-3004

Website: www.publishers.org/home/index.htm

E-mail: ncarew@publishers.org

Members/Purpose: Trade association representing producers of hardbound and softbound general, educational, trade, reference, religious, scientific, technical, and medical books; instructional materials; classroom periodicals; maps, globes, tests, and software.

Training: Conducts seminars and workshops on various publishing topics, including rights and permission, sales, and educational publishing.

Journal/Publication: *AAP Exhibits Directory; AAP Monthly Report; Green Book of College Publishing; International Fairs Calendar.*

Author's League of America
330 W. 42nd St., 29th Floor
New York, NY 10036
Website: www.authorsguild.org
E-mail: staff@authorsguild.org
Members/Purpose: Professional organization of authors of books, magazine material, and plays.
Journal/Publication: *Author's Guild Bulletin.*

Black Women in Publishing
P.O. Box 6275, F.D.R. Station
New York, NY 10021
Website: www.bwip.org
E-mail: bwip@hotmail.com
Members/Purpose: Designers, editors, financial analysts, freelancers, personnel directors, photographers, production managers, and publicists within the print industry. A networking and support group whose purpose is to encourage minorities interested in all sectors of book, newspaper, and magazine publishing.
Training: Sponsors lectures, panel discussions, seminars, workshops, and other programs on a variety of topics.
Journal/Publication: *Interface.*
Job Listings: Provides a placement service, maintains a resume bank.

Friends of American Writers
c/o Eleanor Simmons
1440 N. Lake Shore Dr., Apt. 10A
Chicago, IL 60610
Members/Purpose: Women in the Chicago area who are interested in the study of American literature and in encouraging and promoting high standards among writers of the Midwest.
Journal/Publication: Bulletin; *Friends of American Writers Yearbook.*

National Academy of Television Arts and Sciences
111 W. 57th St., Ste. 1020
New York, NY 10019
Website: www.natasatlanta.org
E-mail: info@natasatlanta.org
Members/Purpose: Persons engaged in television performing, art directing, cinematography, directing, taping, tape editing, choreography, engineering, film editing, music, production, and writing.

Training: Sponsors workshops and seminars.

Journal/Publication: Local newsletter; *NATAS News*; *Television Quarterly.*

National Association of Broadcasters
1771 N St. NW
Washington, DC 20036
Website: www.adweb.com/adassoc24.html
Members/Purpose: Representatives of radio and television stations and television networks; associate members include producers of equipment and programs.
Journal/Publication: Broadcast engineering conference proceedings; *Radio Week*; *TV Today.*

National Cable Television Association
1724 Massachusetts Ave. NW
Washington, DC 20036
Website: www.ncta.com
Members/Purpose: Franchised cable operators, programmers, and cable networks; associate members are cable hardware suppliers and distributors; affiliate members are brokerage and law firms and financial institutions. Represents the cable industry before Congress, the Federal Communications Commission, and various courts on issues of primary importance.
Journal/Publication: *Linking Up*; *Producer's Sourcebook*; newsletter; report; *TechLine*; *Careers in Cable*; *Cable Primer*; *FCC Cable Rules.*

National Writers Association (formerly National Writers Club)
1450 S. Havana, Ste. 424
Aurora, CO 80012
Website: lcweb.loc.gov/loc/cfbook/coborg/nwa.html
Members/Purpose: Professional members must qualify for membership; associate membership is open to anyone seriously interested in creative writing.
Training: Offers home study course in magazine writing for members; sponsors annual workshop.
Journal/Publication: *Authorship*; *Flash Market News*; *Market Update*; newsletter; *Professional Freelance Writers' Directory.*

Poets and Writers
72 Spring St.
New York, NY 10012
Website: www.pw.org
Members/Purpose: Serves as an information clearinghouse for the literary community; works to increase the audience for contemporary literature.

Training: Sponsors readings and workshops.

Journal/Publication: *Directory of American Poets and Fiction Writers*; *Poets and Writers Magazine*; *The Writing Business: A Poets and Writers Handbook.*

Society for Technical Communication, Inc.

901 N. Stuart St., Ste. 904

Arlington, VA 22203

Website: www.stc-va.org

E-mail: stc@stc-va.org

Members/Purpose: Writers, editors, educators, scientists, engineers, artists, publishers, and others professionally engaged in or interested in some phase of the field of technical communications; companies, corporations, organizations, and agencies interested in the aims of the society. Devoted to the advancement of the theory and practice of technical communication.

Training: Committee on education and professional development.

Journal/Publication: *Intercom* newsletter; *ITCC Proceedings*; *Technical Communication.*

Job Listings: Regional chapters provide employment committees and job listings; provides electronic bulletin board for members that lists jobs.

Society of National Association Publications

1650 Tyson Blvd., Ste. 200

McLean, VA 22102

Website: snaponline.org

E-mail: snapinfo@snaponline.org

Members/Purpose: Publications owned, operated, or controlled by voluntary associations and societies, including organizations with licensing and certification functions.

Training: Sponsors seminars and resource networks.

Journal/Publication: Bulletin; *Buyers Guide*; *Snapshot*; *Who's Who in Snap.*

Job Listings: *Snapshot* contains job listings.

Writers Guild of America-East

555 W. 57th St.

New York, NY 10019

Website: www.wgaeast.org

Members/Purpose: Provides script registration service.

Journal/Publication: Directory; newsletter; *Theatrical and Television Minimum Basic Agreement*; agents list.

Writers Guild of America-West
8955 Beverly Blvd.
West Hollywood, CA 90048
Website: www.writersguild.com
E-mail: wga@wga.org
Members/Purpose: Labor union for writers in the fields of motion
  pictures, television, and radio.
Training: Offers seminars.
Journal/Publication: Journal; *Writers Guild Directory.*

CHAPTER ELEVEN

PATH 2: TEACHING

*T*alk to any English teacher you know, and they'll tell you a surprising fact about the teaching profession. They don't teach English, they teach students! The art of teaching and the skill required in the dynamics of student interaction weigh far more heavily in this equation than love of or interest in the subject matter. The subject might be English, but the overriding concerns in this profession are conveying an appreciation of English in all its forms of expression to learners who come to the classroom with different issues, at different ages, from different lifestyles, and with dramatically different degrees of interest in the subject. With all that in the way, simply loving English yourself is not enough, although that is certainly important and desirable. How could you teach something you didn't truly enjoy and expect not to convey that lack of interest through a mechanical approach to the subject?

But teaching something is a unique art and demands skills you probably didn't acquire in your studies of English. It has very little to do with your own proficiency in the subject. The world is full of skillful practitioners who, for one reason or another and often inexplicably, cannot teach someone how they do it. The practice of something is very different from professing it in a classroom.

For example, planning for learning outcomes is critical. Teaching English within an established curriculum, be it high school or college, means corresponding to some state educational goals or course outline. In high school, it may be state standards; in college, it may be a written course description in the catalog. To accomplish this body of learning within a set time requires judicious planning of the material. What will be done each day? How much time will you allow between assignments or readings? Which materials will you require and which will you only recommend? Scores of decisions must be made about how material will be introduced, presented, and ultimately delivered back to you for evaluation.

Add to this the fact that students learn in different ways; some are auditory learners who enjoy listening and gain most of their information in this way. If they are required to take notes while listening, something may have to give, and it may be difficult for them to retain the material. For others, auditory learning is less successful, and they prefer a visual approach with board work, handouts, their own notes, diagrams, books, and many visual materials. They retain these images and can call them up to remember the material.

Others need to participate through reading in class, performing, team projects, and other activities that physically involve them. They learn best this way. These are kinesthetic learners, and they are often forgotten in planning and curriculum design. Professional teachers ensure that their classes satisfy the learning styles of *all* their students through judicious combinations of modalities in teaching. The professional teacher has analyzed his or her own teaching style and seeks to incorporate the elements that come less naturally to maximize learning by every student.

The teaching and learning that takes place in a class is not static. The classroom is an emotionally charged environment for the student and instructor that may call into play questions of self-esteem and competency. People are exploring new definitions of themselves in relation to their capabilities, values, or achievement. A good teacher understands this and encourages a risk-free environment of mutual appreciation and participation. Both teacher and student are allowed to make mistakes and move on. The teacher strives to assist in establishing congruence between the self (who we know we are right now), the ideal self (who we want to be), and the learning environment created in the classroom. The classroom should be a place where our real selves can rise up and begin to touch our ideal selves.

Any mention of competency, self-esteem, or self-worth naturally suggests the subject of grading and the evaluation teachers provide. Grades are an expected and required part of many institutional academic settings. Establishing fair and consistent standards of evaluating your students and assigning grades is a significant challenge to many teachers who otherwise feel perfectly competent in the teaching role. English teachers particularly find that grading the numerous required essays is highly subjective, and they are always seeking better ways to ensure fairness in grading this kind of assignment. Students, too, often complain about grading practices in teachers they, in every other respect, feel positive about.

The teacher of English is called on to play other roles, too. Animating the class and inspiring attention and commitment to the material are all required in teaching. Part of this is the teacher's enthusiasm, part is teaching style, and part is effective use of ancillary materials and the ability to relate this material to a student's life. English teachers, of course, present information and demonstrate periods, schools, and styles of particular writers or poets. They seek to raise relevant questions, prompt dialogues in the class, and develop in students the discipline of self-questioning. They clarify difficulties or obscurities in the material and draw parallels or find relationships between examples.

For a professional teacher, each class is not only an opportunity to teach the subject, English, but to teach how to learn, as well. How to question, how to record information, how to be selective, and how to retain information are ongoing lessons that take place in every classroom to some degree.

A good teacher also uses the class and the material to explain how this material reflects feelings. They will share their own agreement with or support of ideas or emotions in the material under study. Most of all, an instructor will evaluate and by example develop the student's capacity for self-evaluation through careful, caring feedback about both in-class and out-of-class work. The instructor's own example of preparation, organization, personal appearance, evaluation standards, student interest, and enthusiasm will remain an example long after the memory of the actual class content has faded.

Teachers are frequently cited as important factors in one's choice of a career. Teachers often will remember one or two of their own teachers who were strong influences on their decision to teach. Much of that influence was a result of their presence in the classroom. They served as models of people enjoying what they were doing and doing it skillfully. They were professional and correct yet remained natural and approachable. We would watch and listen to them and think, "Maybe I could do that."

DEFINITION OF THE CAREER PATH

We'll look at two possible levels of teaching English: secondary school teaching with a bachelor's degree and college teaching, possibly with a master's degree, but more frequently requiring a doctoral degree as the essential credential.

Following graduation, certified teachers apply for advertised positions in public middle and high schools. Fortunately, and even in spite of stiff competition and an abundance of candidates, teaching positions are well advertised, and all certified teacher graduates are qualified for entry-level English teaching assignments. Actually, in some situations the first-year teacher's inexperience can be a plus. With school budgets under terrific strain, principals, superintendents, and other hiring officials may be more attracted to a relatively inexperienced teacher who will earn a lower salary than to an experienced teacher, perhaps with a more advanced degree, who would take a larger proportion of salary funds.

Is it possible to teach English at the high school level without state certification and with a bachelor of arts in English? Yes, in some public school districts that have had difficulty securing teachers because of location or pay scales, there have been provisions made to grant temporary certification to noncredentialed teachers. This is, however, not very common. Some private high schools also might consider a noncertified teacher, although with the heavy supply of and small demand for secondary English teachers, even private schools can and increasingly do require teaching preparation that equals or is very close to that which public schools require. In fact, at some private schools, it is not uncommon for a majority of the English teachers to have master's degrees, and there exist numerous large city high schools that have attracted Ph.D.s, as well.

A master's degree in English literature may be helpful in securing a private school teaching position at the high school level, especially if the master's specialty work in English corresponds to the school's needs, e.g., twentieth-century British literature or early-nineteenth-century American writers. Graduates with master's degrees and no certification at the bachelor's level may also find employment in junior and community college settings or special college programs for adult learners. These schools may welcome the teacher with a master's degree, again, especially if the specialty is one that corresponds to their curriculum. The following is an actual advertisement for a college-level English instructor with a master's degree:

Community College English Instructor. Full-time, tenure-track faculty position. Minimum of master's degree in English required. Familiarity with computer-based writing, interactive video, Web course instruction, and teaching experience preferred. Applications accepted until position is filled.

The doctoral degree in English opens up the world of college teaching to the prospective educator. Competition here is keen, although at the time of publication of this volume there was not an overabundance of Ph.D.s in the field. Positions are well advertised in vehicles such as *The Chronicle of Higher Education* (www.chronicle.com), a weekly newspaper reporting on higher education issues and containing the most complete list of faculty, staff, and leadership position openings for colleges and universities in the United States and some foreign countries. The following is an ad from *The Chronicle* that would be of interest to a new Ph.D. in English:

Faculty Position English Department. Full-time tenure-track position for a generalist in literature and composition to begin fall 2000.

Requirements: Earned Ph.D. in literature, demonstrated success in college teaching of literature and composition, strong background in composition; American and British literature with supporting work in minority and/or Third World literature; knowledge of critical theories. Six (four-credit) courses constitute the full-time teaching load per academic year.

This ad is interesting for a number of reasons. First, it requires an *earned* doctorate. To apply, you must have your degree in hand. Some advertisements will encourage the application of ABD (All But Dissertation) candidates who have not yet but are soon to complete their degree work. The advertisement also indicates that the successful candidate will be teaching composition classes. An earned doctorate will pay more than an ABD and will lead more directly and quickly to possible tenure and promotion. ABD candidates will also have to decide how they will finish their degree (the dissertation often being the most time-consuming aspect of their academics) while holding down a full-time job.

Teaching freshman composition class is generally part of the teaching load of new college English teachers. Many of these students will be taking English composition because it is a college requirement for graduation and not because they are English majors or have chosen the course. The English department performs a service to the entire college in offering this course. Generally, even senior faculty will teach at least one offering of composition, but as you become more senior in the faculty you can take on courses more directly related to your interests and educational background.

There is also in the ad a request for documentation of teaching success. This could come from teaching assistantships done while working on the doctoral degree. Many students acquire this experience as graduate teaching assistants, part-time faculty, lecturers, or adjunct faculty at other colleges or programs.

The advertisement also calls for Third World literature, critical theories awareness, and composition credentials. These could be substantiated either through a transcript showing course work in those areas, published articles or papers on some aspect of those issues, or recommendations from colleagues stating your expertise in those areas.

The road to a doctorate is fairly long and arduous. It is hard work. Along the way, you'll meet some wonderful people, some who'll be friends and colleagues the rest of your life. Even colleagues separated by long distances have the opportunity to meet at conferences and symposia. You'll have opportunities to write, teach, and perhaps publish—all before you finish your degree.

Take advantage of these opportunities when you can. As the advertisement shown suggests, some of those kinds of qualifications will be asked of you. However, it is possible to become overly involved in some of these areas to the detriment of degree progress.

There has been considerable discussion in academic circles about the number of individuals who begin doctoral programs and do not see them through to completion. In fact, Neil Rudenstein, the president of Harvard College, published a book on the issue of improving and tightening up the time requirements to earn a Ph.D., particularly in the humanities, where his research clearly demonstrated the longest timelines between initiating the degree and earning it, with a correspondingly high rate of mortality (dropouts) in candidates. In the science areas, he found a higher completion rate and less time to degree. This may have something to do with more defined parameters of the fields of science—an emphasis on correct process, formula, and execution—whereas in English, there seems to be less decision making on the part of advisers, doctoral committees, and other participants about the proper timeline and what needs to be accomplished during that period. There were vague suggestions that candidates needed to extend their scholarly preparation as a kind of dues-paying for the forthcoming degree. Consequently, the dropout rate has been disappointingly high.

WORKING CONDITIONS

The working conditions for teachers of English are dramatically different according to the educational setting. The high school English teacher has a full complement of classes, perhaps as many as five or six a day, and may have study hall or lunchroom supervision duties during the week, responsibilities for an after-school detention center, or even a sports activity to supervise. The place of discipline in the secondary curriculum has a major impact in the classroom and is perhaps the single most dominant element of the working conditions for the secondary English teacher. Since the student population in large part is not voluntary, resistance is prevalent and acting out through poor discipline and bad behavior is common.

The effective classroom teacher is one who has successfully mastered classroom management. For many young teachers, these are the most challenging lessons in teaching, and they make for the most interesting stories as they grow in their profession. The balance between teaching English and class-room discipline is seldom in equilibrium and can be particularly frustrating, as when one disruptive student threatens the decorum of an otherwise studious class.

Most public high schools have fairly rigid systems of enforced behavior norms, and the principal agents of that enforcement are the faculty. To elect high school English education as your particular arena is to challenge your ability to maintain your poise and your focus on your subject matter and your interest in training and shaping young people while at the same time requiring you to both enforce and administer the necessary disciplinary elements mandated by your school. These sanctions include grades, dismissal, detention, warnings, parent conferences, and referrals to other helping agencies in or out of the school system.

It is a full day with established starting and ending times and much at-home work. Perhaps among the busiest of at-home schedules are those of the English faculty. So much of their homework involves writing, and giving the valuable feedback students need from the writing involves hours of reading and providing commentary. Staying ahead of text and book assignments is also time-consuming, as is maintaining required records of attendance, grades, warnings, progress reports, and other evaluation instruments that may be required in your school district.

High school English teachers often take on other assignments, such as homeroom duty, field trips, guest speakers, chaperon duties, and advising activities for yearbooks, literary journals, or clubs in the school. These also can demand a great deal of time, and it is important that the teacher entering into secondary English teaching understand that these assignments are not so much additions to but rather a typical part of a high school teaching professional's commitment.

A college teaching environment is significantly different than a middle or high school setting. There is less need to appease a number of outside publics. There is no school board to satisfy, no parents, no parent-teacher groups. The world of the college classroom is closed to outsiders and isn't violated by anyone outside the class. It is, in fact, rare to have a class interrupted by anyone outside of the room, so understood is this convention. Academic free-dom protects the professors in large part and allows them to express them-selves within their class material with far greater pointedness than is the case in high school.

Grading, evaluation procedures, numbers of tests, even the issue of whether to have textbooks or texts is entirely up to the faculty member. If the rationale supports these decisions, the administration does not interfere. An added protection is the granting of tenure to established professors who have documented significant teaching histories and excellent student reviews, publications, campus committee work, and outreach to the community. The granting of tenure gains them an additional degree of job security and further supports their expression of academic freedom. All of these conditions make the classroom environment and the relations of faculty and students very different than what has come before in the student's education.

The actual teaching day in a college or university setting involves fewer class hours taught per day and per week. At an institution that focuses on faculty research, the teacher would be responsible for teaching two to three courses that each meet three to four hours per week. Schools that emphasize teaching rather than research require instructors to teach three to four courses for a total of nine to twelve hours of class meetings per week. These class hours and some mandated office hours for advising students and general advisees are the principal requirements for attendance on the faculty member's part. But as the following ad makes clear, there are other expectations:

> *English Department Tenure-Track Position.* Assistant, tenure track, starting fall 2001. We are looking for a new colleague to teach courses in English education, supervise student teachers, and advise students as a member of a dynamic and growing English program committed to excellent undergraduate and postdegree education. Minimum qualifications: doctorate in English, English education, or equivalent field in hand by August 2001; two years' teaching experience and ability to conduct research. Preference will be given to individuals who have experience working with student teachers in a supervisory position and demonstrate interest in working with a diverse student population. Salary is commensurate with experience. Applicants should submit a curriculum vitae, a statement of interest, a copy of transcripts, evidence of effective teaching, and a sample publication. The applicant should also arrange for three letters of reference to be sent under separate cover.

In addition to courses and advising, scholarly research is an expectation even of those colleges for whom tenure is not based on publication. All colleges want their faculty to contribute to the scholarly dialogue in their discipline, and this is reviewed by chairs of departments and academic deans periodically throughout the instructor's career. It may be a determining element in granting tenure or promotion to that faculty member and may influence issues such as salary negotiations, merit increases, and the like.

Committee work is also important, because the faculty at most colleges are the governing and rule-making bodies who determine and vote on governance and program changes. Committee work can be issue-oriented, such as a commission on the status of women or a pay equity survey; it may be programmatic, such as a committee to study the core curriculum for undergraduates or to devise a new graphic arts major; or it may be related to credentials, as in a committee set up to prepare materials for an accreditation visit.

Some committees are permanent, such as academic standards, curriculum review, promotion and tenure, planning, and administrator review committees, though the members may change on a rotating schedule. Other groups are formed for a limited time or until completion of some task. These committees are essential and are one vehicle for guiding the direction of the school. Having the support of all the faculty and constantly fresh and interested members helps to ensure all voices are heard and many different opinions considered in making what are often far-reaching decisions.

A college day is certainly less rigid than a high school schedule, though it may be just as busy and as long. The difference in content is that for the high school teacher, much of the day and commitment is enforced and required. The college teacher may certainly feel institutional and professional pressure to fulfill certain roles, but exactly how to do that is up to the individual. There will be classes, office hours, meetings, and research work to do. Since college campuses are often wonderful centers of art, music, and intellectual exchange, there are frequently events to attend in the evening. Faculty members may act as advisers to fraternities, sororities, campus newspapers, and clubs, which may also add to their day.

TRAINING AND QUALIFICATIONS

To teach English at the secondary level requires a bachelor of science degree in English education at the secondary level and state certification for the state in which you wish to teach. These programs are well-defined options within the education curriculum of many teacher training colleges and universities. They include a teaching practicum in which you would have the opportunity to leave campus and teach actual English classes under a supervising teacher for an academic quarter or semester. Certification in the state granting the degree is usually part of the degree process and may include the requirement to participate in the National Teacher Examination (NTE). In states requiring the NTE, test preparation is usually well incorporated into the curriculum.

There need not be any mysteries surrounding your eligibility for certification in states other than the state in which you originally earned your teaching certificate. The authors of this book have found the simplest solution to be a phone call to the appropriate office within a state Department of Education. Generally, the folks in those offices have the information you need at their fingertips. There is an excellent website, www.academploy.com /resources.cfm, that has a submenu describing the certification requirements for each state. In many cases, there are links from these listings to the complete documentation provided by those states. You'll find in searching this site that many states have nonstandard options for certification, and you'll learn which states have reciprocal certification agreements with other states.

Another option for the individual with a degree in English who desires to teach but lacks certification would be to enroll in a "conversion" program at a college or university. These programs offer an opportunity to add the necessary state-mandated teaching requirements to an existing degree. Depending on your undergraduate degree and whether a change of institution is involved, this could require twelve to eighteen months of academic enrollment and, in some cases, a full two years.

Such conversion programs can also exist independent of a college or university. Some are the product of a consortium of school districts, such as the Upper Valley Teacher Training Institute in Lebanon, New Hampshire (www.valley.net/~uvttp/index.html). This unique teacher qualifying program takes individuals with bachelor's degrees, many of whom have had other careers or significant work experience, and places them with master teachers in actual classrooms for a full year. Half the year is at one grade level, and the other half of the year is with another grade. The year includes much independent work and follows a contract established at the start of the year. There may be also a requirement to participate in an associated classroom program to meet state reading certification requirements.

College and university teaching requires a completed doctorate or, in some cases, All But Dissertation (ABD). Salary and assignments may be affected by lack of an earned doctorate. In addition to the doctorate, there may be requirements for teaching experience, special depth of research, background in a particular genre or subject area, and some additional competencies. There is almost always the requirement of teaching basic composition classes to first- and second-year students.

EARNINGS

Middle and secondary school teachers of English are paid according to the same salary schedules as other teachers in their school districts. Salaries across the nation vary depending upon location, which affects cost of living and level of support of education as reflected in the school budget. A salary survey published by the National Center for Education Statistics (http://nces.ed .gov/fastfacts/display) in 1999 listed the national average for entry-level teachers at $19,408. Their website is an excellent source of data on all aspects of the teaching profession. Another source of information is the ERIC Clearinghouse on Teacher Education in Washington, D.C. (http://ericeece.org/).

The Chronicle of Higher Education annual faculty salary survey reports that the average faculty salary for English language and literature positions in four-year colleges or universities for instructors (usually people who are ABD) was $26,478 at public institutions and $27,485 at private institutions. New assistant professors earned, on average, $33,949 at public institutions and $32,875 at private institutions. Remember, these are all average figures and some teachers may start at a lower or higher level of pay.

CAREER OUTLOOK

The National Center for Education Statistics cites a number of interesting developments in teacher trends on their website. While the number of teachers in the United States rose during the 1970s and the early 1980s, public school enrollment levels decreased. As a result, the pupil/teacher ratio dropped from twenty-two to one in 1970 to eighteen to one in 1985. Since then, enrollment has risen nearly as fast as the number of teachers, with only a small drop to seventeen to one in the pupil/teacher ratio. Virtually all of the teaching positions approved by public school districts were filled in 1994–95. On average, less than 1 percent of teaching positions were vacant or temporarily filled by substitute teachers because suitable candidates could not be found. So while your teaching degree is a valuable credential, you are entering a highly competitive market and will need to be aggressive in your job search. Your willingness to relocate may dramatically increase your chances of securing your first teaching position.

As for higher education and prospective teachers of English, *The Chronicle of Higher Education* reported in 1999 that not only do English majors take the longest of any degree candidates to complete their doctorates (an average of ten years), but once they achieve their doctorate, they spend an average of 2.8 years in a "holding pattern" working in short-term, nontenure jobs. A recent survey of doctoral students in English who earned their degrees between 1982 and 1985 showed that 75 percent of them had the academic jobs they sought, although 15 percent of that group are in non-tenure-track positions.

STRATEGY FOR FINDING THE PUBLIC SCHOOL JOB

Check with Your Career Office

College, university, and technical school career offices in your region of the state will also be on the mailing list to receive teaching vacancy announcements. Determine which schools' jobs postings you can view through reciprocity agreements with your own college and make these visits part of your regular job search. You will find that you become so practiced at screening newspapers and job postings that it will take very little time to quickly ascertain whether any new openings have been listed.

Directly Contact Schools Where You Would Like to Work

Send a cover letter and resume to schools where you would like to work. State departments of education publish directories of all public schools in the state, listing superintendents, principals, and principal administrators. Names, addresses, and phone numbers are regularly included in these listings. These same departments of education can provide you with similar information for the state university and technical college systems as well. This information is generally provided free of charge and requires only a telephone call. Many libraries and college career counseling centers will have this same information on file.

Surf the Web

Particular websites come and go, but the Internet will always be a good source of job postings for teaching positions. For higher education, *The Chronicle of Higher Education* website (http://chronicle.com) remains the best source of job postings. The website is better than the print version because jobs are clustered on the website by type. In the newspaper edition, you must scan full pages of ads to locate the ones that interest you. For public school jobs, check out these excellent sites: www.ed.gov/Programs/EROD/ERODmap .html, www.ncei.com/State-alt-contact.htm, and www.academploy.com/ resources.cfm.

Scan Relevant Newspapers

The public school teacher candidate is advised to make a regular practice of scanning all newspapers advertising in and around the geographic region being considered for teaching assignments. These newspapers need not be purchased; most libraries subscribe to a generous selection of local papers.

POSSIBLE EMPLOYERS

Public Schools

A 1997 report published by the U.S. Department of Education stated that there were approximately 2,340,443 public school teachers working in the United States in 1993–94. Competition for available positions was then and is still keen. But even when supply far exceeds demand, most teaching positions are advertised. We often speak of the "hidden job market" in business to refer to the large number of positions that are filled without public notification. But in teaching, in an effort to secure the best pool of applicants as well as to respond to school boards and boards of directors, most positions are well advertised.

Department of Defense (DOD) Schools

Since 1946 there have been schools on U.S. military bases around the world for children of military and civilian personnel assigned overseas. Just under 300 schools serve this segment of U.S. public education, and courses of study, eligibility for teachers, textbooks, and programs parallel those of the public schools in the United States. Schools in the DOD system are all accredited by the North Central Association of Colleges and Schools. Application processes are outlined in detail in the annual DOD booklet, *Overseas Employment Opportunities for Educators*.

STRATEGY FOR FINDING THE PRIVATE SCHOOL JOB

Directly Contact Schools Where You Would Like to Work

Send a cover letter and resume to each private school you would like to work for. Private schools are equally easy to identify through sources such as *Peterson's Guide to Independent Secondary Schools* or the *Handbook of Private Schools* published by Porter Sargent Publishers of Boston. Both these reference books are standard fare for comprehensive reference sections of career centers and larger college libraries. *Independent School* is the journal of the National Association of Independent Schools. It is published three times a year and contains articles on issues of concern to private schools as well as a number of display advertisements.

Attend Job Fairs

Find out about job fairs and attend as many as you can. Job fairs for private schools, both in the United States and abroad, are held year-round. Many are administered by recruiting firms. These fairs serve as a major entree for many job seekers into the private school system. You register your materials with a private school placement agency, which then provides access to a private school job fair where you can meet and interact with a number of hiring officials from a regional or national base. Your college career office can put you in touch with some of these private school recruiting firms.

POSSIBLE EMPLOYERS

Private Schools

The U.S. Department of Education reported a total of 2.5 million teachers in the United States in 1996. Of this group, about 10 percent, or 250,000, are private school teachers. Accessing the private school market is a very different process from seeking a public school situation. In general, there is not a significant amount of crossover between the two systems, and teachers in the private school system tend to stay in that educational environment.

Private schools list positions and send out job notices but seldom advertise in newspapers to ensure a more select pool of candidates and maintain a lower profile than their public counterparts. As tuition-driven institutions, they do not have the core franchise market that public schools automatically obtain and must seek students through reputation and advertising.

Private Schools Abroad

Schools abroad can be researched through directories of *Schools Abroad of Interest to Americans,* also published by Porter Sargent Publishers of Boston; the *ISS Directory of Overseas Schools,* published by International Schools Services; and publications such as the *International Educator,* the official publication of the Overseas Schools Assistance Corporation.

Resources for Finding Both Public and Private School Openings

Educational Directories, a major publisher of educational resources, produces *Patterson's Elementary Education* and *Patterson's American Education* each year. They list public and private elementary and secondary schools, school districts and superintendents, postsecondary schools, and others, including nursery schools, YMCA programs, and the like. Use these directories to conduct your proactive job search activities: mailing out cover letters and resumes, networking, and telephone follow-up.

Career offices often carry national job vacancy lists that include teaching positions. Some of these lists include *Current Jobs for Graduates in Education,* the *Job Hunter, Community Jobs,* and *Current Jobs for Graduates.*

In addition, be sure to carefully review the list of professional associations for teachers of English at the end of this chapter. For several associations there is a line labeled "Job Listings"; any activities that the association undertakes to assist its members in finding employment are shown.

The Journal of Employment in Education, a publication of the American Association for Employment in Education (www.ub-careers.buffalo.edu/ aaee/), presents a collection of articles related to job search issues for educators. The 1994 issue contained numerous display ads for teacher job fairs around the country, a complete list of all state departments of education (including addresses and phone numbers), and a guide to teacher vacancy listing subscriptions around the country. *The Journal of Employment in Education* is distributed for a modest fee by education departments and career centers at colleges and universities with teacher training programs.

STRATEGY FOR FINDING COLLEGE AND UNIVERSITY JOBS

Acquiring a college teaching position nearly always demands that you relocate to an institution other than where you received your degree. Higher education has limited openings at any one time, and part-time work or adjunct faculty status at one institution is no guarantee of earning a full-time spot. Most departments have budget lines dedicated to full-time, potentially tenured faculty. This means that faculty who are hired in those budget lines are hired with the expectation they will become a permanent part of the faculty and earn tenure and promotion when they qualify.

Consequently, though there may be schools you would enjoy teaching at or areas of the country you would prefer, the supply and demand of college professorships clearly dictate you must follow the demand and relocate.

Go to "the Source"

The Chronicle of Higher Education (www.chronicle.com) is the weekly national publication listing junior college, four-year college, and university teaching positions in English. Many of these advertisements are large display ads that detail in full the requirements and duties of the positions advertised. This publication is widely available on college campuses, and usually many offices have individual subscriptions. Your career center, department office, and college library will all have copies you can review each week.

Network with Faculty Colleagues

Another excellent source of college-level positions will be your own faculty colleague contacts made as you pursue your advanced degree. There is a well-established network that becomes very active when schools are seeking to fill a position. This network would value the personal recommendation of a friend or former teaching associate. For this reason, it's important to ensure that your faculty mentors and colleagues are well aware of your teaching and research interests and geographic preferences so they can respond for you and move the process along if an opportunity presents itself.

Attend Professional Meetings

Interviews are often conducted at professional meetings, where recent job openings may be announced or posted in a conspicuous place at the registration table. As a graduate student, many of these conferences are available to you at substantially reduced fees or no fee at all. You should take advantage of them for the professional content and the opportunity to meet representatives from the departments of other higher-education institutions.

POSSIBLE EMPLOYERS

Some resources that can be used to identify schools if you are considering teaching English beyond high school include *Peterson's Guide to Two-Year Colleges*, *Peterson's Guide to Four-Year Colleges*, *Peterson's Annual Guides to Graduate Study* (www.petersons.com), and the *College Board Index of Majors and Graduate Degrees*.

POSSIBLE JOB TITLES

For the professional educator, there is not a wide latitude in job title. The term *teacher* is so old and so esteemed that we apply it to professionals from nursery school to the most rarefied levels of postdoctoral research. All are teachers. We see variants from time to time; for example, the resource room teacher in elementary school who works individually with students experiencing difficulties in particular subjects, or the skills application teacher on the college faculty who may have a more narrowly defined teaching role than a staff professor. To students, however, these distinctions may not loom very large, and most are made to indicate bureaucratic distinctions. The teaching role remains the same.

- Bilingual teacher
- Cooperating teacher
- Educator
- International school teacher
- Resource room teacher
- Special education teacher
- Substitute teacher
- Teacher

RELATED OCCUPATIONS

Teaching skills and teacher training lend themselves to innumerable occupations and are seen as universally valuable by all other employers.

The ability to explain, demonstrate, encourage, test, and spark imagination can be transferred to countless settings in business and industry. The introduction of new products, cross-training of staff, planning for change or transition, and responding to crises are all situations that call for a teacher's expertise.

Nuclear power information centers, museum programs for children, historical sites, and public relations organizations all have need of the teacher's training in presentation skills, explanation, and the ability to convey meaning.

Social service programs devote much of their mission to education in the form of new programs and information for their clients that would use teachers in situations not very different from the standard classroom. The following list is a brief and general suggestion of possible related careers for the teacher.

- Counselor
- Education administrator
- Educational consultant
- Employee development specialist
- Employment interviewer
- Environmental educator
- Hospital/community health educator
- Librarian
- Media relations representative
- Museum curator
- Not-for-profit organization administrator
- Personnel specialist
- Preschool worker
- Public relations specialist
- Researcher
- Sales representative
- Social worker
- Trainer

PROFESSIONAL ASSOCIATIONS FOR TEACHERS OF ENGLISH

Finding out about and joining at least one professional association can play an important role in achieving success in your job search. There are many associations that relate to the kinds of jobs available for teachers of English. The following are some groups that can provide valuable information in terms of finding out about actual job listings or talking with members for networking purposes.

American Association for Adult and Continuing Education
1101 Connecticut Ave. NW, Ste. 700
Washington, DC 20036
Website: infolit.org/members/aaace.htm
E-mail: annadarin@dc.sba.com
Members/Purpose: Provides leadership in advancing education as a lifelong learning process. Serves as a central forum for a wide variety of adult and continuing education special-interest groups.
Journal/Publication: *Adult Education*; *Adult Learning Practitioner Journal*; newsletter; membership directory.

American Association of Christian Schools
P.O. Box 2189
Independence, MO 64055
Members/Purpose: Maintains teacher/administrator certification program. Participates in school accreditation program.
Journal/Publication: Newsletter; directory; *The Builder.*
Job Listings: Teacher placement newsletter four times per year.

American Association of Community and Junior Colleges
One Dupont Circle NW, Ste. 410
Washington, DC 20036-1176
Website: www.aacc.nche.edu
E-mail: Same as website
Members/Purpose: Administrators, students, trustees, faculty, public officials, and interested individuals from all segments of postsecondary education. Seeks to clarify and help resolve critical issues in postsecondary education through conferences, publications, and special projects.
Journal/Publication: Bulletin; *Change Magazine.*

American Association of State Colleges and Universities
1307 New York Ave., Ste. 500
Washington, DC 20005-4701
Website: www.aascu.org
E-mail: Same as website
Members/Purpose: Colleges and universities offering programs leading to a degree of bachelor, master, or doctor that are wholly or partially state supported and controlled.
Training: Conducts national and regional workshops.
Journal/Publication: Membership list; *Memo: To the President*; proceedings; studies.

American Association of University Professors
1012 14th St. NW, Ste. 500
Washington, DC 20005
Website: www.aaup.org
E-mail: aaup@aaup.org
Members/Purpose: College and university teachers, research scholars, and academic librarians. Purposes are to facilitate cooperation among teachers and research scholars in universities, colleges, and professional schools for the promotion of higher education and research, and to increase the usefulness and advance the standards, ideals, and welfare of the profession.
Journal/Publication: *Academe: Bulletin of the AAUP; Collective Bargaining Newsletter.*

American Council on Education
One Dupont Circle NW, Ste. 800
Washington, DC 20036
Website: www.acenet.edu
E-mail: web@ace.nche.edu
Members/Purpose: A council of colleges and universities, educational organizations, and affiliates.
Journal/Publication: *Educational Record; Higher Education and National Affairs; ACE/Macmillan Series on Higher Education.*
Job Listings: Job hotline.

American Federation of Teachers
555 New Jersey Ave. NW
Washington, DC 20001
Website: www.aft.org
Members/Purpose: AFL-CIO. Works with teachers and other educational employees at the state and local level in organizing, collective bargaining, research, educational issues, and public relations. Conducts research in various areas.
Journal/Publication: *American Educator; American Teacher; Healthwire; On Campus; Public Service Reporter.*

American Society for Training and Development
1640 King St., Box 1443
Alexandria, VA 22313
Website: www/astd.org/virtual_community
E-mail: Same as website
Members/Purpose: Professional association for persons engaged in the training and development of business, industry, education, and

government. Undertakes special research projects and acts as clearinghouse.

Training: Maintains database of information on more than 100,000 public seminars, workshops, and conferences, and on courseware from more than 100 suppliers.

Journal/Publication: *Buyers Guide and Consultant Directory; Info-Line; National Report on Human Resources; Training and Development Journal; Training and Development Literature Index; Who's Who in Training and Development.*

Job Listings: Check with local chapters.

College English Association
c/o Patricia R. Kelvin and Bege Bowers
CEA Publications
Department of English
Youngstown State University
Youngstown, OH 44555
Website: www.winthrop.edu/cea
Members/Purpose: Members of faculties of English and related disciplines in colleges and universities of the United States and Canada. Studies and works actively to enhance the teaching function of scholars in English and related humanities disciplines.
Journal/Publication: CEA *Critic*; CEA *Forum*; regional groups publish newsletters.

Council for American Private Education
13017 Wisteria Dr., Ste. 457
Germantown, MD 20874
Website: www.capenet.org
E-mail: cape@impresso.com
Members/Purpose: Coalition of national organizations serving the interests of private schools (K–12).
Journal/Publication: *Outlook; Private Schools of the United States.*
Job Listings: List of teacher placement services.

English in Action
16 E. 69th St.
New York, NY 10021
Website: www.english-speakingunion.org/index.htm
Members/Purpose: Program administered by English-Speaking Union of the United States. Volunteers and individual contributors; corporations, foundations, churches, and other institutions. Helps immigrants and foreign nationals visiting, studying, or working in the United States with

conversational English practice and acculturation through weekly person-to-person meetings with American volunteers.
Journal/Publication: *Here and There; Tips on Tutoring English.*

National Association of Independent Schools
1620 L St. NW, 11th Floor
Washington, DC 20036
Website: www.nais-schools.org
E-mail: publicinfo@nais-schools.org
Members/Purpose: Independent elementary and secondary school members; regional associations of independent schools and related associations. Provides curricular and administrative research and services.
Training: Conducts seminars.
Journal/Publication: *Independent School.*
Job Listings: They have a general teacher's packet that consists of recruitment agencies, placement firms, directories, and brochures that help with choosing the right school.

National Catholic Education Association
1077 30th St. NW, Ste. 100
Washington, DC 20007
Website: www.ncea.org
E-mail: nceaadmin@ncea.org
Members/Purpose: Catholic schools and religious education centers from kindergarten through graduate school levels; individuals. Conducts research; works with voluntary groups and government agencies on educational problems.
Training: Conducts workshops and seminars.
Journal/Publication: *Current Issues in Catholic Higher Education; Forum; Momentum; Notes; Update; Parish Coordinator/Directors of Religious Education; Private Law School Digest; Seminary News.*
Job Listings: A job opportunity database: call association for application.

National Council of Teachers of English
1111 Kenyon Rd.
Urbana, IL 61801
Website: www.ncte.org
E-mail: public_info@ncte.org
Members/Purpose: Teachers of English at all school levels. Works to increase the effectiveness of instruction in English language and literature.
Journal/Publication: *College Composition and Communication; College English; CSSEDC Quarterly; English Education; English Journal; Language*

Arts; NOTES Plus; Research in Teaching of English; SLATE Newsletter; Teaching English in the Two-Year College.

National Educational Association
1201 16th St. NW
Washington, DC 20036
Website: www.nea.org
E-mail: BobChase@nea.org
Members/Purpose: Professional organization and union of elementary and secondary school teachers, college and university professors, administrators, principals, counselors, and others concerned with education.
Journal/Publication: *ESP Journal; ESP Progress;* handbook, *NEA Today.*

National University Continuing Education Association
One Dupont Circle NW, Ste. 615
Washington, DC 20036
Website: www.nucea.edu
E-mail: postmaster @nucea.edu
Members/Purpose: Institutions of higher learning, both public and private, with active extension and continuing education programs; professional staff at member institutions.
Journal/Publication: *Continuing Higher Education Review; Guide to Independent Study Through Correspondence Instruction; NUCEA Newsletter; Guide to Certificate Programs.*

Teachers of English to Speakers of Other Languages
700 S. Washington St., Ste. 200
Alexandria, VA 22314
Website: www.tesol.edu/index.htm
E-mail: tesol@tesol.edu
Members/Purpose: School, college, and adult education teachers who teach English as a second or foreign language; students and professional people in the field; colleges and schools are institutional members, and publishers are commercial members. Aims to improve the teaching of English as a second or foreign language.
Journal/Publication: *Directory of Professional Preparation; TESOL Journal; TESOL Matters; Membership Directory; Quarterly; Training Program Directory.*
Job Listings: Placement bulletin.

CHAPTER TWELVE

PATH 3: ADVERTISING AND PUBLIC RELATIONS

*T*here is certainly an attractive mystique surrounding the fields of advertising and public relations, and not only for the English major. They are seen, and justifiably so in most instances, as glamorous, high-visibility industries. Not only are advertising and public relations omnipresent in today's society, but we are also fascinated with the mechanics of how they are accomplished and what works and what doesn't. Advertising campaigns become the subject of morning-after conferences in the workplace, and the latest spokesperson's financial deal is the subject of newspaper headlines. Working in these fields seems to convey to the employee a halo of quickness, creativity, and imagination—not all of which may be warranted. We associate advertising with celebrity, which may or may not be justified. Advertising is not only omnipresent in society; it can be (and has been) the subject of great controversy, subsequently attracting enormous press coverage in and of itself.

Advertising continues to be a medium of social change in the United States. Increasingly, ads are targeted at very specific audiences. The music, setting, and choice of actors all combine to create a message directed at a very specific group of the buying public. With so many advertising messages constantly being aired, individual advertisers will frequently "push the envelope" of taste and/or discretion to have their product noticed in hopes the public will be provoked to some kind of reaction.

Public relations has also come into the common vocabulary as we become more aware of how organizations, products, and personalities manage their public presence in our lives. An incident that emphasized the importance of public relations to the viability of a product was brought to our attention as a result of the tragic series of deaths brought about by, as we now know, illegal tampering with Tylenol capsules. The company's decision to remove all of its product from store shelves nationwide, to grant refunds for those who requested them, and to withdraw all advertising for an extended period were seen as highly responsible, ethical corporate actions and did much to lay the groundwork for the successful revitalization of this product. Although the company suffered horrendous financial losses, the product's current preeminence as an analgesic choice of both consumers and medical professionals is seen as a coup for the company's skillful handling of public relations during this crisis.

Much is written and broadcast about the behind-the-scenes work of both public relations and advertising managers. Not all of it is positive, and occasionally we see instances of downright duplicity, but both fields remain centers of creativity, originality, and impact. Because of that, they justify being called "glamour" jobs.

For the English major interested in a graphic illustration of the shifting importance of language in both public relations and advertising, a fascinating comparison would be to look at advertising from the 1950s and advertising from the present. You'll notice in the older advertisements a far greater reliance on textual material. People read ads, and there was a significant amount of straightforward text. Today, people view ads and respond far more to color and photographic images than to factual detail. Our increasing fascination with photographs means they are used far more often than the printed word to convey meaning. Today, we only see "text-heavy" copy in advertisements for very costly or highly complex products, such as expensive cameras or luxury automobiles. Generally, commercial advertising has become a visual medium, and product presentation through the use of words has taken second place to art, atmosphere, and personalities.

Public relations has also undergone a revolution over the past few decades. In the 1950s, public relations may have simply meant responding to a consumer's letter of compliment or complaint and answering inquiries about product composition or manufacturing processes. American society was enjoying a booming proliferation of consumer goods, variations on product themes, and even packaging. This was a far cry from our concerns today, where much of that is being rejected or subjected to intense scrutiny. But during the '50s, the public was largely an adulatory audience to the manufacturer and wanted more, not less.

Today public relations departments have many more interested observers and critics carefully watching the organization's performances from the vantage point of whatever special-interest group they represent: environmental, nutritional, child protective rights, gender equity issues, product quality, or full-disclosure concerns. These groups recognize the impact corporations can have on our quality of life and the influence they can exert on public opinion, social structure, moral issues, and values. Many argue that just the prevalence of these messages sends a disturbing signal about acquisitiveness and self-indulgence. More than ever before, a business must be prepared to answer numerous publics on equally as many issues.

Some organizations have learned a difficult lesson from not having a crisis management team to deal with threats from the outside that might have permanent negative effects on the organization's product, image, or continued existence. Now, corporations frequently have departments or at least teams who handle crisis management. These personnel are trained to provide information to the public about the crisis, organize and manage product recall (if necessary), and create mechanisms to prevent reoccurrence (if possible).

Public relations has become increasingly complex, the situations are often serious, and the concerns of the public are legitimate and insistent. Public relations must become increasingly proactive; therefore, the field is more in need of good writers and communicators than ever before. Both advertising and public relations still welcome the English major who is interested in the field of persuasive communications. There are a number of avenues possible in both fields, and both offer much creativity and opportunity to touch the lives of people in meaningful and unexpected ways.

DEFINITION OF THE CAREER PATH

Public relations and advertising are often linked, but in fact they are two very different fields of public communication with different aims, techniques, and intentions. Nevertheless, we usually refer to them in one phrase, and with good reason. Most firms that buy advertising and use it to promote their corporate image, products, or ideas will probably at some time need public relations to explain, clarify, or deal with sectors of the public that take issue with the organization over some aspect of its operation.

Public relations is that function of an organization that seeks to maintain good relations with any number of "publics" it must interact with in doing business. A good example may be the popular American fast-food chain McDonald's. The publics McDonald's must stay responsive to include environmentalists who are concerned about such issues as packaging; nutritionists who want consumers to understand the caloric, sodium, fat content, and nutritional composition of products and who have wider-ranging concerns about the general homogenization of taste in America; city and town planners who worry about issues such as signage and sign height, curb cuts to allow entrance and exit to parking lots, and the physical impact of a restaurant on their municipality; school officials who may be concerned that the restaurant not become a hangout or who fear many children will work excessive part-time hours and diminish their school performance; and zoning officials who worry about spot-rezoning planned neighborhoods to accommodate a McDonald's restaurant. The list could go on and on. Each of these groups has issues over this internationally famous restaurant chain's operation. Public relations officials seek not only to understand the points of view of these groups, but also to have these groups understand McDonald's point of view on the concerns they may hold particularly important.

You may have noticed that customers were not in the list of publics. Customers are not part of the public in the term public relations. Customers are certainly the focus of advertising, marketing, operations, and product delivery. The customer is the "business" that a firm is about. It is in doing business with the market that certain publics may take issue with the organization, and public relations is the arm of an institution that takes that responsibility. The public relations department may respond to individual consumer concerns by providing needed technical data, but, as a group, consumers are categorized separately.

It isn't just commercial enterprises that have need of public relations. It must be emphasized that public relations exists in any large institution; even colleges and universities have need of public relations. Perhaps neighbors are upset over clogged streets every time there's a football game on Saturday at a major university, or about shifting property values as students take over city dwellings for apartment buildings. Public relations officers are used to handling these situations and helping both parties reach solutions. They also draw the public's attention to the new city park built and financed through student efforts, or the care for elders provided by a fraternity or sorority house. No public relations staff member expects all assignments to be positive ones, but part of the job is to ensure that we, the public, have the full picture of an organization.

Our McDonald's example hardly exhausted the range of publics that a public relations department deals with, however. Other aspects of public relations include public information provided to concerned groups and individuals to explain changes in operations, product quality information, or initiatives undertaken by the corporation. This may seem relatively static, but part of good public relations is being able to document this kind of consistent public disclosure to prevent accusations of conspiracy or undue secrecy. Most firms issue regular press releases that announce expansion plans, new factory sites, potential layoffs, new products, product recalls, and a host of other events of at least some interest to the public.

Investor relations is a public relations function organized to meet the needs of individuals who have invested through stock purchases or other mechanisms and who tend to be among the most vocal and active of publics. These members have a right and obligation as investors to thoroughly understand company operations and policy. Public relations produces informative material to keep these investors abreast of profits, losses, future plans, personnel, and the financial stability of the firm.

Whenever a corporation makes information public by press release; newsletter; a mass mailing to customers, clients, or investors; television announcement; or major newspaper display ad, this is the realm of the corporate communications department that knows best how to present the message of the organization to the public at large. Mobil Corporation, which has certainly had ample opportunity to test the merits of its own corporate communications department, pioneered the "advertorial," a paid piece of advertising designed and written to resemble an editorial piece. These are thoughtful and thought-provoking pieces of writing to keep the public thinking about the role of oil energy and the impact of that product in our lives.

Consumer services is yet another public relations division that answers customers' questions about product handling, quality, manufacturing processes, safety, and even student requests for company information to do research reports. In fact, some organizations provide quite extensive consumer services, and many now maintain websites and toll-free numbers. As with all public relations efforts, the purpose is two-fold. In satisfying consumer requests for information and by being accessible, the company increases the probability of a positive relationship and assures its continued presence in the marketplace.

A research department of a large public relations division might support public relations by providing the necessary factual data to most accurately and honestly respond to a variety of situations. They can ascertain how much of a product is sold, where in the world certain raw materials used in the manufacturing process are obtained, the origin of the labor pool, the origin of specific parts used in making the product, and any other information required by the public relations department. A consumer may be sensitive to a chemical or ingredient that is not listed and does not need to be listed on the ingredients of a particular product because it occurs in such small amounts. Nevertheless, there may still be an allergic reaction and perhaps serious health consequences. If the public relations department does not immediately know the answer to such a query, it could direct the problem to the organization's research arm.

Employees staff the organization, but they are also a public that needs to understand the corporation's mission because they serve as its ambassadors in their personal lives. Likewise, they need to be understood by management so that an effective team is formed and sustained as products or services are produced and delivered to the consumer. Corporate newsletters, picnics, interest-free Christmas loans, or on-site child care or elder care are all projects in which public relations team members might participate. You might have seen television commercials showing various employees in an organization going about their jobs. General Electric has been notable in this regard. Such commercials certainly put an individual face on a large corporation for average consumers, but they also serve to instill pride and loyalty in the workforce that is being featured.

The following advertisement is an actual job posting for a public relations staff member that would be particularly attractive to a college English major. See what it can begin to tell you about the job and the organization:

Corporate Communicator. _____, a growing & dynamic financial services organization, has opening in Service Excellence dept. for corporate communicator who will coordinate company communications projects with clients and inside/outside suppliers. This person will be responsible for writing, editing & formatting internal & external company communications including client communiqués, letters from the president and upper management, year-end publications & monthly employee newsletter. This is highly visible position within our organization & we're looking for proficient communicator who can think on their feet & work equally well alone or in a project team. Candidates should possess a degree in English (master's preferred) as well as two yrs professional work experience in corp communic, training or work experience in fine arts/graphics plus a strong working knowledge of desktop publishing software. Must understand print & video production & be able to direct suppliers in bidding & project execution. Forward resume to . . .

Advertising is the world of paid, persuasive communications that reach consumers through the mass media. The design, production, and execution of an advertisement for a website, magazine, newspaper, or TV or radio spot are designed to remind customers of a product, to highlight a need for that product, to inform the audience of a product's availability and location of the seller, or to detail product features and compare them to the competition. Advertisers like to create excitement around their products by developing an image and identity that will clearly separate the product from that of the competition.

As products and their uses change over time, advertisers often need to create advertising to demonstrate to the public new ways of thinking about and using their products. The classic example of such "repositioning" might be the condom. For most of its product history, the condom was used to prevent pregnancy. However, with the arrival of AIDS, condom use began to be advocated as a method of disease prevention and condom manufacturers responded with advertising that featured this product advantage.

Before ads reach the public, much activity has already taken place. Most of the planning for advertising is done with written communications that outline ideas, document various proposals, and suggest possible themes. Ultimately this written work is realized in formal presentation documents that put forth a commercial idea and its associated costs before the officials who provide the goods or services being advertised and who will fund the cost of the advertising.

Account executives will present numerous ideas and rationales on paper to company agents suggesting possible advertising campaign themes, such as scripts for TV advertising, radio spots, in-theatre commercials, telemarketing activities, and print advertising. This is the work of the copywriter. Although the copywriter's work is the most obvious and creative use of words seen by the commercial consumer, there is much behind that work in the building of an advertising concept, in the creation of a Unique Selling Proposition to the public that will help to separate this product from its peers, in the rationale for a filmed piece, and in the preparation of ideas, proposals, and presentations to advertising agencies, artists, and owner representatives. Ad agencies are built on words. Advertising people care deeply about words, enjoy them, and value people who can use them dramatically and effectively. But they are not precious about language; they listen to the language of the market they hope to talk to. They mimic the vocabulary, syntax, and phrases of that market. When the market sees or hears this work, consumers should think, "They're talking to me!" Then the writer has been successful.

Advertising departments include creative services, which can realize packaging, logotypes, design concepts, slogans, signature lines, and any kind of concept or visual to enhance the impact of the product that appears before the public. Although much of this work may be subcontracted to smaller "boutique" type agencies, especially in cases of music services, voice-overs, etc., there is creative control exercised from the agency and the account executives managing that particular client's account. These account executives have helped to develop the concept and will ensure that any participating services, performers, designers, and copywriters who become involved serve to further enhance the original ideas and maintain a fidelity to that concept. Much of the integrity of those ideas and the adjusting of advertising to match them are the subject of countless memoranda, letters, and notes exchanged between account executives and the providers of individual services, who may be at some distance from the original concept.

Media services is a common area of entry into an agency and involves the scheduling and buying of media time for an account. How commercial messages are "timed" for frequency in any particular time period (month, season, year) can have a tremendous impact on the public's response. The buying of media is a sophisticated art blending knowledge of the market, understanding the best media approach to that market, knowing the optimum listening or viewing times for the market, desired length and content of message, and repetition frequency. Too little and the impact is weak, too much and there actually may be a negative reaction to the product. Each additional dollar spent on media should ideally add customers. Media buying requires creativity to work effectively.

Perhaps you are promoting a movie about a mother and daughter, both parts being played by actresses popular with their own age group. Running a movie commercial featuring the mother during daytime or late afternoon talk-show time slots (a documented time period favored by mature women) and a different commercial featuring the younger actress during prime-time situation comedy slots would attract both audience segments.

The senior account executives who manage individual client accounts are drawn from across all agency departments and have the experience to manage general oversight of a client's total advertising effort with the agency. They schedule and conduct meetings and presentations for the client, interact with subcontractors, decide on billing, and, most importantly, work with the client to achieve the most distinctive campaign or advertisement possible for the medium and cost. These individuals are excellent communicators, both verbally and on paper. Many an advertising executive is also a short-story writer, novelist, poet, playwright, or screenwriter. Legions of published writers have been incubated in advertising agencies.

It is an exciting, fast-paced career position with frequent changes of jobs between agencies as executives seek new arenas to exercise their talents. Clients also frequently change agencies, even when their current agency does superior work. After some lengthy associations with an agency, a client may simply wonder if someone else couldn't "spark" them in a unique way. This kind of movement of both executives and clients should suggest the need for a high tolerance of risk and low need for job security.

Not all advertising is done in a professional advertising agency. Many firms have their own advertising departments, which replicate in many aspects the functions of a full-fledged agency. Often these in-house agencies will do everything up until the actual purchase of print or broadcast media time.

Consumer goods firms also have individuals charged with brand management. These executives have the responsibility for all activities surrounding a particular branded product, such as Minute Maid orange juice, Folger's ground decaffeinated coffee, or Hellmann's mayonnaise. They manage all aspects of production, product sizing, sales promotion, and advertising. They exercise a strong influence on advertising initiatives for their product line and work closely with in-house and contracted outside agencies to produce effective advertising for their product.

We have made a distinction between the fields of advertising and public relations, but the question remains, why group them together if they are, in fact, so different? It's a reasonable question with a logical answer. Both advertising and public relations are essentially communication efforts. The advertiser has a message, and it wants to convey that message to the public. To do that most effectively means understanding who the public is, how they think, and what language, images, ideas, and words they are most likely to respond to.

Another shared dimension of the communications of both advertising and public relations is that it is persuasive in tone. Advertising seeks to move the market to excitement, change of attitude, and ultimately purchase. The public relations approach may be more subtle, but it also seeks to influence public thinking and behavior about an organization. Public relations communications seek to persuade us to perceive the organization in a certain way; to understand its position, mission, and goals; and to appreciate its contribution to our life and society in general.

In fact, in both fields the precise word, tone, and nuance of the message can have significant reverberations for the organization being represented. These fields both require not only a masterful grasp of English, but also a real sense of the sweep of English language, both historically and in its most recent incarnations. Along with these language skills must come a very high level of general information. Advertisers need to know at least something about almost everything, and public relations people have to be equally in tune with their audience. For example, if a public relations department were sending out correspondence regarding environmental issues, sending that message on recycled paper (labeled as such) and printed with environmentally approved soy-based ink would be much appreciated by the audience and would help to condition the audience's response to the message.

It is through these "connections" that they base their messages. So it isn't enough to know about only sports and athletes if your next client is a music producer representing a violin virtuoso. Pest exterminators, AIDS activists, microchip manufacturers, department stores, ladies' dressmakers, insurance companies, and thousands of other organizations seek advertising and public relations assistance. Your limitations in terms of awareness of and appreciation for their products and services could be your biggest liability.

The need for computer skills, especially desktop publishing and graphics familiarity, is particularly acute for both the advertising and public relations fields. If you are contemplating either of these careers and are still in college, take advantage of your computer science or graphic arts department course offerings and build some expertise in this area to add to your desirability as a job candidate.

Personal characteristics of advertising executives have tended to overstress the need for creativity. Certainly there is a demand for quickness, the ability to generate ideas, and the ability to be intuitive about a product and how best to present that product. But most advertising professionals will say that their best efforts are actually born from a deep understanding of the product and marketplace. The concepts and appeals they "create" develop quite organically from their research on the market and the product. Advertising has become a highly quantitative business; people spending money on advertising expect some reasonable quantification of return on their investment. How many people will see a particular print ad or view a commercial? What percentage of sales increase might be realized in a geographic market as the result of special advertising programs? What would be the net effect of in-store promotions versus broadcast media for a product?

For those in public relations, personal characteristics would include a sense of poise even under pressure and a good sense of humor, even of the absurd! The ability to remain cool and collected in stressful situations is important to ensure that any communications you give out in times of stress (crisis management, unusual incidents, natural disasters) are statements you can live with long after the incident. Diplomacy, thoughtfulness, and a real sensitivity to the concerns of interested publics are also important. If you are helping to stage a reception for some distinguished foreign guests, should you serve cuisine of their country or American food or perhaps some combination? What would suit the audience and the situation? Public relations professionals are masters of anticipation. They are constantly thinking of how any action, statement, or initiative on the part of their organization may be perceived or misperceived by the public.

Much of both advertising and public relations is teamwork, so the ability to work in groups is quite important to success. It is difficult to generalize about other desired characteristics in the successful advertising executive and public relations official. Both have room for a great many personalities with as many skills and talents. Both will tolerate an extreme range of personalities if they can produce effective work. Most, however, probably are curious about people's behavior and values and the marketplace itself. Many are widely read and enjoy staying current with literature, art, music, the theatre, and athletics. They are intensely aware of social and political events and how these can affect the public's collective consciousness. They are often predictors of trends and fads.

Entry into either advertising or public relations can be discouraging because, as with so many "glamour" jobs, most of the glamour is misunderstood. The lines of applicants are long, however, and competition is stiff. Some kind of related experience would be helpful. Meeting practitioners and learning their experiences and views of the business would also be of immense value. For advertising, it may be best to think not in terms of a job in advertising, but a job in one of the media, for example, radio, TV, or print. Build your expertise in a department such as scheduling or sales and then bring that experience to an advertising agency.

Public relations shares a similar emphasis on this grooming process. From our discussion, it is apparent to speak with authority and credibility for the organization, you need significant experience at a senior level to know what to say and how to say it. It is not uncommon for senior public relations officials to have been leaders of a number of different divisions. It is through long experience that the trust an organization must place in its spokesperson is born. He or she has earned this trust over time and in many roles.

Because advertising and public relations have become rather predominant in American society, many organizations have done very well through their advertising efforts, and even small organizations have taken it upon themselves to buy advertising services. Public relations has also grown as an industry, although as a specialty it has not achieved the stature of advertising because a firm needs to reach a certain size in terms of output, staff, and impact to feel the need to respond to its publics in a formal, planned manner. Likewise, the public doesn't seem to demand a professional level of response from a smaller firm. Consequently, you will find fewer public relations opportunities with small firms than are found in advertising.

Careers develop in both advertising and public relations in a somewhat similar fashion. Advertising careers are made by how well you do for a particular account. This means not only how much your advertising is noticed, but also how effectively it moves consumers to do what you hoped they would, which might be simply to remember the product's name. Public relations success is accelerated when you are helpful in responding to a difficult situation for an organization or managing a successful change in image or a repositioning of the organization in the public's mind.

Often practitioners of both public relations and advertising see career growth by moving to larger and larger clients and increasing the size of their staffs and budgets in the process. Issues and challenges become correspondingly larger, and the opportunity for great success or public failure is an element of risk. Even the most skilled advertisers with extensive staffs and budgets can produce advertisements that not only don't do what they set out to accomplish, but might, in fact, attract negative publicity. Likewise, skilled public relations professionals can misjudge the significance of a situation and fail to exercise judicious damage control at the proper time, letting a difficult situation go from bad to worse. It is just this risk—this potential for failure or success—that so many in advertising and public relations find exciting. It is highly dependent on the professional's "reading" of the public's attitudes and disposition toward the organization.

What are the rewards of working in public relations or advertising? Both involve teamwork; consequently, those who enjoy working in tandem with other individuals and the camaraderie and esprit de corps that develops will enjoy this aspect of the work. Using your intelligence, creativity, understanding of the public, intuition, artistic sense, critical judgment, and analytical ability can allow people to feel an exciting sense of "stretch" and personal development. Both fields test the individual's skills and attributes. If you enjoy that kind of testing in a work environment, you will find advertising and public relations stimulating and challenging.

Salaries for established professionals usually depend on the span of control, budgetary authority, and educational and experiential background. Senior positions in corporate settings can be highly paid situations.

The following are some sample entry-level and just above entry-level positions in both fields.

Marketing Associate. Manufacturing company. Market rsrch, project mgmt, external communications. Req. BA/BS, excel comm skills, analytical skills. Resume to . . .

Public Relations Associate. Fast-paced public affairs dept for major natl agricultural org seeks cand for entry-level public affairs/public relations pos. Light clerical & assist w/public relations activ incl writing, media monitoring & research & press events. Tremendous growth potential. Need strong writing & org skills, extensive computer tech exper & coll deg in journalism, public rel, commun, or related field. Agriculture background & exper pref. Exc bene, sal & metro access. Fax lttr & resume to . . .

Ad Account Coordinator. Position is core of account team. Entry-level requires coll deg, pref in business, communications, English. Manage databases, research editorial opportunities, track projects & assist team in all client activities. Solid position from which to grow. Send resume & lttr to . . .

continued

continued

Account Associate. Current opening for account assoc w/degree in English, commun, public rel, journalism or rel field & 2–3 yrs relevant exp. Exc media rel contacts & solid business writing skills req. High-tech & PR agency exper a plus. Develop media materials, schedule media & analyst tours, develop & maintain long term relationships with local & trade media. Become product expert & develop & execute product PR plans; responsible for logistics & management of projects. Serve as second-level pt of contact with clients. Fax/send resume & letter to . . .

WORKING CONDITIONS

Advertising

Advertising working conditions are centered around the product and the market for the product. Advertising professionals need to be aware of the news and social trends, for in any of these events may come an indication of change that may impact how a product should be presented or how a product's reception may change. For example, the AIDS crisis has been a terrible blow to humanity, and medical researchers are struggling to find some cure. However, condoms have become a public product because of this tragic disease and have seen dramatic changes in product presentation, product take-up by the market, and in why and how the product is used. In the recent past, it had largely been one method of birth control—a product seldom discussed and even less seldom advertised. The process of actually purchasing a condom was often the subject of comedy routines because so many people found it embarrassing and awkward. That would hardly be the case today, and some major manufacturers are now publicly traded firms on the New York Stock Exchange.

So advertisers must stay current on social thinking and trends. Consequently, advertising offices and departments are social centers with much collaboration and shared idea generation. Everything is grist for the advertising mill. Much planning goes into advertising, but different ideas are welcome and risks are often taken in the hopes of increasing market share for a product. For established products of stable demand, advertisers simply try to create the most effective distribution of their message through the appropriate media for the budget they have been allotted.

Advertising offices exhibit all kinds of energy levels, from frantic activity to intense concentration, depending on what stage of the process or what kind of account the workers are focusing on at the time. They are fast-paced, active, "let's do it" climates with high energy levels that require a high tolerance for stress.

Public Relations

Public relations offers two different work conditions. For most public relations, there is significant ordered planning to build and achieve rapport with any number of publics. Formal presentations, responses to letters or complaints, court cases, consumer disputes, company expansion plans, or new product launching are all situations that require research, careful thought, and solid preparation to ensure the organization's goals and mission are presented accurately and that material is available to meet the questions and concerns of interested publics.

This proactive work may involve placing informative messages in major media publications, direct mailings to customers or investors, telemarketing, press conferences, or press kits to the media. In most instances, public relations are ongoing, although there may be short-term goals for a particular reason (price hikes or a product recall).

Sometimes, however, plans don't go as they are intended. Accidents occur, violence takes place, nature intervenes, production lines fail, or any of a million possible negative situations occurs. Then the public relations department is called in to react and set things right: alert the public to alternative product sources, describe how to file a reimbursement claim, or explain how to return a damaged product. Some of these situations could be classified as crisis management. Most public relations experts will tell you that although you cannot anticipate a crisis, you can plan for it by suggesting certain scenarios and determining in advance what might be the best response alternative for the organization in such an eventuality. The more alternatives and situations that you can anticipate, the faster and more effectively any response you make will be judged by the publics who are interested.

Even though you may have planned for a particular crisis, it is still a time of stress if it actually develops and, for the duration of the problem, the public relations department may find itself the press headquarters of an organization—giving news stories, press releases, and details, all of which must be carefully considered to maintain public confidence in the product or service and the organization.

TRAINING AND QUALIFICATIONS

A review of some of the actual advertisements for entry-level positions in advertising and public relations will clearly demonstrate that with your

English degree you have the basic qualifications for work in these fields. If you have a strong grasp and are a skillful user of English both verbally and in written formats, you'll be even more competitive. Add some computer familiarity (word processing at least; desktop publishing is a plus), and you'll find you fit the bill for most entry-level positions.

This is good news for English majors. However, there is a caution attached! The basic skills and a little more may get your foot in the proverbial door, but from that point on, the qualifications become less specific and more difficult to pin down.

Both industries demand a high level of general information. Because these fields are essentially barometers of social trends, the qualified candidate needs to be a highly aware individual. You cannot afford to ignore or deny awareness of certain fields of human activity. For example, perhaps you find professional wrestling childish, contrived, and repellent, so you have always ignored it and its personalities. However, as an advertising executive, you may be managing the promotion events for a line of toys or clothing or board games based on this sport. In public relations, you may have secured the services of a currently popular children's TV star to promote your client's product.

The people who populate the fields of advertising and public relations are marked by their diversity, their wide range of interests, and their encyclopedic knowledge of current events, human activity, politics, and personalities. They can talk on the latest medical developments in the cure for cystic fibrosis and move on to experimental opera. They are, and you should be, too, inveterate readers. They watch television and go to films, theatre, car rallies, rodeos, concerts, and other events.

To communicate effectively with the public, you need to understand all human activities, not just those that you personally prefer. You will need to appreciate varying public tastes, needs, wants, and desires and how they are expressed in order to effectively communicate through the medium of advertising or public relations.

A valuable test of your own preparedness for these fields as well as a qualifying training experience in and of itself is the internship. This will be an education in what professionals do in these fields as well as a close-up observation of the personalities that inhabit them. You'll learn some skills, practice many others, and take stock of how well you measure up to expectations and norms.

Most importantly, given the intense and unrelenting competitive demand for positions in these fields, the internship provides yet another notch in your handle of experience. Examine some of the excellent annual internship directories, such as the *National Directory of Arts Internships* (National Network for Arts Placement), *Internships* (Peterson's Guides), and the *National Directory of Internships* (National Society of Internships and Experiential Education). The *National Directory of Internships* alone lists 100 sites from coast to coast offering public relations opportunities in museums, social service agencies, theatres, festivals, university settings, environmental organizations, women's centers, juvenile courts, TV and radio stations, and zoos. Look for these directories in your career-office library or public library. You will find internships listed on the Internet as well. Simply use your favorite search engine and start looking!

EARNINGS

Advertising

The Internet can be a useful resource for finding the latest earnings information for jobs in the advertising industry. Career websites like www.career mosaic.com and commercial sites like *Advertising Age*'s site (www.adage.com) provide lots of useful information, including salaries. Keep in mind that salaries will vary by type of agency, billing size, and region of the country. At the time of this writing, the following ranges of entry-level salaries were shown:

- ❑ Assistant account executive: $21,200–26,500

- ❑ Assistant editor: $23,850–29,150

- ❑ Marketing assistant: $23,850–29,150

Public Relations

The *Public Relations Journal* regularly publishes salary surveys. It reports entry-level salary information for assistant account executives by type of employer. Be sure to check the latest information available. At the time of printing, *Princeton Review*'s website (www.review.com)—under the "career" option and searching on "public relations"—reported the average starting salary as $21,000; the average salary after five years at $36,000; and the average salary after ten to fifteen years at $54,000. Sites like this may also contain information on current major employers and current job openings.

CAREER OUTLOOK

Employment of public relations specialists, according to predictions made in the *Occupational Outlook Handbook* published by the U.S. Department of Labor, Bureau of Labor Statistics, is expected to increase as fast as the average for all occupations through 2006, but because entry into the field is very competitive given the number of graduates with relevant degrees, your work experience (in the form of internships, related summer work) and relevant course work will affect your standing in the applicant pool. Employment prospects with public relations firms are brighter than those in the corporate or nonprofit sector. New growth will occur through attrition of aging workers and in the industry of health care, corporations, associations, consulting firms, and professional groups.

Advertising-industry employment is expected to grow steadily in the next few years, according to the *Occupational Outlook Handbook*. Three factors affecting advertising employment are a shifting emphasis to regional marketing and media, rapid globalization, and increased use of the Internet. As consumers draw from both domestic and international markets, there will be a corresponding demand on advertisers and marketers to master the promotional, communications, and advertising strategies needed to succeed in this evolving business environment.

Of course, employment rates will vary by industry. While manufacturing may present only moderate growth in advertising positions, service industries such as computer and data-processing firms as well as, interestingly enough, public relations, will see very rapid growth in advertising jobs.

STRATEGY FOR FINDING THE JOBS

Hit the Streets!

Most job listings in both advertising and public relations that you come across will be for specialized experience (which you do not yet have) or will be low-level clerical/administrative jobs that you may not enjoy and, more importantly, may not learn from. The wisdom on the street for jobs in these fields is direct contact with an agency or organization for whom you want to work.

Review Job Advertisements

Read listings on the Internet and in the papers, nevertheless, because you will learn job titles, duties, and responsibilities for those jobs and get some sense of salary levels. Respond to job advertisements that mesh with your interests and background. It is important to know what's out there, both the good and the not so good. But the best cover letter and resume in advertising and public relations is the one that's hand delivered. The supply of candidates in advertising and public relations so far outweighs demand for available positions that people literally go straight to the employers. The standard is so developed that employers ignore resumes that arrive by mail. They don't need to answer letters that suggest the agency call the job seeker if interested.

Keep Checking with Potential Employers
If an agency principal is looking to fill a position, chances are they don't have to do much more than wander out to their office lobby and see who is at the reception desk trying desperately to see someone about a job. There is a logic here, as well. The kind of assertiveness, persistence, and "go for it" drive that would bring an individual to the agency in person are just the qualities that are called for in advertising and public relations. If you want to get a job, yours will be the face that the receptionist sees on a fairly regular basis.

POSSIBLE EMPLOYERS

There is a range of possible employers for those interested in working in advertising or public relations. The list includes advertising agencies, TV stations, radio stations, specialty advertisers, outdoor advertising agencies, magazines, newspapers, public relations firms, utilities, sports organizations, the U.S. government, state and local governments, educational institutions, medical institutions, and associations. Let's review a series of possible employer types with an accent on the English major. Because many of the employer directories and job listings sources cover all or many of these employer types, we'll provide a basic library of listings and resources to locate these employers. Give each type of employer your full consideration and begin your job search by contacting the type of employer you are most interested in working with.

Advertising Agencies
Advertising agencies continue to break new ground in communicating with the public, despite the continuing proliferation of products and "noise" surrounding each of those products. Although advertisements have become increasingly visual, there is still writing opportunity for copy used in print ads, voice-overs in films and videos, and product packaging. Even in the

purest visual advertisement, the effectiveness is achieved because behind and supporting that ad is a position paper outlining the intent, scope, and focus of the proposed piece of advertising. Communications remains the mainstay of the independent advertising agency. The demand is still crucial for strong and creative communication that will arrest the public's attention and move them to some desired response.

TV Stations

TV stations are supported by the advertising that is placed with them. Advertising departments for TV stations work to attract and hold potential advertisers by offering them time and day slots for their advertising that will best deliver the correct market for the advertiser's product. Because of these stations' ability to mount and film commercials, they are frequently called on to produce commercial messages as well as air them, and opportunities to function similarly to a full-fledged advertising agency also exist in television.

Radio Stations

Radio has become particularly specialized over the last few years, with stations making market-oriented decisions to go all classical or country or talk or news and weather or pop psychology or soft rock. The intent here is that by focusing on the needs of a particular market profile, the station will also be better able to attract advertisers whose products speak to that narrow market, and the station will create a definite niche in the radio spectrum. This represents a sharp break from the past, when station programming tried to provide a little bit of everything throughout the day. Now, the trend is to provide a narrow focus and hope that it brings in a deep audience. English majors working in radio today will need to understand the particular market they are writing for so that they can communicate using language, including style, syntax, metaphors, and tone, that says to the audience, "That's talking to me!"

Specialty Advertisers

Specialty advertising is all around us. The printed yardstick from the lumberyard. The free mini-flashlight from the hardware store with the store's address and hours of operation. The credit card case imprinted with a printer's logo. Most businesses cannot afford broadcast or print media advertising, but almost every firm can afford some kind of imprinted article that reminds people who it is and where the business is located. Specialty advertising actually far outweighs broadcast advertising in dollars spent each year, because it is used by far more businesses. Creative opportunities abound in this area as the specialty advertiser and the client come together to plan a promotion, event, or anniversary. Often, items, slogans, themes, and messages are expressly designed for the client. For the English major who enjoys the creative use of language, specialty advertising offers possibilities.

Outdoor Advertising Agencies

With a renewed interest in the aesthetics of public spaces, including highways, outdoor advertising has undergone some restructuring and reframing of purpose. Although restrictions proliferate, there are still ample opportunities for billboards, spectaculars, and other forms of outdoor advertising, including signs, blimps, skywriting, and tethered inflatables. These agencies often work with an advertiser and its agency to add outdoor ads to a complete campaign. The outdoor specialists can provide the best information on site selection, copy length, and copy/visual balance.

Magazines

Today's magazine advertising departments have assembled more information on their readership than ever before. They can tell a prospective advertiser how old their readers are, how many cars they own, how often they travel abroad, and how much money they make. The magazine uses this information to recruit the kind of advertiser its readers want to see and have need of. It will assist advertisers with designing winning appeals to the market and can advise on successful placement of the ad within the publication. Some magazine product runs allow for creative "split ads" on opposing pages or can incorporate some product samples in the assembling and stapling process.

Newspapers

Newspapers depend heavily on advertising to support the publication. Newspaper advertising departments often work very closely with clients of all sizes to assist in producing ads that are effective, often under pressures of time and space limitations. The use of color in newsprint has attracted new advertisers. English majors interested in this particular area of employment will find their talents constantly stretched.

Public Relations Firms

Public relations organizations take on individuals, institutions (churches, corporations, not-for-profit firms, etc.), products, and even ideas and work to improve, alter, reposition, or change public opinion about them. They use every opportunity at their disposal, including the placement of news stories, photo opportunities, charity work, public appearances, and one-on-one meetings to build support for whatever position or platform they are trying to affect. Considerable written work is involved, and public relations organizations issue a steady stream of position papers, news releases, background stories, biographies, and fact sheets to support their efforts. The writing task is a demanding one, because the final product must meet severe public scrutiny.

Utilities

Another symptom of a shrinking planet and the public's interest and concern is the need for utilities to have public relations offices. Once a very quiet sector of the economy, firms that deal in oil, gasoline, natural gas, hydroelectric power, and nuclear energy are constantly being called on to explain and document their impact on the environment. In an era of rising costs that outstrip rising paychecks, there is also concern for the economic impact of ever-escalating energy costs on the individual. Public relations professionals must be excellent listeners, able to understand and empathize with others' points of view, while at the same time articulating company policy. They can play a significant role in bringing disparate viewpoints together and building bridges for cooperation. English majors looking to do PR work in the utilities need to be equally at home on the word processor and in front of the microphone. They need to be able to produce a newsletter or field angry questions from consumers. This job requires a unique blend of skilled communicator and negotiator.

Sports Organizations

Promotion of individual sports, specific sports leagues, and unique competitions are all part of the working day for public relations specialists in sports organizations. Increased attendance brings increased sponsorship and results in bigger prizes and more public attention for events. Creating excitement, raising public awareness about a sport, and attracting advertisers are all the responsibility of the sports organization public relations staff. If you have an English education and a love for sports, you may want to investigate the extensive possibilities in sports organization public relations.

Federal Government

Many job seekers would be surprised to find that the government employs public relations professionals. However, whether it's controversy surrounding federal money mismanagement, cheating at a major military college, or a positive news story about military assistance during civilian disasters, the government needs qualified public relations professionals who can communicate effectively with all those interested in government activites. Because the U.S. government is our largest employer and has numerous departments, agencies, and divisions, the entry-level public relations aspirant would do well to spend some serious investigative time on opportunities in government public relations.

State and Local Government

The same public scrutiny that necessitates federal public relations is present for state, city, and local governments to a lesser degree. Depending on the size of the locality and the issues present, the concerns may be taxes, zoning, preservation of wetlands, redistricting, highway tolls, state lotteries, and similar issues that need to be addressed in the press, on television and radio, by personal communication, and in news conferences. A high level of general information about the locality and its issues, poise under pressure, and the gift of diplomacy are all helpful attributes.

Educational Institutions

Perhaps a college campus is reacting to news reports of private corporate advertising on the college's website. Or it may be a story concerning "town-gown" relations between the college and the community in which it is located. These are some of the issues that a public relations staff member would be planning for and responding to in educational institutions today. The very nature of these examples is evidence enough of the need for the kind of skilled communications and education a trained professional can bring to such volatile situations.

Medical Institutions

Questions of medical ethics, the prolongation of life, the acceptance or denial of certain classifications of patients, the movement of patients from one facility to another, and the high-risk areas of experimental surgery and drug treatment are often the focal issues for public relations in hospital administration. Working in this field means acquiring a specialized medical vocabulary and gaining familiarity with hospital procedures, because public statements must be carefully worded to avoid confusion or misstatement.

Professional Organizations

A growing number of associations have a critical need for a public relations practitioner. Staffs for these groups may be small and include many volunteer workers, but there is a need for skilled personnel to answer press queries and personal letters and to issue press releases on possible news stories. Some organizations find, over time, that their activities are perceived differently, and they seek help to reeducate the public about their true intents and aims as an organization. Others want public support in terms of time and financial contributions and need professional help through public relations to elicit that support. Although only large, well-funded associations can maintain a professional public relations staff, this is in no way a limitation for the job seeker. Directories of associations list thousands of organizations whose size and financial structure allow them to employ PR staff.

POSSIBLE JOB TITLES

The two following lists are an attempt to give you some idea of possible job titles in both advertising and public relations. This is not an exhaustive list. Many other titles exist that might not directly suggest an advertising or public relations function. For example, on some college campuses, there is a Director of News Services. A significant component of this job is public relations. Use this list as a rough guide, and add to it those job titles you discover through your own investigations.

Advertising	
Account Coordinator	Media Buyer
Account Director	Media Director
Account or District Manager	Media Planner
Account Executive	Media Supervisor
Account Supervisor	Press Secretary
Advertising Director	Producer
Art Director	Production Assistant
Assistant Account Executive	Production Manager
Assistant Planner	Production Supervisor
Associate Media Director	Project Director
Associate Research Director	Research Director
Broadcast Supervisor	Research Supervisor
Copywriter	Researcher
Creative Director	Sales Assistant
Executive Research Director	Sales Planner
Group or Regional Manager	Sales Representative
Junior Buyer	Traffic Assistant
Management Supervisor	Traffic Controller
	Traffic Manager

The division of these lists is somewhat arbitrary because the two functions of advertising and public relations walk hand in hand most of the time. Many of these positions overlap responsibilities frequently. Some practitioners would be hard put to tell you definitively if they were, in fact, advertising or public relations specialists because the two roles are so intertwined in some organizations. Nevertheless, the following list indicates some titles peculiar to public relations.

Public Relations	Industrial Public Relations
Account Assistant	Executive
Account Coordinator	Internal Communications
Account Specialist	Staffer
Account Trainee	Investor Relations Officer
Communications Specialist	Junior Account Executive
Community Affairs	Media Placement Specialist
Coordinator	Media Relations Executive
Consumer Affairs Specialist	Office of Civic Affairs
Coordinator, Event Creation	Representative
Corporate Communications	PR Writer
Director	Public Affairs/Information
Crisis Manager	Officer
Director, Investor Relations	Public Relations Assistant
Director of Internal	Shareholder Relations
Communications	Coordinator
Director of Public Affairs	Staff Writer
Editor	Supervisor of Educational
Employee Publications	Affairs
Specialist	Washington Representative
Governmental Relations	
Staffer	

RELATED OCCUPATIONS

The fields of advertising and public relations are welcoming to the generalist such as the English major because although the emphasis is on written and spoken communication skills, there is also a need for a high level of general information, responsiveness under pressure, the ability to present to large groups, and the ability to be endlessly responsive and creative as situations present themselves. It's difficult for an employer to know ahead of time who will be a success in this field. This brief related occupation list suggests that these skills, so valued in public relations and advertising, will be valued anywhere there is a need for someone to act as an intermediary between the organization and outside publics, formally or informally. Each of these has been selected because they draw on the same attributes to a greater or lesser degree.

Caterer	Patient Relations Specialist
Cruise Director	Police Officer/Community
Development Specialist	Relations
Function Sales Manager	Promotion Manager
Fund-raiser	Real Estate Salesperson
Interior Designer	Religious Administrator
Lobbyist	Shopping Mall Manager
Membership Services	Spokesperson
Director	Volunteer Coordinator
Patient Relations Director	

HELP IN LOCATING THESE EMPLOYERS

Advertising and public relations agencies know the value of potential customer awareness. As you would expect, they are masters of self-promotion. There are a number of excellent websites and directories and lists available to identify where these employers are situated, how big their staffs are, what specialties each offers, and how much and what kind of business they are doing. The following list represents a beginning library of job sources for each of the possible advertising and public relations employers listed in this chapter. Ask to see these resources when you visit local libraries.

Adweek (Weekly)
Box 1973
Danbury, CT 06813
Website: www.adweb.com/adpub3.html

Advertising Age (Weekly)
Crain Communications
220 E. 42nd St.
New York, NY 10017
Website: www.adage.com
E-mail: webinfo@adage.com

Advertising Career Directory
Magazine Publishing Career Directory
Public Relations Career Directory
Gale Research Inc.
P.O. Box 33477
Detroit, MI 48232-5477

Gale Directory of Publications and Broadcast Media
(Formerly *Ayer Directory of Publications*)
Gale Research Inc.
P.O. Box 33477
Detroit, MI 48232-5477

Moody's Public Utility Manual
Moody's Investors Service
99 Church St.
New York, NY 10007
Website: www.moodys.com/fis/source/proddesc/public.htm
E-mail: fis@moodys.com

The National Ad Search
National Ad Search, Inc.
P.O. Box 2083
Milwaukee, WI 53201
Website: www.nationaladsearch.com

O'Dwyer's Directory of Public Relations Firms
J. R. O'Dwyer Co. Inc.
271 Madison Ave.
New York, NY 10016
Website: www.odwyerpr.com
E-mail: jackodwyer@aol.com

Public Relations Journal
Public Relations Society of America
33 Irving Pl., Third Floor
New York, NY 10003-2376
Website: www.prsa.org
E-mail: ppc@prsa.org

Standard Directory of Advertisers (The Advertiser Red Book)
Reed Reference Publishing
121 Chanlon Rd.
New Providence, NJ 07974
Website: www.adweb.com/adpub34.html

Standard Directory of Advertising Agencies (The Agency Red Book)
Reed Reference Publishing
P.O. Box 31
New Providence, NJ 07974
Website: www.redbooks.com
E-mail: redbooks@prod.lexis-nexis.com

PROFESSIONAL ASSOCIATIONS FOR ADVERTISING/PUBLIC RELATIONS

The following list will begin to give you some idea of the variety and spe-
cializations of professional associations supporting the fields of public relations and advertising. As you begin your own job search, you'll find many
other professional groups, some with quite specialized purposes. With just a
simple telephone call, these groups often will send you materials that open
up career vistas you had not imagined.

Advertising Council
261 Madison Ave.
New York, NY 10016-2303
Website: www.adcouncil.org
E-mail: info@adcouncil.org
Members/Purpose: To conduct public service advertising campaigns.
Journal/Publication: *Public Service Advertising Bulletin*; *Report to the
American People.*

Advertising Women of New York
153 E. 57th St.
New York, NY 10022
E-mail: awnyplayer@aol.com
Members/Purpose: Professional development for women in advertising,
publicity, marketing, research, or promotion.
Training: Annual career conference for college seniors.
Journal/Publication: *Advertising Women of New York.*
Job Listings: A notebook of listings.

American Advertising Federation
1101 Vermont Ave., Ste. 500
Washington, DC 20005
Website: www.aaf.org
E-mail: aaf@aaf.org
Members/Purpose: To promote a better understanding of advertising
through government relations, public relations, and advertising education
in order to further an effective program of advertising self-regulation.

Training: Sponsors National Student Advertising Competition.
Journal/Publication: Annual report to members; *Communicator*; college newsletter.

American Association of Advertising Agencies
405 Lexington Ave., 18th Floor
New York, NY 10174-1801
Website: www.aaaa.org
Members/Purpose: To foster, strengthen, and improve the advertising agency business; to advance the cause of advertising as a whole; to aid its member agencies to operate more efficiently and profitably.
Training: Sponsors member information and international services.
Journal/Publication: Bulletin, media newsletter; roster; booklets.

Association of National Advertisers
155 E. 44th St.
New York, NY 10017
Website: www.ana.net
E-mail: rwebster@ana.net
Members/Purpose: National and regional advertisers.
Training: Conducts surveys, studies, workshops, and seminars. Provides specialized education program.

Institute for Public Relations Research and Education
3800 S. Tamiami Trail
North Sarasota, FL 34239
Members/Purpose: Sponsors and conducts research in field of public relations.
Training: Annual lectures and competitions.
Journal/Publication: *Managing Your Public Relations*; series of guides for nonprofits; *R&E Report*; newsletter.

National Council for Marketing and Public Relations
c/o Becky Olson
364 N. Wyndham Ave.
Greely, CO 80634
Members/Purpose: Communications specialists working within community and junior colleges in areas including public, community, media, government, and alumni relations; publications; marketing; and coordination of special events. Promotes improved relations between two-year colleges and their communities.
Training: Annual conference with exhibits, national surveys, needs assessments.
Journal/Publication: *COUNSEL.*

Public Relations Society of America
33 Irving Pl.
New York, NY 10003
Website: www.prsa.org
E-mail: ppc@prsa.org
Members/Purpose: Professional society of public relations practitioners.
Training: Professional development programs.
Journal/Publication: *PRSA News*; newsletter; *Public Relations Journal*;
Public Relations Journal Register.
Job Listings: Job listings contained in journal.

Specialty Advertising Association International
3125 Skyway Circle N
Irving, TX 75038-3526
Website: www.adweb.com/adassoc33.html
Members/Purpose: Promotes industry.
Training: Speakers bureau, conducts research, holds executive training and
development seminars.
Journal/Publication: *Ideasworth*; newsletter; *Specialty Advertising Business*;
many educational publications.

CHAPTER THIRTEEN

PATH 4: BUSINESS ADMINISTRATION AND MANAGEMENT

Majoring in English has been fun. Hard work, sure, but lots of fun as well. Fascinating courses, interesting books, poetry and literature to read and discuss, and the company of like-minded people who also enjoy the many forms of expression in English. You've loved all the reading and will probably spend the rest of your life as an avid reader, but how does that qualify you for a job? No one is going to pay you just to read.

Is your love of reading of any use to an employer? Absolutely! The ability to read and the enjoyment of reading are highly valued in business administration and management careers. Whether it's the mountainous volumes of memoranda, letters, magazines, or professional reading that comes across a desk each day or books and articles that help one to see the big picture or learn a new management technique, all of this reading and the ability to accomplish it will come in very handy to you in management/administration. You'll be more knowledgeable, you'll have a higher level of general information, and you'll be able to refer colleagues and subordinates to information of interest to their particular concerns. Your awareness of and grasp of your reading material makes you a valuable resource, especially to others who might read less.

Writing was also very important to your degree. Short papers, long papers, documented research papers, free writing, and journals became regular items in your bag of tricks. Unlike some students in other majors, writing became so practiced for you that these assignments were enjoyable challenges rather than onerous tasks. You became quite adept at writing under pressures of time and space limitations. You learned to condense or expand, depending on what was needed or allowed. You might have even had the opportunity to contribute to a literary journal or college newspaper or help a professor with research for a scholarly article. You learned how practice and critical feedback improved your writing, and you experimented with different writing styles. You know writing is an important skill and valued by the world of work, but how exactly will you put your writing experience to work for you?

There is perhaps no single more valued gift in the world of employment than the ability to write well and easily. The amount of correspondence alone is staggering, and business writing requires an excellent vocabulary, clarity of expression, and some special stylistic techniques of directness, collaboration, and persuasion. And business writing is not lacking in opportunities for creativity, either. New business ventures, advertising proposals, international ventures, and new products all present opportunities to do something different. Not-for-profit organizations need to produce a never-ending stream of materials to help people understand and appreciate what they do and then be willing to support them. Business is constantly changing and responding to the marketplace, and business writing reflects that.

Your college required some degree of word-processing skill, and you probably found it useful in your major to know how to work on a computer: moving texts, cutting and pasting, changing formats, and using the dictionary, thesaurus, and search-and-replace options on your word processor to improve your writing presentation. Maybe you got to try your hand at some desktop publishing software as well and gained some familiarity with this increasingly popular technology. In fact, you probably saved much of your college writing output on diskettes and now have a nice portfolio of work assembled and ready to print. But you don't want to be a secretary; won't your word-processing and desktop publishing skills be seen as just clerical?

A quick review of available job openings for management level, college graduate positions in business administration and management, both profit and not-for-profit, display overwhelmingly the need for at least word-processing competency and a variety of word-processing software familiarity. Beyond this, many positions are interested in candidates having some desktop publishing skills, knowledge of graphics packages, and awareness of spreadsheet software. Regrettably, many English curriculums are quite divorced from the computer science field, except for perhaps core curriculum computer courses required of all undergraduates. In the reality of the workplace, there is an overt link between the practicing business writer and communicator and the computer. Here's an excellent example of this requirement in an advertisement from *Community Jobs,* a specialized job posting newspaper for the not-for-profit sector. This is the qualifications section of a want ad seeking a program assistant for Africa for the family-planning management division of a health organization:

Qualifications: Bachelor's degree and/or office experience required. Ability to operate various software packages; ability to learn new software packages. Strong office, organizational, and administrative skills. Ability to learn complex project procedures, meet deadlines, prioritize, and manage a variety of tasks simultaneously.

Note how much the technical demands in their specificity overshadow the general requirement of a four-year degree.

Try to expand your computer skills while still in school in the areas suggested and, if you have graduated, see about some continuing education courses in desktop publishing or spreadsheet analysis software. Don't let this kind of easily acquired technological skill come between you and a job that lets you use many of your English major skills.

⋯⋯⋯⋯⋯⋯⋯⋯⋯⋯⋯⋯⋯

Here's yet another advertisement, for a development officer for a nonprofit organization:

Development Officer. Support foundation & corporate fund-raising incl writing grant proposals, visit donor institutions, & help produce nwsltr/fund-raising materials/annual report. BA in English/related field. Resume/ltr to . . .

Certainly the requirement for a BA in English is clear in this ad, but that is hardly enough to be competitive. Familiarity with grant writing, fund-raising, newsletter production, and other written materials is also required. It's an excellent example of the kinds of demands an employer believes it can make on an English graduate today. The degree by itself is simply not enough for this organization.

....

Maybe your interest is in business, not in teaching, but you had some great teachers who taught you to listen, to express yourself in a complete and reasoned way, and to understand that being critical is not being negative, but rather evaluative. This evaluative skill will be particularly useful in business, where much work is done in groups and individuals come to the table with differing perspectives. There may be someone who will look at a proposal from a quantitative perspective. Another may bring the history of the organization to bear on a situation. Yet another may have a public relations or marketing approach. You may look at the logic, the tone, and the bigger picture of the concept and bring a valuable and completely different perspective to the meeting.

Your teachers taught you about styles, periods, and the nuances of particular writers. You learned from them the value and power of specific choices in vocabulary. From hour upon hour in the classroom you came to appreciate the well-developed lecture or thoughtful presentation and understood the mechanics of public presentation skills. You will frequently find yourself called upon in meetings, both with and without advance notice, to speak on certain subjects, sometimes at length. The modeling you received from your classroom presentations is sure to influence your own presentation style. You'll understand how to speak to the audience and what they are interested in hearing. You will have learned to modulate your voice and include everyone with eye contact. You'll have a sense of when visual aids would be a compelling addition.

When you consider writing and reading and word-processing skills, do these open any doors for you? Absolutely! If there is one constant refrain from the world of organized business, large and small, it is "we need people who can think and speak and write—we'll teach them everything else they need." English majors, take a look at administration and management careers.

DEFINITION OF THE CAREER PATH

Because an English degree program focuses on educating the student about the traditions of the English language and its contemporary reflection in modern literature, poetry, theatre, video, art, and film, it's common for an English major to have an immensely successful college career, graduate with honors, and yet feel ill-equipped to find a good job. We've indicated that although some wonderful skills and training *have* been received, it's necessary for the job seeker to learn to *extract* those skills from the context of an education in English and transform them into a context an employer will find attractive.

This means taking a skill out of the academic context, for example, writing research papers on topics in English literature. For the business employer who isn't in need of English-literature research writing, that particular skill may be difficult to fully appreciate. Some employers would do the necessary generalization and understand its value, but it's more effective and certain if you do it. So instead of indicating on your resume that you know how to write and research papers on subjects in English literature, you might better indicate that you are comfortable with research methods and resources. You can assemble pertinent data on a subject using a variety of reference materials and transform that data into a piece of valuable information. Now, the employer thinks, "Yes, that is something I can use." It's easy to do!

••••••••••••••••••••••••••••••••••••••

The best way to begin to understand how valuable your English degree might be to the world of administration and management is to review some current job postings. Look at Internet job listings and Sunday papers with want ads. It doesn't matter if they are out of date; you're reviewing them to learn how employers request people with your kind of talent. These job postings will educate you in a couple of different ways. What phrases do they use and what kinds of skills do they expect? Where do your talents match up with what's requested, and where do you fall short? Some will directly ask for English skills; others will speak of writing and verbal presentation ability. As you read the job descriptions, you will begin to become familiar with menus of duties and responsibilities you might be performing. Another bonus of this exercise is that you will discover job titles. Even when we have a good idea about what we want to do with our lives and the employment environment we want to find ourselves in, we often don't know what they call what we want to do. This exercise helps you to learn about and build your own personal library of job titles to explore. And if you need further information on any particular job, you can research it in the *Dictionary of Occupational Titles.*

Your college career office or library may have some additional job posting newsletters with listings of entry-level jobs for liberal arts graduates in a number of fields directly and indirectly related to English. Check those out as well.

• •

Following is an excellent example of a position for which English majors would be well qualified but that they might not be aware of or might not expect to refer to skills they possess.

> *Program Analyst.* Evaluate strategic planning management, report and track regional accomplishments. Requires excellent analytical skills, writing and communication skills, computer skills including database and word processing. Min. $22,717.

This kind of job could exist in both the commercial and not-for-profit sectors and within each of them in numerous kinds of organizations: medical, sales, agriculture, banking, etc.

We've established that the English major is well-grounded in analytical skills and should have solid writing and communication skills. So you fit the bill for the example position on that score. Your research experience would have allowed you training in the kind of tracking and reporting of data that is being requested in this advertisement. The subject matter may be different, but the procedures and evaluative process are identical. It's just a new vocabulary.

Certainly the advertisement is not requesting anything outside the range of the average English major, except perhaps some software familiarity. As we have mentioned, computer skills have been stressed throughout all the English-major career paths cited, so if time remains in your degree, use that time to acquire as many computer skills as you can in desktop publishing, spreadsheets, and word processing. It will stand you in good stead in the employment market.

Here's another example, again with some computer skills required and a specific interest in the arts.

> *Communications Assistant.* Help program director develop Arts
> Wire (nat'l online network), produce variety of pubs,
> press/publicity. Req knowledge/interest in arts, orgz skills, admin
> skills, IBM/MAC computer skills. Resume & letter to . . .

This ad may seem typical of what you would expect for an English major seeking entry-level employment. It focuses on communications (even in the job title); it involves publications, writing, and publicity; and it's in the arts. But the humanities are not the only places for such a communications assistant job. The clone of the job could exist in the sciences, medical, financial, or management research fields and in U.S. government positions as well. The material you would be working with would be different in each area, but the tasks and processes would be similar.

Management trainee ads for any number of employers often simply ask for a four-year graduate because they are looking for a broad range of skills and will do most of the specialized training in company and product awareness on the job. They prefer college graduates for their education, intelligence, and exposure to a broad range of subject fields. They especially appreciate English majors for their emphasis on communication skills. Jobs as diverse as production assistant for a TV station, sales account manager in industry, research associate, political campaign manager, assistant director for personnel services, and a host of equally interesting and varied positions seek an English or other appropriate four-year degree with good written and verbal communication skills, analytical ability, perhaps some research experience, and almost always computer literacy and often familiarity with particular software.

··

So you will certainly be using the skills you practiced in acquiring your degree and some new ones besides. The context won't be literature, but it almost certainly will be prose, and you will play a major role in ensuring that writing is clear, direct, correct, and has some style as well. Letters, memoranda, policies, procedures, and short and long business reports are the currency of the workplace. The quality of this writing is a direct reflection on the organization sponsoring it. Consequently, individuals who can write, edit, and present these materials are valued for those skills.

Here's a fund-raising position with an emphasis on issues and skills and not on the particular degree:

Development Specialist. Assist development director. Req BA/BS, fund-raising exp. Sensitive to gay/lesbian/ minority issues, excel oral/writ comm skills, computer skills incl WP/spreadsheet. Resume/ltr to Box B.

Think about the different talents you are developing in your English major and try to picture yourself using them in some employment context. Which do you enjoy the most and which the least? Which could you not do without in a job and which will you not miss? The study of English as a major is comprehensive enough to ready you for a variety of worthwhile occupations in which you can justifiably say you are using your degree to the fullest.

•••

In your job as a manager or administrator, you'll eventually begin to have people under your leadership, and you will be involved in staff supervision, perhaps some budgetary control, and evaluation of your staff. From time to time there'll be hiring decisions as well. These are all important skills in any job, and all require leaving a "paper trail": a formal letter offering someone a position, a sick leave or vacation time policy, a proposal for reorganizing a department or division, or introducing a new product to an existing product line.

Even if you feel assured from reading this book that an employer needs your skills, you might recognize that your education in English seldom focused on the world of employment. You had opportunities to listen to poets and novelists read their work. You might have had a journalist visit your class. But did you ever have a visit from a manager/administrator who wanted to share with you how he or she uses his or her degree in English? Probably not. You legitimately feel somewhat ill informed about the world of business. What do various organizations do? What are the functions of different departments and the roles of the people who staff those departments? As you go about your job search, you'll want to fill in the gaps in your knowledge about business by doing some basic research about organizations and specific firms. With your educational background, this will be a piece of cake!

Company literature can be a gold mine of information about organizational structure. Internet sites, brochures, and pamphlets describe departments, show organizational charts, and may contain photographs of individuals at work. Some organizations break down along functional lines: accounting, personnel, finance, marketing, etc. Others use their products as the division: boilers, generators, transformers, cables.

If, for example, you are looking at a management trainee position for a fruit juice manufacturer, you could check out the food processing industry at your library or college career center or on the Internet. Learn about the basic operation of the industry, possible departments, staffing, and raw materials sourcing. Next seek out information about the particular company that you are applying to.

Organizations such as Very Fine, Snapple, or Ocean Spray describe their products and their manufacturing process. Some firms publish human resources brochures that profile selected workers and their jobs. These descriptions can give you an even better sense of what this organization is doing and who works there.

As you begin to realize how widely attractive the English major is to many kinds of employers, you'll soon build up quite a knowledge base about certain fields. You can then focus your research more on specific organizations and less on the sector they are part of. Becoming so aware of the world of employment is part of any job search, but for the English major, there are many more doors available to open and, consequently, more to learn.

Perhaps you chose English as a degree simply because you love to read and think. These corporate jobs sound interesting to you, and it may be comforting to realize that so much of American business would value your skills. But some of these jobs may sound more active, more extroverted than fits your personality. They suggest lots of interpersonal communication, high degrees of interaction, and potentially some conflict or dissonance. You worry that perhaps, although you have the skills, the environment will be wrong. Could there be corporate jobs for people who like to just read and think?

The answer to this reasonable question is a complicated one. First, there are jobs in business, industry, and nonprofits that involve significant amounts of reading and thinking. That work may be solitary and introverted as the reader wrestles with concepts or ideas. Ultimately, however, the results of such work must be presented publicly, either to a supervisor, a committee, or a team. That presentation may be verbal, written, or a combination of techniques.

The kinds of jobs that are this autonomous and self-directed are almost always fairly senior positions in terms of rank and salary. It would be unusual in an entry-level position to just send the new employee off to read or think with no understanding of the organization and its mission, goals, or history.

With such senior responsibility (and commensurate salary) come additional duties beyond one's primary task of reading and thinking. The organization has the right to use the skills of this thinker/reader for the general good. It would demand that this good thinking be brought to bear on decision making and goal setting. So while such positions do exist, they exist at senior levels for experienced staff who often have other equally important ancillary duties that put them on the line again and again.

WORKING CONDITIONS

Corporate working conditions and norms of behavior may also inspire some hesitation. You may sense that business and industry and even some larger, more organized not-for-profit organizations have more rules about conduct, appearance, manners, and hierarchy than you have been used to or would enjoy. After all, part of your decision to major in English might have been a rejection of some of the same work orientation or profit motive that led some of your peers to major in business or computer science. Now you're also considering the world of commerce and justifiably wondering, will I fit in?

Rest assured that the world of work is as diverse as the population in general. It is populated with people of differing interests, political persuasions, lifestyles, values, and talents. There is certainly room for you. Your skills are valued and needed, and most organizations realize that along with your talent and education comes a particular philosophy and lifestyle.

But that is not to suggest that some changes will not have to be made. After all, a corporation is a public entity represented by its employees. How they look, act, and communicate affects the business and, ultimately, their livelihood. Publicly traded companies with shareholders may feel this responsibility to a greater degree than does a private company or family-held business. Nevertheless, a business's success rises and falls on its ability to maintain good relations with its publics.

Businesses today have become much more sophisticated about their staff and their needs. Some offer flexible time scheduling with varying arrival and departure times for different workers. Some will allow two people to "share" a job, each splitting it in half. This kind of benefit has been helpful for parents who are interested in staying home more with young children. Some larger organizations offer on-site child-care or elder-care—a real recognition of home and scheduling problems. An increasing number of firms are offering benefits to gay couples and even recognizing same-sex couples in invitations to social functions. Drug/alcohol and emotional issues are more out in the open. Firms often offer counseling and referral services for these problems and do so discreetly and without the stigma these problems earned employees in corporations of the past.

Many firms now offer memberships in health/fitness clubs or actually have those kinds of clubs on-site as part of their benefit program. Of course, this emphasis on exercise and diet has beneficial effects on productivity and reduced absenteeism. Even more than that, it builds self-esteem; people become prouder of how they look and feel and return that pride in their work. It increases camaraderie and cuts across all hierarchical lines as different kinds of workers meet in the gym and weight rooms.

Many organizations have trips to the ballet, theatre, sports events, and museum openings for employees and their families at greatly reduced prices. You are sure to find many, many like-minded individuals at work with equally as many opportunities to share your enthusiasms and interests in work-sponsored activities.

It might be easy to believe that because a nonprofit organization is involved in doing good in the world, many of the conditions so entrenched in a corporation would not exist in the not-for-profit. Although some nonprofit organizations have relaxed norms, a great many others know that to gain the private and public dollars needed to run these organizations and inspire public trust, they need to present in every way the same picture of organization, sophistication, and determination as a corporation.

Another reasonable concern is the issue of competitiveness. Are corporate climates as competitive as they are portrayed? Certainly as an English major you competed for grades and against your own past performance, but you were also in a sense competing with a class standard set by all members. Business is no different. While most competitive initiative is *outwardly* directed, toward other firms, there are certainly performance norms established over time by the general level of expertise in the firm. Because you are hired in large part with these norms in mind, and your resume and experience were evaluated on criteria already established for success in the organization, you will probably do fine. What is important is that you stay "tuned in" as an employee to performance standards and do your best to maintain your contributions.

You will participate in periodic evaluations with your direct supervisor to review your accomplishments and set appropriate goals for yourself for the next evaluation period. These evaluations will be the proper setting to discuss your understanding and appreciation of your job, your desire for additional training, or your ideas for job modification.

TRAINING AND QUALIFICATIONS

Our review of some sample advertisements has made it clear that along with your fine English education, some computer familiarity would be well advised. It is impossible to anticipate all the potential demands of the marketplace, but certainly word processing, some spreadsheet software, some IBM-compatible hardware familiarity, and desktop publishing techniques would be attractive additions to your resume. If you have some of the skills on this list, you would at least be able to negotiate to learn the rest on the job. Without any of these skills, an employer has no way of judging whether you are computer literate or whether you will turn out to be difficult to train. If you have at least some computer experience, there is less risk in spending training dollars on your computer education as an employee.

If your curriculum allows, a general introduction to business course would also be helpful, especially if it touches on accounting principles, management, and operations. This information would help you to understand your employer's situation, improve your communication at interviews, and speed up your research activities when investigating certain industries or specific companies. Some schools offer an introduction to not-for-profit organizations, which would be of help to anyone interested in that employment sector.

Any kind of business internship would also assure an employer of your interest in applying your English skills in the public arena. You might look at internships in communications, research, office administration, development, membership services, event coordination, program planning, or in rotating assignments where you have the opportunity to spend some time in all the departments of an organization. You'll come away from such an experience with a strong sense of what you could do for a firm and how an organization functions.

EARNINGS

This is a broad employment category, and starting salaries are a function of both the general salaries in the industry you are looking at (salaries in industry will be higher than in service firms) and your particular set of skills. The more specific skills (computer, math, research, etc.) you bring in addition to your degree, the higher your initial salary range. Entry-level salaries start at about $24,000–25,000 and can rise to $35,000–36,000.

CAREER OUTLOOK

The kinds of positions we have been discussing are sometimes referred to as "generalist" positions. They are not technical jobs, and the educational background required is rather broad. Additionally, with these generalist positions there are no firmly established criteria for entry-level positions. Much depends on the employer being approached and the particular combination of skills, talent, and personality of the applicant and how that combination fits. The hiring outlook has much to do with the general trend of the economy and the size and location of the hiring organization, as well. These types of positions often follow trends. If, for example, an industry and the employers within that sector are not doing well, the funds employers have to spend on hiring new employees will probably first go toward technical expertise to improve efficiency and product quality and then to financial management staff to ensure fiscal control and solvency. The general administrator with "soft" or untried skills is not an attractive commodity at such times.

When personnel staffing funds are more freely available, it is easier to find and win these positions. A corollary of this is that these positions are also more likely to be early casualties during a downturn in the economy through layoffs, reductions in force, enforced leaves of absence, or outright dismissals. To prevent this situation, you are encouraged to use your employed time to acquire more specific skills that would significantly alter your resume.

A good example of this would be how you self-manage for growth in an entry-level position as a human resources associate for a large company. Perhaps you have been hired as an assistant benefits administrator, briefing new employees on benefit program choices and assisting in managing the smooth flow of paperwork and forms surrounding the filing and paying of claims. You could do this job in an exemplary manner for three years and yet still only be qualified for an identical job somewhere else.

Or you could request cross-training in OSHA (Occupational Safety and Health Administration) guidelines for workers, participate in professional development programs to learn more about pay classification guidelines, volunteer to work on the team producing a new benefits brochure and pick up copywriting and graphics experience, and participate in every training opportunity provided. Ask your boss if you can sit in on contract negotiations when benefit packages are up for renewal. Soon you will discover you have built a substantial body of expertise in your field. No longer are you a generalist with only your degree to recommend you; now you are qualified as a payroll specialist, benefits officer, employee trainer, or even director of personnel for a smaller organization.

STRATEGY FOR FINDING THE JOBS

As an English major seeking employment in the areas of business administration and management, you need to do three things to be successful. First, you need to become skillful at transforming descriptions of your academic skills and successes into skills and attributes that the workplace will find valuable. Second, you must know who the employers are. Third, you must reflect what you have learned on your resume.

Help Businesses Appreciate Your Skills

Candidates need to be able to document each of their strengths with anecdotes and examples that will have meaning to an employer who is far removed from the world of college academics. So if one of your particularly strong skills is project planning, you will want to express that to the employer as a usable skill. Perhaps you acquired project planning skills in terms of research paper writing or end-of-semester presentations. This won't make much of an impact on an employer. But if you suggest to the employer that you have project planning skills that can help in opening new branches or making client presentations or preparing for a sales conference, that will have more impact. You can then talk about attention to detail, assembling all relevant materials, coordinating with involved staff, and producing the necessary ancillary materials. You have taken your skills out of one context and placed them in another.

Know Something About the Organizations You Are Contacting

The second ingredient for success follows naturally from the first. To convincingly express the importance of your skills to a business employer, you will need to know something about the organization's product, personnel, and operations. It has always been a watchword of the job search process to know something about the employer you are contacting for work. This is especially important for the generalist coming from an English major to work in business or administration. It's up to you, not the employer, to express where in the organization you can be most effective and what kinds of contributions you can make. You cannot do that effectively without understanding your potential employer's operation.

Obtain company literature from the firm's home page, or from your college career office. In addition to annual reports, you'll find product line information, human resources literature, and statements of philosophy of business and mission. Look at more general sources, including current periodicals, to gain a sense of current strengths and challenges to the industry. As an English major, you know the value of specialized vocabularies from reading Shakespeare or Dickens. Entering the world of business and administration requires the same kind of diligent application to feel at home.

Reflect Newfound Knowledge on Your Resume

It is especially important for the English major's resume to say to a business audience, "I'm trained to contribute to your organization." You can do this in the way you describe your objective and history. Use the tips we've described here to set yourself apart from other liberal arts students who haven't figured out that their resume should focus on their audience rather than on themselves.

POSSIBLE EMPLOYERS

It is no exaggeration to say that the accomplished English graduate holds a degree that is an accepted passport across the borders of every industry. Employers know and value the educational background of an individual who has studied English in college. Moreover, they appreciate the contribution that such an individual can make to their organization.

Let's take the world of work and divide it up into some general categories. We'll profile each of these sectors for you and provide both general and specific resources to help you explore on your own. You'll be looking for employers that are doing things you're interested in and who hire people in the job title categories you've identified.

Not-for-Profit Organizations

Profile. All too often, the words *employment, job,* and *career* fail to call up images that include the large and diversified group of employers in the not-for-profit sector. Many of these simply cannot afford to spend for advertising what their counterparts do in the for-profit zone. Often, because these organizations benefit by and are supported by targeted markets, such advertising would not be a wise expenditure. Nevertheless, it would behoove the job seeker to investigate this rich and varied group of employers.

Not-for-profit employers can be segmented into six broad categories: health services, education, religious organizations, social services, arts, and culture. There is an incredible range of concerns that have precipitated the formation of innumerable not-for-profit organizations. Just a few of these issues are animal rights, government funding for the arts, child advocacy, consumer advocacy, education, energy use and the environment, government oversight, homelessness, hunger, legal aid, influence of the media, peace and disarmament, people with disabilities, social action, social work, sustainable agriculture, and women's issues.

Where You Might Fit In. A common characteristic of the not-for-profit organization is that one employee wears many hats. This means that when an organization hires a worker for one job, it seeks someone who can fill other roles as well. So an administrator may be called on at various times to serve as a trainer or an editor or a telemarketer. The English major is versatile, and not-for-profit employers will find that especially attractive.

For the English major or graduate seeking employment, these nonprofit organizations offer equally as many opportunities as the commercial sector. Not-for-profits have a similar organizational structure, including positions relating to the following administrative functions: human resources, office management, field staff direction, accounting, public relations, government relations, legislative relations, marketing, membership services, management information systems, development, outreach, and volunteer management.

Help in Locating These Employers. A personnel professional in the not-for-profit sector recommends that job seekers investigate policy changes, grant-making trends, and local initiatives to stand the best chance of finding job openings. *Community Jobs* is a newspaper published by Access: Networking in the Public Interest, an organization providing comprehensive resources for the job seeker in not-for-profits. In addition to the newspaper, which contains extensive job listings, Access offers a nonprofit organizations search, career development workshops for the nonprofit sector, and a resume bank. Access is located at 50 Beacon Street, Boston, MA 02108.

Some other organizations that can provide information include the Foundation Center, New York; National Training and Information Center, Chicago; Environmental Support Center, Washington, D.C.; and Society for Non-Profit Organizations, Madison, Wisconsin.

Institutions of Higher Education

Profile. Institutions of higher education can be reasonably included in any not-for-profit listing, but they deserve their own category for several reasons. First, they encompass a vast range of employment levels from gardeners to professors; second, they value skill and care in written and spoken English because it is a reflection of the institution; and third, they are often both institutions of learning and complete communities that produce an enormous range of activities, programs, and literature, providing unusual scope in terms of job titles and activities.

Where You Might Fit In. Junior and community colleges, vocational/technical colleges, and four-year colleges and universities are all institutions of higher education, and they offer many entry-level jobs that require at least a bachelor's degree. These jobs are found primarily in the student services and business units of schools. Consider this range of departments: admissions and records, career planning and placement, commuter student programs, counseling, financial aid, international student programs, judicial programs, minority student services, orientation programs, residential life programs, student activities and organizations, student union, business, development, and alumni relations.

The size of the institution will affect the number of positions available in these units; you can expect that larger colleges and universities will hire many staff members to meet the needs of their students, faculty, and staff.

Help in Locating These Employers. Each of these categories of academic institution is easily located, and a large supply of directories provide classifications by school size, type, academic majors offered, size of student population, and geographic locale. As a result, they are relatively easy to identify for your job search. Some of the standard reference sources through which you may locate academic employers include job listings in *The Chronicle of Higher Education* (www.chronicle.com) and Peterson's guides listing two-year colleges, four-year colleges, and graduate programs (www.petersons.com).

Professional Organizations

Profile. As you have noticed in reading this book, there is an association or professional organization to support every possible human endeavor. Reading through a directory of associations can be fascinating, educational, alarming, and amusing as you encounter groups of people organized around other people (James Dean Memory Club), products (North Atlantic Seafood Association), activities (Foreign Car Haters Club of America), political persuasions (Monarchist Alliance), and job categories (Academy of Dispensing Audiologists) that meet the needs and interests of nearly any type of worker. There are 23,000 U.S. national associations and 102,000 U.S. regional, state, and local associations. Nearly every association of this type has a not-for-profit structure, but because there are so many professional associations, they deserve separate attention.

Where You Might Fit In. The activities of most of these organizations revolve around year-round direct mail correspondence with their members punctuated by regularly scheduled conferences or annual meetings. Many organizations also publish directories, journals, and newsletters. Consequently, there are significant amounts of employment in preparing written materials: regularly scheduled letters and mailings to members, newsletters and newspapers, informational packets and membership services brochures to potential members, meeting packets, and educational materials.

Additionally, these organizations hear from nonmembers seeking information and answers to questions about the organization, its members, and its aims. Home pages, pamphlets, and brochures are often made available to answer these questions. Some even have targeted career information available for their industry.

In reading through the entries shown for each organization in a reference such as the *Encyclopedia of Associations,* look for the number of staff members employed there. Directory entries will indicate publications and services as well. Also be sure to read about the purpose of the group to see whether it is something you are interested in. Many people who work for professional organizations are expected to feel strongly about what the organization is trying to accomplish.

Help in Locating These Employers. If you haven't visited a career library or the career section of a public library, be sure to do so, and look for the *Encyclopedia of Associations* or *National Trade and Professional Associations of the United States.* As of this printing, neither publication was available on the Internet. Both of these resources list organizations that need workers with the skills you have to offer. Both have a geographic index to allow you to locate potential employers in any state you are hoping to live in.

Federal Government

Profile. The federal government, even with promised budget cutbacks, is still the largest employer in the country. Future budget cutbacks will affect the number of entry-level government positions available, and competition for those jobs will be keen, but there continues to be a need for federal employees.

Federal government agencies that hire graduates who are considered generalists include the Air Force; Army Information Systems Command; Training and Doctrine Command; Bureau of Alcohol, Tobacco, and Firearms; Bureau of Labor Statistics; Defense Investigative Service; Employment and Training Administration; Employment Standards Administration; Equal Employment Opportunity Commission; Federal Aviation Administration; Federal Deposit Insurance Corporation; Federal Highway Administration; General Services Administration; Immigration and Naturalization Services; Department of Labor; Library of Congress; Maritime Administration; Military Traffic Management Command; Mine Safety and Health Administration; National Science Foundation; Occupational Safety and Health Administration; Office of Inspector General; Office of Personnel Management; Office of the Secretary; Health & Human Services; Railroad Retirement Board; Department of State; U.S. Marshals Service; U.S. Postal Service; and Department of Veterans Affairs.

Where You Might Fit In. Each of these government units has an organizational structure that provides job opportunities ranging from generalist to specialist. The Library of Congress, for example, hires people with Ph.D.s in biology for biological science analyst positions and people with B.A.s in the liberal arts as research assistants; the General Services Administration looks for English majors to work as contract specialists and seeks law-degree holders to work as attorneys.

Many of these federal government agencies have their own administrative staff responsible for various functions including personnel, procurement, and reporting. Some resources to help familiarize you with the operations of these various units include VGM's *Opportunities in Federal Government Careers, Complete Guide to Public Employment,* and *Government Job Finder.*

Help in Locating These Employers. A good place to start looking for actual job listings is on the U.S. government's website (http://www.usajobs. opm.gov/index.htm). This site explains the federal employment process and lets you look at current job openings, get general information on federal agencies, and submit an on-line application.

If you select the option "Current Job Openings" and then "Entry-Level Professional," you can begin exploring the possibilities. Select options relating to job type, geographic area, and date of job listing. Submit your search criteria, then select any of the entries and a detailed job description is provided, including information on who to contact for more information and how to apply for the specific position.

State and Local Government

Profile. State and local governments offer a variety of administrative positions in departments that include corrections, court systems, education, fire protection, health, highway and street construction, housing and community development, hospitals, libraries, natural resources, parks and recreation, police, sanitation, transportation, utilities, and welfare and human services.

Where You Might Fit In. As with the federal government, there is a range of agencies and job titles that you should consider. Many specialists are hired, but generalists such as the English major will fit in comfortably in many places. Resources such as VGM's *Opportunities in State and Local Government Careers, Careers in State and Local Government, Government Job Finder,* and *Complete Guide to Public Employment* detail the many possibilities.

Help in Locating These Employers. Use your favorite search engine and enter "State of (put state name here)". You will find references to state departments;

look for Employment, Personnel, or Human Resources, then look for job listings, opportunities, etc. You will also find application procedures and contact names, and some sites will allow you to apply on-line.

Expand your search by using published directories to uncover government units you were not aware of. Directories such as the *Municipal Yearbook, Braddock's Federal-State-Local Government Directory, Municipal Executive Directory, Directory of City Policy Officials, County Executive Directory, State Executive Directory, State Government Research Directory,* and *Regional, State, and Local Organizations* are all useful for identifying possible employers.

For-Profit Businesses

Profile. If you have or are getting a degree in English and you are thinking about working in a for-profit setting, the possibilities for employment occur in every area of human endeavor. You may not have considered some of these industries: agriculture, forestry, fishing, mining, construction, manufacturing, transportation, public utilities, wholesale trade, retail trade, finance, insurance, real estate, and business and personal services.

You may find it difficult to imagine all the possible categories of employment available to you, so here's an easy exercise. Pick up your local yellow pages telephone directory. Advertisers are listed under general headings: contractors, desktop publishing services, hospitals, mortgage services, paper manufacturers, resorts, transportation, and video production services. A walk through the phone book is a reminder of all the employment possibilities around us that are duplicated in nearly every locality.

Where You Might Fit In. For-profit employers spend most of their energy in connecting their product or service with a potential market. The essence of that "connection" is communication. Of course, this may involve written and oral communication as well as the media. But even more than public communications, there is a demand for individual talent to focus and define an organization's mission, to clarify goals, to set agendas, and to enunciate strategies to reach those goals.

A never-ending stream of both public external and private internal communications is the hallmark of the for-profit employer. They have a message, a product, or a service that must be communicated clearly to an audience if they are to survive. In surviving, they have the opportunity to improve the quality and delivery of that product, whatever it may be. The English major who can write and speak clearly, who can analyze and solve problems, who can research and transform data into meaningful information, and who can persuade people to take action is vitally important to organizations in this sector of the economy.

Because these organizations must continually respond to the marketplace, the English major can expect to be stretched, to grow, to be challenged, and to play a major role in the ever-changing definition of the competitive organization.

Help in Locating These Employers. If you're looking locally or regionally and are including small and midsize organizations in your search, begin with your telephone book. Search the Web for a local chamber of commerce—many sites include member directories, the state Department of Business and Industry, and the regional Small Business Administration.

For more comprehensive searches and to include major employers, you'll want to consult some of the larger directories published for just such a purpose. Most of this directory information is *not* available on the Internet, so you'll need to use printed resources. These include *Ward's Business Directory of U.S. Private and Public Companies, Directory of Corporate Affiliations, Business Rankings Annual,* and *Hoover's Handbook of American Business.*

POSSIBLE JOB TITLES

Whether an organization is a for-profit or a not-for-profit entity, you will see similar job titles, because there are basic functions necessary to run both types of organizations. Have you been watching for advertisements for jobs such as personnel officer, communications assistant, marketing manager, public relations assistant, office manager, program manager, account representative, field staff director, financial assistant, project director, research assistant, or production assistant? Some job titles that may be seen more frequently in the nonprofit sector include event manager, outreach worker, director of volunteers, counselor, or membership coordinator.

Don't be frightened off by the title of counselor. Many nonprofit organizations are seeking people with a willingness to learn these skills in addition to people who may already possess them. Sometimes, however, a counseling job really doesn't involve "counseling" in the strict sense of the word.

There are some jobs, like office manager or administrative assistant, that many people associate with secretarial work. In fact, there are many highly paid people in these types of jobs who do very little secretarial work, for example, managers of large medical facilities or law firms. You may want to look more closely at the job descriptions for this type of work the next time you review the classified ads.

In higher education, often-seen job titles unique to the functions of a college or university that are associated with student affairs divisions include admissions representative, career adviser, program coordinator, administrative aide, financial aid representative, international student coordinator, minority student programmer, orientation coordinator, residential life adviser, student activities coordinator, student union administrator, and special programs coordinator. The business division of a college or university would include job titles such as development associate, grants administrator, technical assistant, trainer, and financial aid officer.

Any government unit, whether at the federal, state, city, or local level, is involved in such a wide range of activities that it would be difficult to enumerate all of the possible job titles. The following list is provided as a teaser: outdoor recreation planner, public-health program specialist, technical writer, appraiser, communications specialist, financial examiner, industrial specialist, traffic manager, computer specialist, personnel manager, contract representative, import specialist, archivist, geographer, social scientist, and park ranger. If you would like to gain a deeper understanding of the range of possible job titles, the following resources should be used: *Occupational Outlook Quarterly, Opportunities in State and Local Government Careers,* and *Federal Civil Service Jobs.*

Use the industry index in the *Dictionary of Occupational Titles* to expand your list of interesting job titles in the various industries. Before long, you'll have a much deeper understanding of the range of possible job titles that you are interested in and qualified to apply for.

PROFESSIONAL ASSOCIATIONS FOR BUSINESS AND ADMINISTRATION

A variety of associations are listed here. We have tried to include at least one for each of the types of employers described.

American Association for Higher Education
One Dupont Circle, Ste. 360
Washington, DC 20036
Website: www.aahe.org
E-mail: info@aahe.org
Members/Purpose: Administrators, students, trustees, faculty, public officials, and interested individuals from all segments of postsecondary education.
Journal/Publication: *AAHE Bulletin; Change Magazine.*

American Business Association
292 Madison Ave., Seventh Floor
New York, NY 10017

Members/Purpose: Owners of businesses and individuals in executive, managerial, and sales capacities. Provides financial services to business professionals.
Journal/Publication: *ABA Business Brief.*

American Federation of State, County, and Municipal Employees
1625 L St. NW
Washington, DC 20036
Website: www.afscme.org
E-mail: webmaster@afscme.org
Members/Purpose: AFL-CIO.
Journal/Publication: *AFSCME Leader; Public Newsletter; Women's Newsletter.*

Civil Service Employees Association
P.O. Box 125, Capitol Station
143 Washington Ave.
Albany, NY 12210
Members/Purpose: AFL-CIO. Members are state and local government employees from all public employee classifications.
Training: Conducts training and education programs.
Journal/Publication: Newsletter; *Public Sector.*

National Association of Government Employees
2011 Crystal Dr., Ste. 206
Arlington, VA 22202
Website: www.nage.com
E-mail: on Web
Members/Purpose: Union of civilian federal government employees with locals and members in military agencies, the Internal Revenue Service, Postal Service, Veterans Administration, General Services Administration, Federal Aviation Administration, and other federal agencies, as well as state and local agencies.
Training: Offers seminars.
Journal/Publication: *Fednews.*

National Business Association
P.O. Box 700728
Dallas, TX 75370
Website: www.nationalbusiness.org
E-mail: nbal2@airmail.net
Members/Purpose: Self-employed small businesspeople. Promotes and assists the growth and development of small businesses.
Training: Sponsors seminars.

Journal/Publication: *NBA News; NBA in Partnership with the Self-Employed; How to Start Your Own Business.*

Non-Profit Management Association
315 W. 9th St., Ste. 1100
Los Angeles, CA 90015
Website: www.cnmsocal.org
E-mail: main@cnmsocal.org
Members/Purpose: Individuals who directly manage or provide management or technical assistance to nonprofit groups.
Journal/Publication: *NMA Bulletin Board; NMA Members Directory.*
Job Listings: In San Francisco Bay Area, check *Opportunity Knocks,* published by the Management Center.

Society for Non-Profit Organizations
6314 Odana Rd., Ste. One
Madison, WI 53719
Website: Danenet.wicip.org/snpo
E-mail: snpo@danenet.wicip.org
Members/Purpose: Executive directors, staff, board members, volunteers, and other professionals who serve nonprofit organizations.
Training: Sponsors seminars and workshops on nonprofit management and leadership.
Journal/Publication: *National Directory of Service and Product Providers to Non-Profit Organizations; Nonprofit World: The National Nonprofit Leadership and Management Journal;* resource center catalog.
Job Listings: Suggests job seekers review *Community Jobs.*

CHAPTER FOURTEEN

PATH 5: TECHNICAL WRITING

We live in an increasingly technological age. Technology changes the speed at which we communicate, the devices we use to communicate, and even the language we employ to express ourselves. Cell phones, pagers, answering machines, fax machines, word processors, videophones, and portable computers have all dramatically altered the movement of words, ideas, and images. Not only is there more information to deal with each day, but we may also need help both to acquire the information we need (getting the automated teller to produce a statement of our account balance) and to interpret the information we have (understanding the directions to program a CD recorder system).

Most of us see only the commercial and consumer-oriented products of this technological revolution. But there is an industrial revolution of even greater magnitude going on as well: laser imaging, patient-administered intravenous analgesics, and digital recording equipment. Entire assembly lines for major products such as automobiles being built by robots usher in a new kind of worker that needs to be understood and managed just as any human workforce does.

In addition to our own active participation in this revolution, we rely on words, both written and spoken, to explain the world to us. But what happens when the world becomes so complicated that words aren't sufficient to help us understand or the words themselves are almost like a foreign language?

We need a new kind of interpreter, someone who can take the complex and make it digestible for those of us without a technical background.

We need an intermediary between this increasingly technocratic world and our own lives. But we also need people who can communicate in these new technical "languages," people who write, speak, and communicate with each other in dialects of their own devising to continue producing the products, services, and enhancements of life that come with technology. These are technical writers.

DEFINITION OF THE CAREER PATH

The term *technical writing* is subject to various interpretations. Anyone close to the field will have his or her own favorite definition of the job and its duties. Two interpretations seem to be among the most prevalent. One states that technical writers are responsible for taking material that is difficult for the layman to understand and rewriting it in a more comprehensible form and style. This may involve writing manuals, directions, installation guides, repair instructions, books, film scripts, training programs, or any number of factual pieces. There is even some commercial work for technical writers in advertising, press relations, and industrial sales. Technical writers use a potent combination of strong writing skills and a grounding in at least one technical field (including computer science, engineering, medicine, or aerospace).

The other common definition states that technical writers are responsible for writing technical material for others who are versed in this material to read. The medical technical writer might take the results of a number of studies and write a review of the material comparing the studies. The computer science technical writer might help prepare a paper for delivery at a major software conference. The engineering technical writer might produce a document reviewing stress and fatigue studies on a particular kind of steel I beam. Both definitions express the role of a technical writer, and many technical writers do both kinds of jobs all the time.

The very existence of this profession may be a result of advances in technology moving exponentially faster than the pace of human utilization. The tremendous developments in the computer industry in the past decade alone in terms of speed of processing argue for someone to help us bridge the gap between what exists and what we can understand based on our own experiences and education. Without the assistance of technical writers, there might be a frightening and divisive gap between science and everyday life.

So we have come to need the services of technical writers; in fact, we rely on them to a great extent. We hear about a new digital camera. We may not entirely understand how it works, but we know that if we acquire it, it will come with instructions to allow us to incorporate it into our lives.

The intensive care nurse on the neonatal ward of a children's hospital places the same trust in the installation and operating instructions that accompany a new infant incubation unit. Although the nurse may appreciate the features and understand the need for them, without a technical manual on how to program, troubleshoot, and operate the system, the equipment would be useless.

There have always been technical specialists who wrote, but with the proliferation of technology, the field has shifted from technical specialists who write to writers who are grounded in technology. A skilled writer with a technical background can be a powerful member of a team developing any kind of structured systems design product that requires written documentation. Of course, end users will need this documentation and the training it provides to use a new system, whatever that system may be. But, increasingly, the technical writer is involved during product development. A good technical communicator can be indispensable in helping to analyze user requirements, clarify the documentation process, and solve increasingly complex communication problems with information systems management staff. The insightful technical writer can help enhance the efficiency of a design.

To fully understand how technical writers can contribute to systems design, a shift in thinking is needed. Technical writers included in a design team early on in planning can help the firm turn out a higher-quality product while reducing time and costs of systems development, testing, revision, and documentation. There are several reasons why a technical writer might make a good designer. Traditionally, it is a writer's skill to determine what a user needs to know and when. This helps them to create a logical flow of information. Technical writers can combine this user's perspective with their own experience and ability to emphasize logic, simplicity, usability, and consistency.

The change in role here is dramatic. Rather than functioning solely as the software documenter at the end of a development process, the technical writer now joins the team early on in product development to bring an end-user perspective that may have dramatic implications for product design, development, and features.

Fortunately for those aspiring to be technical writers, this proliferation of technology has not been limited to one or even a few sectors of the economy. For example, the growth of air, land, and sea defense systems and new radar capabilities in the military; the movement toward a permanent space station and the routine launching of shuttle missions (many with commercial payloads) in the aerospace industry; the dramatic changes in the pharmaceutical industry as it works overtime to challenge the threats of Alzheimer's and cancer; the computer industry and its continued appearance in every aspect of our lives; robotics in manufacturing; dramatic new procedures in surgical technique and postsurgical care in medicine; and research work in communications, energy, and precision instruments are but a few of the countless developments signaling employment for the technical writer.

Writers document procedures such as how to grow bacteria, build complex viruses, develop artificial insulin, and cleanse cholesterol. Many advances in science, especially biology and chemistry, suggest that these may be promising backgrounds for future technical writers. Robotics will also provide a fruitful proving ground for new advances in engineering and hydraulics. Some of this growth seems to be localized geographically in familiar regions such as California's Silicon Valley, the Pacific Northwest, Atlanta, central Florida, New Jersey, and Washington, D.C.

The growth of technology has led to many new, smaller, start-up organizations, many of which need technical writing expertise but not on a full-time basis. Technical writers who are entrepreneurially inclined might enjoy freelancing for a number of different organizations. What they lack in benefits and stability, they may recover in higher fees and the pleasure of an ever-changing workload.

Technology is complex, and the need for technical writers was born out of that complexity. The technology sector of our economy remains the largest employer, both currently and prospectively, for aspiring technical writers. But life in general has grown increasingly complex, and technical writers can also be found in colleges, universities, and even in advertising agencies. Technical writers can work for book, magazine, and newspaper publishers as well. Some technical writers work for the U.S. Government Printing Office producing brochures and pamphlets that cover many different fields: activities of various government agencies and reports on government work in agriculture, medicine, science, and aerospace.

Some technical writers work in nonscience areas, as well. There are technical writers in large insurance companies who explain terms and procedures to field agents, claims adjusters, and others who work for the firm. Technical writers can produce contracts, policies, and procedural manuals for any field from commercial shipping to banking.

In seeking entry into a field that might lead to a technical writing position, look for job descriptions that emphasize work that will provide opportunities to acquire the knowledge base you will need to attain a technical writing position. To better understand the varied duties and responsibilities inherent in a technical writer's job, let's look at the complete description outlined in the *Dictionary of Occupational Titles*:

Develops, writes, and edits material for reports, manuals, briefs, proposals, instruction books, catalogs, and related technical and administrative publications concerned with work methods and procedures, and installation, operation, and maintenance of machinery and other equipment: receives assignment from supervisor. Observes production, developmental, and experimental activities to determine operating procedure and detail. Interviews production and engineering personnel and reads journals, reports, and other material to become familiar with product technologies and production methods. Reviews manufacturer's and trade catalogs, drawings and other data relative to operation, maintenance and service of equipment. Studies blueprints, sketches, drawings, parts lists, specifications, mock-ups and product samples to integrate and delineate technology, operating procedure, and production sequence and detail. Organizes material and completes writing assignment according to set standards regarding order, clarity, conciseness, style, and terminology. Reviews published materials and recommends revisions or changes in scope, format, content, and methods of reproduction and binding. May maintain records and files of work and revisions. May select photographs, drawings, sketches, diagrams, and charts to illustrate material. May assist in laying out material for publication. May arrange for typing, duplication, and distribution of material. May write speeches, articles, and public or employee relations releases. May edit, standardize, or make changes to material prepared by other writers or plant personnel and be designated Standard Practice Analyst. May specialize in writing material regarding work methods and procedures and be designated Process Description Writer.

Technical writers emerge from two possible entry-level sites. The college graduate with an English major and sufficient technical background or willingness to acquire such background may begin as a technical writing research assistant or a technician in any of the employment sectors hiring technical writers. They would spend this entry-level time acquiring increasingly sophisticated technical information about their organization and its product. Larger firms may contribute substantially to a promising employee with courses, workshop attendance, seminars, and professional conference invitations.

Other entry-level positions are for technicians with an interest in developing writing skills as technical writers. These individuals are most often already employed within an organization and seek either job change or job modification to explore this possibility. In most cases they would be assigned to work closely with an established staff technical writer who would give them research assignments and pieces of writing to edit and use as a training tool to improve the quality of the trainee's writing efforts.

The promotion ladder next moves up to full-fledged technical writer and from there to technical editor. The technical editor assigns tasks, monitors work flow and deadline dates, and has overall responsibility for quality. This individual, as a department head, might also evaluate employees, manage the department budget, make equipment purchases, hire new staff, and participate in other organizational efforts.

The following actual advertisements are illustrative of established technical writing positions and detail not only desired backgrounds and qualifications but also suggest the variety of settings in which technical writing takes place:

Technical Writer. Entry level, supply writing services to all div of pharmaceutical co. Write user & tech manuals, etc. Req BA/BS English/journalism/creative writing. Good writing, proofreading & editing skills. MAC, Framemaker, Microsoft exper. Send writing samples & resume to . . .

Automotive Technical Writer. Write diagnostic and repair manuals. Req BA English/tech communications/rel field, 2 yrs automotive service pubs exp, engineering/tech bkgrnd, pref ASE cert. Resume/writ samples to . . .

Marketing Technical Writer. Market rsrch services, decision support software. Write procedural manuals/reference guide/scripts for training videos. Req BS/equiv, excel writ/edit skills, pref exp writing market research surveys/questionnaires. Resume/sal hist to . . .

Bilingual Technical Writer. Req native Spanish speaker, 1 yr exp writing mechanical/electrical documentation in English. Resume/sal hist to . . .

Technical Writer. Software firm marketing products in health-care and self-insurance industries. Testing, user documentation, manuals, more. Req 2 yrs software documentation exp. $25K–$35K. Resume to . . .

Biomedical Engineering Technical Writer. Major New York hospital seeks self-starter with excellent writing, communications, and interpersonal skills and understanding of technical material. Write/edit technical letters, evaluations, and reports. Maintain technical libraries and manuals, pursue technical research and investigative projects on scientific and medical instrumentation. Maintain files on instrumentation incident reports, medical alert notices, and manufacturer recalls. Send resume with salary to . . .

WORKING CONDITIONS

Most technical writers live in or near major metropolitan areas. Jobs are available around the country, but they are concentrated in the Northeast, Texas, California, the Northwest, Atlanta, central Florida, New Jersey, and Washington, D.C.

Working conditions will depend on the industry and type of specialty required. Many technical writers are employed in the software industry, which tends to provide more flexible hours and allows more casual dress, although many hours of overtime may be required as release dates and publishing deadlines approach.

Some technical writers handle pieces of machinery or operate computer programs in order to determine the best way to explain the procedures. For many other technical writers, their day is sedentary as they sit at a personal computer or terminal to produce their written product. Freelance technical writers often work odd hours to fit this work into another full-time work schedule.

The most important aspect of technical writers' working conditions is that they must constantly be learning new technologies and developments in their field of expertise in order to remain attractive to their employer or contractor. Most begin any new project with extensive research, so some of their time is spent on the Internet and in libraries and research facilities. But not all their research is on the Web or with books and manuscripts. They may be called on to do some interviewing as well. Both research activities and interviewing assignments can provide some travel opportunities and variety to the working conditions of a technical writer.

TRAINING AND QUALIFICATIONS

Technical writing positions require at least a four-year degree, and it can take up to six additional years of training or schooling to acquire the specialized knowledge necessary to work in some areas. Students graduating with a degree in English must begin as early as they can to build an area of technical expertise. Choosing a minor in a science, computers, etc., is one way to accomplish this.

Effective communication skills are required in this occupation. Many would wrongly assume that this job is solitary or suitable for an introverted person. In fact, as a technical writer you will interact with countless other professionals and will need to be a superb communicator at all levels. The writer must be prepared to extract information from others who use a highly specific and technical vocabulary.

Though technical writers come from any number of educational backgrounds, including English, they share many basic skills. They are required to be logical, disciplined, accurate, and detailed in their writing. They often must thoroughly research their subject matter before beginning to write and confer early and frequently with other authorities in the field to ensure accuracy and quality of information. They must have strong research skills, and they frequently employ research in their preparation to write. In this preparation, they may encounter technical diagrams, blueprints, schematics, flowcharts, and any number of highly specialized and technical aids, which they must then interpret.

Accuracy and attention to detail are critical. It cannot be stressed enough that "attention to detail" for technical writers is of an entirely different order than our everyday use of that phrase. Some might say it needs to be almost pathological because the detail in technical writing is the essence of the work. Poise under pressure and the ability to work with deadlines make aspects of this job similar to news reporting. Curiosity and aggressiveness about acquiring information suggest that some qualities of a detective would be helpful.

In addition to consultations throughout the writing process with other experts in the field, the technical writer's work is subject to final review by professionals in the subject area. In fact, much technical writing is collaborative, and the technical writer must be comfortable working and creating in a team environment.

The foundation of the technical writer's skill, however, is not just excellent writing, but a thorough grounding in some technical specialty. For this reason, entry-level technical writing positions are not often found. Technical writers almost always gravitate to this profession after some years of work in a technical specialty. Writing skill can be developed and polished in the general writing assignments that we encounter in the work environment, but technical writing is founded on knowledge and expertise gained through experience. Aspiring technical writers often begin by doing some research or working alongside an established technical writer, helping with drafts and editing.

This skill is more than simple "translation" of the material from technospeak to plain English; it is, in fact, the transformation of material that is too obtuse to be useful into information that can be easily understood and appreciated by the intended audience. So the writing, while crucial, cannot really be separated from the technical skill and grounding in the science. The explosion of information, especially technical information, available on the Web has led the Manitoba chapter of the Society for Technical Communications to reopen its on-line Special Interest Group (SIG). This SIG's purpose is to provide a forum for technical communicators to share ideas and concepts related to the development and structure of on-line information.

It is certainly understandable in reading about the technical expertise and attention to detail required of a technical writer that some individuals interested in this career may feel that this isn't really writing, but rather some kind of robotic translation. Nothing could be further from the truth. Peter J. Hager and Ronald J. Nelson, in a 1993 article in *IEEE Transactions on Professional Communication* that is still relevant today, point out that as far back as Geoffrey Chaucer's "A Treatise on the Astrolabe" we have marvelous models for how technical writers can incorporate into their works rhetorical components such as coherent organization, appropriate content, accurate descriptions, personable tone, varied sentence structure, and even humor.

Although even practicing technical writers may find it difficult to inject humor into their writing, it has been argued that the use of humor as part of a technical writing text gives documentation several advantages, including the suggestion that both the writer and designer are genuinely engaged in the subject. That engagement is compelling to the reader and lightens what might otherwise be an overly heavy approach to the subject. There's no question that most documentation is seen as dreary in style and content. The argument here is not humor for the sake of humor, but rather humor judiciously used to enhance, not obscure, the documentation. The continuing dialogue on this and other stylistic matters shows there certainly is a place for the thinking, stylistically concerned writer in the field of technical writing.

It will come as no surprise to aspiring technical writers that their command of computer technology must be substantially more than simple word-processing skills. Desktop publishing familiarity would be considered a basic skill, as would some computer graphics, analysis software, spreadsheet capability, and any number of other programs for the manipulation of data. All of these would be helpful to the technical writer and add to a candidate's attractiveness in this market.

The following phrases from recent job descriptions are representative of nearly every ad that was examined, and they highlight the importance of building experience in a range of software applications: "The more computer skills the better." "Required: course work in PC computer applications." "Essential knowledge: familiar with layout of technical documentation using desktop publishing systems." "Working knowledge of word-processing, spreadsheet, and database software is required." "Essential skills: knowledgeable in the use of Microsoft Word and Power Point software applications."

EARNINGS

As reported by the Society for Technical Communications on its website (http://www.stc-va.org/Default.htm), as of this writing salaries for technical writers and editors continue to rise. The average salary for entry-level technical writers and editors in the United States is $36,100, and in Canada the figure is $37,530. Be sure to check the Society's website for the most current information available.

Earnings information taken from another source, U.S. News Online (http://www.usnews.com/), listed "technical writer" as a hot job in communications and showed an average entry-level salary of $35,500, a midlevel salary of $41,300, and a top salary of $54,510. Salary information changes each year; check the websites mentioned for the latest information.

How much freelancers earn varies widely and has much to do with their experience, subject matter specialty, and reputation as well as the nature and originator of whatever assignment they are working on. Since they are self-employed, they must provide their own benefits. Many job postings were found on the Web. Be sure to check the website of the Society for Technical Communications and other major sites for freelance writer earnings.

CAREER OUTLOOK

The outlook for technical writers is excellent. The U.S. Department of Labor, Bureau of Labor Statistics, reports faster than average growth of technical writers due to the proliferation of scientific and technical information and the need to communicate that information.

Approximately 286,000 writers and editors, including technical writers, were employed in the U.S. in 1996, and that number is projected to grow to 347,000 in the year 2006. The federal government employs a number of these workers. Nongovernment workers are employed in a wide range of industries, and the employment outlook will vary with the industry in which you hope to be employed.

Revolutions in the personal computer market, networking capabilities, and the use of laptops, notebooks, personal digital devices, and pen-based computers all suggest that the need for technical writers in the computer hardware industry will grow. Existing and emerging technologies in virtual reality and object-oriented software will also provide opportunities for growth in the software industry, traditionally one of the largest sources of employment for technical writers.

The increasing use of on-line retail trade, especially in the customer service area, provides many job opportunities for technical writers. They assist in developing product information and technical information that is posted on a company's Internet site. This information allows companies to efficiently manage customer relations and improve customer satisfaction. Growth is also projected in the biotechnology industry, which introduces breakthrough processes and products in medicine, agriculture, and the environment.

Some industries do not hold as much promise, however. Be sure to do some basic research on any industry you are considering. A good resource for exploring this subject is the latest edition of the *U.S. Industry and Trade Outlook,* published by the U.S. Department of Commerce and McGraw-Hill. This information is not available on the Internet, but the book is available at many career and public libraries. It includes discussions of long-term industry prospects, including employment trends.

STRATEGY FOR FINDING THE JOBS

Target the Type of Technical Writing You Want to Do

Technical writers possess a technical knowledge base in at least one field, so your job search will be affected by the depth of your specialized knowledge at this point. You might already have a solid background in a given field or industry. Perhaps you have a minor in computer information systems and have done an internship with a software manufacturer. In this case, you'll want to network with employers and use the job listings made available by professional associations. Two examples of these associations are the American Medical Writers Association (www.amwa.org) and the National Association of Science Writers (www.nasw.org). Some sites will allow you to access job listings at no cost, but others will only allow access to those people who have joined the organization.

Target Specific Industries

If you have not yet had an opportunity to build a level of technical expertise, begin your job search by identifying industries that truly interest you. The next few years will be a continuation of your education as you increase your knowledge in a given field, so choose something you can get excited about. Once you identify an industry, begin reviewing entry-level job postings in that field to develop a list of potential employers. If you have the funds, join a professional organization that serves this type of worker. Once you develop a list of employers, contact them and conduct informational interviews with as many you can. Between your review of the job listings and your networking activity, you will quickly gain an understanding of the job possibilities in your chosen sector of the economy and for the geographic location you are targeting.

Identify Useful Resources

Begin your search for actual job listings for technical writing positions, or positions that will allow you to begin building a technical expertise, by using the Internet. Just a few of the major Internet career sites that will lead you to these types of position advertisements include www.careermosaic.com, www.jobbankusa.com, and www.monster.com. As you spend more time exploring career sites, it will become easier to find the kind of job description and listing you are looking for.

POSSIBLE EMPLOYERS

As you discovered in previous sections of this chapter, the employment opportunities for technical writers can be found anywhere there is technical information that needs to be relayed to other professionals working in the industry, or where there is information that needs to be simplified for a lay audience. These needs cross nearly every industrial and geographic boundary. Industries needing and hiring technical writers include the following:

- Natural resources and energy
- Construction and related industries
- Industrial materials and components
- Production and manufacturing equipment
- Information and communications
- The consumer economy
- Transportation and travel
- Health care
- Financial services
- Business and professional services
- Public administration

Remember, it is important to build a knowledge base in at least one technical area, so you may want to begin your search for employment by looking for entry-level jobs that will allow you to begin gaining the required expertise.

Listed under each employer category are resources you can use to develop a list of potential employers. Our purpose in listing these resources is simply to help you understand where you can find employers who typically hire in a given industry. Use the information in Chapter 3 to help you identify additional employers who hire technical writers.

Natural Resources and Energy

Profile. This industry includes metals and industrial minerals mining, coal mining, crude petroleum and natural gas, petroleum refining, and electricity production and sales; technical writers are needed in each of these areas. For example, companies that operate oil and gas fields use complex equipment and procedures to make oil and gas marketable. Field technicians must have a complete understanding of the equipment and procedures so that they can work efficiently and handle any problems or disasters that may arise.

There is great risk of accident and natural disaster in all aspects of the natural resources and energy field. Mine cave-ins, oil-well blowouts, and underground fires call for quick response and creative use of highly complex equipment. Instructions and associated visuals must be crystal clear for situations such as these when tension adds to the difficulties. Technical writers help to create manuals and emergency procedure directions so that these high-risk situations can be brought under control in a time- and cost-efficient manner. It is no exaggeration to say that, in these cases, their work can mean the difference between life and death.

Help in Locating These Employers. There are so many hiring companies in this industry that it would be nearly impossible to list them all here. Resources such as *Standard and Poor's Industry Surveys* and *Moody's Industrial Manual* provide lists of companies by type of industry. Use these kinds of references to build your list of companies in this industry. Once you identify actual company names using paper-based resources, using the Internet to search for jobs at these companies becomes an easy task to undertake.

Some of the professional organizations that can provide useful information on the petroleum industry include the American Petroleum Institute (www.api.org), Washington, D.C.; the Coordinating Research Council, Atlanta (www.crcao.com), which includes the Association of Petroleum Writers; and the Gas Research Institute, Chicago. There are similar professional associations for each of the various natural resources and energy subindustries.

Construction

Profile. The construction industry includes private residential, private non-residential, publicly owned, and international construction. The skills of the technical writer are needed here, too. The blending of the aesthetic demands of the architect, the building codes required in a particular locality, cost and energy constraints, and the overriding pressure of labor costs associated with protracted construction schedules all place heavy demands on the technical writer to produce materials that not only synthesize all these competing entities but also provide readable guidelines in the field.

Help in Locating These Employers. Associations and organizations related to this sector of the economy include Associated General Contractors (www.agc .org), Associated Builders and Contractors (www.abc.org), and National Association of Homebuilders. All are in the Washington, D.C., area.

Industrial Materials and Components

Profile. When you think about textiles, paper and allied products, chemicals (including drugs and pharmaceuticals), plastics and rubber, metals, general components like valve and pipe fittings, and microelectronic components, you're thinking about activities and products related to the industrial materials and components industry.

Each time a new drug is allowed on the market, specifications on the use of that drug must be provided to doctors, pharmacists, and patients alike. Dosage requirements, administration protocols, and contraindications for existing conditions or combinations with other drugs require the clearest kind of information. The skill of the technical writer in documenting and presenting this information in an organized and logical way could mean a lifesaving difference for the patient.

Help in Locating These Employers. If you are interested in working as a technical writer in the pharmaceuticals industry, you may want to begin by researching some of the larger companies. Explore various Internet sites that provide industry information, or check manuals such as *Ward's Business Directory* or the *Business Rankings Annual* for the names of these companies. Not too long ago an entry-level technical writing position for a large pharmaceutical company was found at www.careermag.com.

Several organizations that can provide information on pharmaceutical companies and associated jobs include the Pharmaceutical Manufacturers Association, Washington, D.C.; National Association of Pharmaceutical Manufacturers, Garden City, New York (www.napmnet.org); and the Nonprescription Drug Manufacturers Association, Washington, D.C.

Associations for other products included in this industry are the American Electronics Association, Santa Clara, California (www.aeanet.org); Northern Textile Association, Boston, Massachusetts (www.textilenta.org); the Publishing Mall website (www.pub-mall.com); Printing Industries of America, Alexandria, Virginia (www.printing.org); Society of the Plastics Industry, Washington, D.C. (www.socplas.org); Association of American Publishers (www.publishers.org); and the Valve Manufacturers Association, Washington, D.C. (www.vma.org).

Production and Manufacturing Equipment

Profile. This industry covers a range of manufacturers, including metalworking equipment, production machinery, electrical equipment, environmental technologies and services, aerospace, ship building and repair, industrial and analytical instruments, and photographic equipment and supplies.

If we look more closely at the aerospace industry, we find that it includes aircraft, missiles, and space-launch vehicle production and manufacturing. If you are interested in being involved in technical writing somehow associated with this industry, employment is projected to grow, so technical writers continue to seek employment here.

Help in Locating These Employers. You could begin your search for employment by finding out which employers manufacture equipment needed to keep space-launch programs operational. Most states' manufacturing activity is summarized in *Directory of Manufacturers,* which is available at most public libraries and college or career office libraries. These directories list manufacturers by their Standard Industrial Classification (SIC) code; the SIC for this industry is 376. For each manufacturer listed, you will usually find contact information (address and phone number), a summary of products, sales information, company officers, and number of employees.

If you are interested in finding out more about employment in the aerospace industry, the Aerospace Industries Association in Washington, D.C. (www.aia.aerospace.org), can provide information, as can the General Aviation Manufacturers Association, also in Washington, D.C. (www.generalaviation.org).

Information and Communications

Profile. When you think about printing and publishing, information services, computer equipment, computer software and networking, telecommunications services, telecommunications and navigation equipment, and entertainment and electronics, you are thinking about the information and communications industry.

Many technical writers are employed in this sector of the economy, especially in computer software and networking. One dynamic segment of this industry is CAD/CAM/CAE or computer-aided design, computer-aided manufacturing, and computer-aided engineering. Engineers, designers, and draftspeople all use these types of software, and, as new products come onto the market, technical writers must create new instruction manuals to help users effectively incorporate these tools into their work.

Help in Locating These Employers. There are many large as well as smaller start-up companies that offer employment prospects. The Internet is really the best place to look for industry information, employer names, and job listings. Use any of the major sites (www.careermosaic.com, www.jobbank usa.com, www.monster.com, or www.ahandyguide.com) and begin exploring. And don't hesitate to submit your resume via the Internet when seeking a job in the information and communications industry.

A comprehensive website that will help you link to associations, employers, and jobs is that of the Computer Information Center (http://www.comp info.co.uk/index.htm). Some industry-specific organizations include the Software and Information Industry Association (http://www.siia.net/), Telecommunications Managers Association (http://www.tma.org.uk/home.htm), and Electronic Industries Alliance (http://www.eia.org/).

Consumer Economy

Profile. The consumer economy provides many opportunities to the aspiring technical writer. Wholesaling and retailing of food and beverages, apparel, motor vehicles, household furniture and appliances, and sporting and athletic goods are all a part of this sector of the economy. Nearly every item sold, no matter how simple or complex, is accompanied by a set of user instructions. If you've just purchased a new answering machine, you want to be sure that you have set it up correctly to respond to calls that come in. So you get out the instruction manual. You find the instructions easy to understand and, in just a few minutes, the machine is ready to answer incoming calls. Say thanks to the technical writer!

Help in Locating These Employers. There are a myriad of both employers and professional associations connected with the consumer economy. You may be especially interested in one type of product, so let your search begin there. Use the *U.S. Industry and Trade Outlook* to find out more about long-term prospects for that sector, and then use the *Encyclopedia of Associations* to locate related professional organizations. Each association will tell you whether it includes job listings in its newsletter and can advise you on the best sources for additional job listings. Don't hesitate to check their websites for job listings and other career information.

Transportation

Profile. Transportation includes airlines, railroads, trucking, water transportation, and domestic shipping. Each of these sectors uses complex computerized information systems tailored for their specific use, and technical writers are needed to explain the mechanics of these systems. One of the largest and most complex computerized information systems in place today is the airline reservation system. Computer programmers, computer operators, system managers, airline executives, reservations operators, and travel agencies are all linked together, and each must understand how to use this system. Translations from technical to lay terms are needed when different kinds of system users interact.

Help in Locating These Employers. There are many well-known employers in the transportation industry, and each uses information systems, equipment, and procedures that need to be clearly explained to employees. If you are interested in working in this industry, develop your list by reviewing *Moody's Transportation Manual* at your career office, college, or local public library.

Some of the professional associations related to the transportation and travel industry include the Air Transport Association of America, Washington, D.C. (www.air-transport.org); Association of American Railroads, Washington, D.C.; American Trucking Association, Alexandria, Virginia; Lake Carriers Association, Cleveland, Ohio (www.lcaships.com); and the ENO Transportation Foundation, Landsdowne, Virginia.

Health Care

Profile. The quality of health care and the way it is delivered in the United States is in the forefront of the news. If you want to be employed in this ever-changing industry, the industrial groups to consider are health and medical services and medical and dental instruments and supplies.

Caring for aging parents using currently available health-care options is one topic receiving a lot of press. Understanding the options—home care, congregate housing, assisted living, continuing-care facilities, and nursing homes—and associated costs is of great import to today's families. The skill of the technical writer is used to document and present this information. Decisions are often made in a time of crisis. An organized, logical, and clear explanation to consumers who will be placing parents in these facilities could mean a real difference in the quality of life for all those involved.

Help in Locating These Employers. If you are interested in working as a technical writer in the health care industry, you may want to begin your search by going on-line to find current information on the industry, companies, and associations as well as links to actual job listings. For example, searching the HandiLinks site (www.ahandyguide.com) using the words *health care* immediately pulls up a generous number of entries to examine and job-listing links to explore.

Several organizations that can provide information on health care include the Health Industry Manufacturers Association, Washington, D.C.; National Association for Home Care, Washington, D.C. (www.nahc.org); American Association for the Continuity of Care, Hartford, Connecticut; and the Nursing Home Advisory and Research Council, Cleveland Heights, Ohio.

Financial and Business Services

Profile. You will find commercial banking, international commercial banking, savings institutions, mutual fund companies, securities firms, commodities futures trading companies, and insurance companies in the financial and business services industry. As this industry has grown more complex, its documentation has grown equally complicated, with some surprising results. Consumers, angry about their inability to understand the complexities of legal documents used by these industries, have frequently sued and won court cases over issues of obscure language. Technical writers have been asked to replicate the essence of these complex agreements for financial services in "user-friendly" language that still conveys all the required legal points of culpability, responsibility, and ownership.

Help in Locating These Employers. Some resources that can be used to generate lists of potential employers include the *American Bank Directory, Credit Union Directory, Directory of American Savings and Loan Associations, Directory of Bond Agents, Security Dealers of North America,* and *Best Insurance Reports.*

Many professional associations are in place for this industry. Just a few of the larger associations include the American Bankers Association (www.aba. com), Washington, D.C.; Futures Industry Association, Washington, D.C.; National Association of Mutual Insurance Companies (http://www.namic. org/); and the Insurance Industry Internet Network (http://www.iiin.com/ index_frames.html).

Professional and Business Services

Profile. Professional and business services include equipment leasing, accounting, auditing, bookkeeping, advertising, legal services, management, consulting, and public relations. Business associations, professional organizations, and labor organizations are also included in this category.

One of the great success stories of American business has been the restaurant franchise. Many enterprising businesspeople have become millionaires through buying and successfully managing a branch of a national restaurant chain such as Pizza Hut, McDonald's, Burger King, Hardees, etc. To ensure consistent quality of its products, each of these chains provides every owner with a specification document for each product it sells. If they can duplicate that product, according to these specifications (written by the technical writing staff), they may buy locally. If a local vendor cannot meet these exacting specifications, they must purchase from the franchise owner. The specifications for McDonald's sesame seed buns even document the density of sesame seed coverage!

Help in Locating These Employers. As you begin to develop a list of potential employers to contact, some references to check include *Who Audits America, Standard Directory of Advertising Agencies, Directory of Management Consultants, Consultants and Consulting Organizations Directory, O'Dwyer's Directory of Corporate Communications,* and *O'Dwyer's Directory of Public Relations Firms.* There are many industry specific career guides available that also list specific company names.

You can contact the American Association of Advertising Agencies, New York (www.aaaa.org); American Bar Association, Chicago (www.abanet.org); American Institute of Certified Public Accountants, New York (www.aicpa.org); Institute of Management Consultants (www.imcusa.org); and the Public Relations Society of America, New York (www.prsa.org), to get more specific information on technical writing and other career opportunities available with that type of employer.

Public Administration

Profile: Federal Government. The procedures for shredding and destruction of classified documents, the safe storage procedures for confidential material, the arming of a security system on a naval base, the fire-control trajectory instructions for a shipboard missile assembly, and directions for assembling and heating field rations are just some of the countless ways in which technical writers provide needed skills in the federal government.

Help in Locating These Employers. There are many federal agencies that employ technical writers; a few of the largest agencies include the Department of the Interior, Department of Agriculture, Health and Human Services Department, National Aeronautics and Space Administration, Department of Defense, Nuclear Regulatory Commission, Environmental Protection Agency, National Institutes of Health, Centers for Disease Control, and the

Department of Energy. Most of these agencies operate their own personnel/ human resources function, so contacting them directly is a good way to begin. A place to start looking for actual job listings is on the U.S. government's website (http://www.usajobs.opm.gov/index.htm). This site explains the federal employment process, and lets you look at current job openings, get general information on federal agencies, and submit an on-line application.

If you select the option "Current Job Openings" and then "Choose a Specific Series," one of the options is "1083—Technical Writing and Editing." Select this option, search for "All" jobs, and a list will appear on your screen. Select any of the entries and a detailed job description is provided, including information on who to contact for more information and how to apply for the specific position.

Profile: State and Local Government. State and local governments continue to be impacted by a variety of federal legislation in every area of government. Social services, wetlands conservation, schools, hospitals, and taxes have all become increasingly complex and the subject of intense public scrutiny and emotion. In every case and at every level, directives and policies must be reinterpreted and tailored to the region, locality, or government level involved. This is the job of the technical writer.

Help in Locating These Employers. Some state and local governments provide both entry-level positions that can help you build your technical knowledge base and actual technical writing jobs. Start by contacting the state or city human resources department in the geographic area where you would like to work. Talk with someone there about departments and offices that hire technical writers. Many state and local government jobs are listed in each state's larger newspapers, and websites contain job listings. Use your favorite search engine and enter "State of (put state name here)." You will find references to state departments; look for Employment, Personnel, or Human Resources, then look for job listings, opportunities, etc. You will also find application procedures and contact names, and some sites will allow you to apply on-line. Don't hesitate to directly contact government units that you discover have a need for technical writing skills. Be proactive and let the directors of those government units know you have skills they can put to use.

POSSIBLE JOB TITLES

Technical writing jobs are usually advertised as such, but you will also see technical communicator, medical writer, technical editor, publications specialist, and science writer used.

As you begin to consider entry-level jobs that could be used to gain expertise in a specific industry or discipline, the range of job titles to consider expands. Look for job titles that might include media associate, marketing associate, proposal writer, associate editor, editorial assistant, copywriter, museum assistant, research assistant, field technician, lab technician, designer, computer programmer, systems analyst, or reporter.

RELATED OCCUPATIONS

There are three often-mentioned job titles that relate to technical writing: researcher, science journalist, and public information writer. A brief description of each follows.

Researchers conduct studies and gather verbal or statistical information. They then analyze the data and prepare reports to describe their findings. Researchers work in nearly any discipline you can imagine, including law, medicine, politics, genetic engineering, physics, animal care, food science, agronomy, geology, meteorology, soils, oceanography, and psychology.

Science journalists translate technical information into a public interest format and relate that information via newspaper and magazine articles, press releases, radio and TV scripts, trade books, textbooks, information booklets, and encyclopedia entries.

Public information writers usually work for high-technology industries, public research agencies, or colleges and universities. These writers help the outside world understand research efforts going on within their organization. They may use the written word, photographs, videotapes, or audiotapes to convey their message to various audiences, including chief executive officers, members of the general public, alumni, or representatives from news organizations.

PROFESSIONAL ASSOCIATIONS FOR TECHNICAL WRITERS

Many associations can provide information valuable to your job search in technical writing, but there are a few that you especially should consider contacting. Find out about membership benefits as you request more general information from the group. Joining any of these associations will increase your knowledge of current industry trends and issues, all of which affect hiring prospects.

American Medical Writers Association
9650 Rockville Pike
Bethesda, MD 20814
Website: www.amwancal.org
E-mail: amwa@amwancal.org
Members/Purpose: Medical writers, editors, audiovisualists, public
relations, and pharmaceutical personnel; publishers; and others concerned
with communication in medicine and allied sciences.
Journal/Publication: Journal; membership directory; freelance directory.
Job Listings: Members can list their names in the freelance directory; job
market sheet sent to members nine times per year.

American Podiatric Medical Writers Association
P.O. Box 50
New York, NY 10044
Website: www.apma.org
E-mail: askapma@apma.org
Members/Purpose: Podiatric medical writers; promotes improvement of
writing on podiatric topics.
Training: Conducts writing seminars.
Journal/Publication: Membership directory; newsletter.

Associated Business Writers of America
1450 S. Havana, Ste. 424
Aurora, CO 80012
Members/Purpose: Professional freelance writers who specialize in
business writing. Objective is to serve as a marketplace where business
editors can locate writing talent.
Journal/Publication: Directory; newsletter.

Aviation/Space Writers Association
17 S. High St., Ste. 1200
Columbus, OH 43215
Members/Purpose: Aviation/space writers and editors of newspapers,
magazines, books, radio, television, and press services; public relations
representatives and other writers associated with the aviation/space
industry.

Computer Press Association
7000 Bianca Ave.
Van Nuys, CA 91406
Website: www.computers.org
E-mail: nchase@nwu.edu

Members/Purpose: Journalists and other individuals who write or report regularly about the computer industry.

Journal/Publication: *Computer Press Association Network News*; directory.

Job Listings: Operates job listings service; provides computerized database providing job listings and access to a clearinghouse for writing assignments.

Construction Writers Association

P.O. Box 5586

Buffalo Grove, IL 60089

Website: www.constructionwriters.org

E-mail: office@constructionwriters.org

Members/Purpose: Writers and editors for media, public relations, and advertising in the construction field.

Journal/Publication: Newsletter.

International Association of Travel Journalists

P.O. Box D

Hurleyville, NY 12747

Members/Purpose: Newspaper and magazine writers covering the fields of aviation, travel, tourism, and airports. Promotes accurate reporting of these subjects.

National Association of Science Writers

P.O. Box 294

Greenlawn, NY 11740

Website: www.nasw.org

Members/Purpose: Writers and editors engaged in the preparation and interpretation of science news for the public.

Journal/Publication: Awards; newsletter.

New York Financial Writers Association

P.O. Box 21

Syosset, NY 11791

Website: www.nyfwa.org

Members/Purpose: Financial and business editors and writers whose publications are located in metropolitan New York.

Training: Sponsors annual seminar for college students interested in the financial journalism field.

Journal/Publication: Directory.

Scientists' Institute for Public Information, Defense Writers Working Group

355 Lexington Ave., 16th Floor

New York, NY 10017

Members/Purpose: Fosters dissemination of objective scientific data on current social issues linked to science and technology. Provides toll-free number for journalists seeking science/technology, environmental, defense, child health, and public policy information.

Training: Conducts seminars and symposia.

Journal/Publication: *SIPIscope.*

Society for Technical Communication
901 N. Stuart St., Ste. 904
Arlington, VA 22203-1854
Website: www.stc-va.org
E-mail: webmaster@stc-va.org
Members/Purpose: Primarily concerned with the education, improvement, and advancement of technical communicators.

Training: Society offers seminars, lectures, workshops, international symposia, and an annual conference to keep technical communicators informed of latest techniques and methods in communication.

Journal/Publication: *Technical Communication;* newsletter; proceedings.

Job Listings: Regional chapters provide employment committees. Most employment committees have managers who provide information about jobs. Members can also use the bulletin board service.

ADDITIONAL RESOURCES

ABI/Inform On Disc
UMI-Data Courier, Inc.
620 S. Fifth St.
Louisville, KY 40202

Advertising Career Directory
Gale Research Inc.
P.O. Box 33477
Detroit, MI 48232

America's Corporate Families
Dun & Bradstreet Information Services
899 Eaton Ave.
Bethlehem, PA 18025
Website: www.business-sales-leads.com
E-mail: mrktngtlsl@mail.dnb.com

American Bank Directory
McFadden Business Publications
6195 Crooked Creek Rd.
Norcross, GA 30092

American Bar Association Directory
American Bar Association
750 N. Lake Shore Dr.
Chicago, IL 60611
Website: www.abanet.org
E-mail: info@abanet.org

ARTSearch
Theatre Communications Group, Inc.
355 Lexington Ave.
New York, NY 10017

ASCUS Annual
Association for School, College & University Staffing
1600 Dodge Ave., S-330
Evanston, IL 60201

Audio Video Market Place
R. R. Bowker Co.
245 W. 17th St.
New York, NY 10011

The Best Towns in America
Houghton Mifflin Co.
222 Berkeley St.
Boston, MA 02116
Website: www.hmco.com

Best's Insurance Reports
A. M. Best Co.
Oldwick, NJ 08858
Website: www.ambest.com

The Boston Globe
The Globe Newspaper Co.
135 Morrissey Blvd.
P.O. Box 2378
Boston, MA 02107
Website: www.thebostonglobe.com
E-mail: gould@globe.com

Braddock's Federal-State-Local Government Directory
Braddock Communications
909 N. Washington St., Ste. 310
Alexandria, VA 22314

Broadcasting and Cable Market Place
R. R. Bowker
121 Chanlon Rd.
New Providence, NJ 07974

Burrelle's Media Directory
Burrelle's Media Directories
75 E. Northfield Rd.
Livingston, NJ 07039

Business Rankings Annual
Gale Research Inc.
P.O. Box 33477
Detroit, MI 48232

The Career Guide: Dun's Employment Opportunities Directory
Dun & Bradstreet Information Services
899 Eaton Ave.
Bethlehem, PA 18025

Career Information Center
Macmillan Publishing Group
866 Third Ave.
New York, NY 10022

Careers Encyclopedia
VGM Career Horizons
NTC/Contemporary Publishing Group
4255 W. Touhy Ave.
Lincolnwood, IL 60712

Careers in State and Local Government
Garrett Park Press
Garrett Park, MD 20896

The Chronicle of Higher Education
1255 23rd St. NW
Washington, DC 20037
Website: www.chronicle.com

College Placement Council Annuals
62 Highland Ave.
Bethlehem, PA 18017

College to Career: The Guide to Job Opportunities
Joyce Mitchell
The College Board
P.O. Box 866
New York, NY 10101

Community Jobs:
The National Employment Newspaper for the
Non-Profit Sector
ACCESS: Networking in the Public Interest
50 Beacon St.
Boston, MA 02108
Website: www.accessjobs.org
E-mail: commjobs@aol.com

Companies That Care
Hal Morgan and Kerry Tucker
Simon & Schuster/Fireside
Simon & Schuster Building
Rockefeller Center
1230 Ave. of the Americas
New York, NY 10020

The Complete Guide to Public Employment
Ronald Krannich and Caryl Krannich
Impact Publications
4580 Sunshine Ct.
Woodbridge, VA 22192

Consultants and Consulting Organizations Directory
Gale Research Inc.
P.O. Box 33477
Detroit, MI 48232

County Executive Directory
Carroll Publishing
1058 Thomas Jefferson St. NW
Washington, DC 20077

Credit Union Directory and Buyer's Guide
United Communications Group
4550 Montgomery Ave., Ste. 700-N
Bethesda, MD 20814

Current Jobs for Graduates
Current Jobs for Graduates in Education
Current Jobs in Writing, Editing & Communications
Plymouth Publishing, Inc.
P.O. Box 40550
5136 MacArthur Blvd. NW
Washington, DC 20016

Dialing for Jobs: Using the Phone in the Job Search (video)
JIST Works, Inc.
720 N. Park Ave.
Indianapolis, IN 46202
Website: www.jist.com

Dictionary of Occupational Titles
U.S. Department of Labor
Employment and Training Administration
Distributed by Associated Book Publishers, Inc.
P.O. Box 5657
Scottsdale, AZ 86261
Website: www.wave.net/upg/immigration/dot_index.html

Directory of American Savings and Loan Associations
T. K. Sanderson Organization
1115 E. 30th St.
Baltimore, MD 21218

Directory of Bond Agents
Standard and Poor's Corp.
25 Broadway
New York, NY 10004

Directory of City Policy Officials
National League of Cities
1301 Pennsylvania Ave. NW
Washington, DC 20004

Directory of Directories
Gale Research Inc.
P.O. Box 33477
Detroit, MI 48232

Directory of Management Consultants
Kennedy and Kennedy, Inc.
Consultants News
Templeton Rd.
Fitzwilliam, NH 03447
Website: www.kennedyinfo.com/mc/dc.html

DISCOVER
American College Testing
Educational Services Division
P.O. Box 168
Iowa City, IA 52244

Effective Answers to Interview Questions (video)
JIST Works, Inc.
720 N. Park Ave.
Indianapolis, IN 46202
Website: www.jist.com

Employer's Expectations (video)
JIST Works, Inc.
720 N. Park Ave.
Indianapolis, IN 46202
Website: www.jist.com

Encyclopedia of Associations
Gale Research Inc.
P.O. Box 33477
Detroit, MI 48232

Environmental Opportunities
Environmental Studies Department
Antioch/New England Graduate School
Keene, NH 03431

Equal Employment Opportunity Bimonthly
CRS Recruitment Publications/CASS Communications, Inc.
60 Revere Dr.
Northbrook, IL 60062

Federal Career Opportunities
Gordon Press Publishers
P.O. Box 459
Bowling Green Station
New York, NY 10004

Federal Jobs Digest
Breakthrough Publications
P.O. Box 594
Millwood, NY 10546
Website: www.jobsfed.com

Folio: The Magazine for Magazine Management
Six River Bend Center
911 Hope St.
P.O. Box 4294
Stamford, CT 06907
Website: www.foliomag.com

Foundation Grants to Individuals
The Foundation Center
79 Fifth Ave.
New York, NY 10003
Website: www.fdncenter.org/marketplace/catalog/gti.html

Gale Directory of Publications and Broadcast Media
P.O. Box 33477
Detroit, MI 48232

Government Job Finder
Daniel Lauber
Planning/Communications
7215 Oak Ave.
River Forest, IL 60305

Graduate Management Admissions Test
Graduate Management Admission Council
P.O. Box 6108
Princeton, NJ 08541
Website: wwww.gmat.org
E-mail: gmat@ets.org

Graduate Record Exam
Graduate Record Examinations Board
Educational Testing Service
P.O. Box 6000
Princeton, NJ 08541
Website: www.gre.org

Handbook for Business and Management Careers
VGM Career Horizons
NTC/Contemporary Publishing Group
4255 W. Touhy Ave.
Lincolnwood, IL 60712

The Handbook of Private Schools
Porter Sargent Publishers, Inc.
11 Beacon St., Ste. 1400
Boston, MA 02108

Harrington-O'Shea Career Decision Making System
American Guidance Service
4201 Woodland Rd.
P.O. Box 99
Circle Pines, MN 55014

Hoover's Handbook of American Business
The Reference Press
6448 Highway 290 E., Ste. E-104
Austin, TX 78723
Website: www.hoovers.com/hooc/store/storefront.htm

How to Write a Winning Personal Statement for Graduate and Professional School
Richard Stelzer
Peterson's Guides
P.O. Box 2123
Princeton, NJ 08543

Humor & Cartoon Markets
Writer's Digest Books
1507 Dana Ave.
Cincinnati, OH 45207

Independent School
National Association of Independent Schools
1620 L St. NW
Washington, DC 20036

Index of Majors and Graduate Degrees
College Board Publications
P.O. Box 886
New York, NY 10101

Infotrac CD-ROM Business Index
Information Access Co.
362 Lakeside Dr.
Foster City, CA 94404

The International Educator
Overseas Schools Assistance Corp.
P.O. Box 513
Cummaquid, MA 02637

International Television Association Membership Directory
International Television Association
6311 N. O'Connor Rd., LB 51
Irving, TX 75039

ISS Directory of Overseas Schools
International Schools Services
P.O. Box 5910
Princeton, NJ 08543

Job Bank series:
Atlanta Job Bank
Boston Job Bank
Chicago Job Bank
Dallas–Ft. Worth Job Bank
Denver Job Bank
Detroit Job Bank
Florida Job Bank
Houston Job Bank
Los Angeles Job Bank
Minneapolis Job Bank
New York Job Bank
Northwest Job Bank
Ohio Job Bank
Philadelphia Job Bank
St. Louis Job Bank
San Francisco Job Bank
Seattle Job Bank
Washington, D.C., Job Bank
Bob Adams, Inc.
260 Center St.
Holbrook, MA 02343

Job Hotlines USA
Career Communications, Inc.
P.O. Box 169
Harleyville, PA 19438
Website: www.americasemployers.com

The Job Hunter
The National Bi-Weekly Publication for Job Seekers
Career Planning and Placement Center
University of Missouri-Columbia
100 Noyes Building
Columbia, MO 65211
Website: www.collegerad.com/employers

Job Seekers Guide to Private and Public Companies
Gale Research Inc.
P.O. Box 33477
Detroit, MI 48232

Million Dollar Directory: America's Leading Public and Private Companies
Dun & Bradstreet Information Services
899 Eaton Ave.
Bethlehem, PA 18025

Moody's Manuals
Moody's Investors Service
99 Church St.
New York, NY 10007

Municipal Executive Directory
Carroll Publishing Co.
1058 Thomas Jefferson St. NW
Washington, DC 20077
Website: www.carrollpub.com

The Municipal Yearbook
International City Management Association
777 N. Capitol St. NE, Ste. 500
Washington, DC 20002

Myers-Briggs Type Indicator
Consulting Psychologists Press, Inc.
3803 E. Bayshore Rd.
Palo Alto, CA 94303
Website: www.meyers-briggs.com

National Center for Education Statistics
"America's Teachers: Profile of a Profession"
U.S. Department of Education
Office of Educational Research and Improvement
Washington, DC 20208
Website: www.nces.ed.gov/index.html
E-mail: NCESWebmaster@ed.gov

National Directory of Accounting Firms and Accountants
Gale Research Inc.
P.O. Box 33477
Detroit, MI 48232

National Directory of Arts Internships
National Network for Artist Placement
935 W. Ave. 37
Los Angeles, CA 90065

National Directory of Internships
National Society for Internships and Experiential Education
3509 Haworth Dr., Ste. 207
Raleigh, NC 27609

National Directory of Weekly Newspapers
National Newspaper Association
1627 K St. NW, Ste. 400
Washington, DC 20006

National Job Bank
Bob Adams, Inc.
260 Center St.
Holbrook, MA 02343

National Teacher Exam
Educational Testing Service
P.O. Box 6051
Princeton, NJ 08541
Website: www.ets.org
E-mail: etsinfo@ets.org

National Trade and Professional Associations of the United States
Columbia Books Inc.
1212 New York Ave. NW, Ste. 330
Washington, DC 20005

NewsLinks: The Newspaper of International Schools Services
15 Roszel Rd., P.O. Box 5910
Princeton, NJ 08543

The Newspaper Guild
8611 Second Ave.
Silver Spring, MD 20910
Website: www.newsguild.org

Newspapers Career Directory
Gale Research Inc.
P.O. Box 33477
Detroit, MI 48232

Non-Profit Job Finder
Planning/Communications
7215 Oak Ave.
River Forest, IL 60305

Novel & Short Story Writer's Market
Writer's Digest Books
1507 Dana Ave.
Cincinnati, OH 45207
Website: www.writersdigest.com
E-mail: wdweb@fwpubs.com

Occupational Outlook Handbook
Occupational Outlook Quarterly
U.S. Department of Labor
Bureau of Labor Statistics
Washington, DC 20212
Website: www.dol.gov

Occupational Thesaurus
Lehigh University
Bethlehem, PA 18015

O'Dwyer's Directory of Corporate Communications
O'Dwyer's Directory of Public Relations Firms
J. R. O'Dwyer Co. Inc.
271 Madison Ave.
New York, NY 10016

The 100 Best Companies to Sell For
Michael Harkavy and the Philip Lief Group
John Wiley & Sons
605 Third Ave.
New York, NY 10158

The 100 Best Companies to Work for in America
Robert Levering and Milton Moskowitz
A Currency Book published by Doubleday
Bantam Doubleday Dell Publishing Group, Inc.
666 Fifth Ave.
New York, NY 10103

101 Challenging Government Jobs for College Graduates
An Arco Book
Prentice Hall Press
New York, NY 10023
(Out of print, but it can be found in many career libraries.)

Opportunities in Banking Careers
Opportunities in Publishing Careers
Opportunities in Government Careers
Opportunities in Insurance Careers
Opportunities in Journalism Careers
Opportunities in Marketing Careers
Opportunities in Nursing Careers
Opportunities in Sports and Fitness Careers
Opportunities in Psychology Careers
Opportunities in Television and Video Careers
VGM Career Horizons
NTC/Contemporary Publishing Group
4255 W. Touhy Ave.
Lincolnwood, IL 60712

Overseas Employment Opportunities for Educators
Department of Defense
Office of Dependents Schools
2461 Eisenhower Ave.
Alexandria, VA 22331

Patterson's American Education
Patterson's Elementary Education
Educational Directories Inc.
P.O. Box 199
Mount Prospect, IL 60056

Peterson's Grants for Graduate Students
Peterson's Guide to Four-Year Colleges
Peterson's Guide to Independent Secondary Schools
Peterson's Guide to Two-Year Colleges
Peterson's Guides to Graduate Study
Peterson's Internships
Peterson's Guides
P.O. Box 2123
Princeton, NJ 08543

Places Rated Almanac
Prentice Hall General Reference & Travel
15 Columbus Circle
New York, NY 10023

Poet's Market
Writer's Digest Books
1507 Dana Ave.
Cincinnati, OH 45207
Website: www.writersdigest.com
E-mail: wdweb@fwpubs.com

Professional Career series:
Advertising
Business
Communications
Computers
Health Care
High Tech
VGM Career Horizons
NTC/Contemporary Publishing Group
4255 W. Touhy Ave.
Lincolnwood, IL 60712

Professional's Job Finder
Planning/Communications
7215 Oak Ave.
River Forest, IL 60305

Public Relations Journal
Public Relations Society of America
33 Irving Pl.
New York, NY 10003
Website: www.prsa.org
E-mail: hq@prsa.org

Publishers Weekly
P.O. Box 1979
Marion, OH 43306

Regional, State, and Local Organizations
Gale Research Inc.
P.O. Box 33477
Detroit, MI 48232

Schools Abroad of Interest to Americans
Porter Sargent Publishers
11 Beacon St., Ste. 1400
Boston, MA 02108

Security Dealers of North America
Standard and Poor's Corp.
25 Broadway
New York, NY 10004

SIGI PLUS
P.O. Box 6403
Rosedale Rd.
Princeton, NJ 08541

The Skills Search (video)
JIST Works, Inc.
720 N. Park Ave.
Indianapolis, IN 46202
Website: www.jist.com

Social and Behavioral Sciences Jobs Handbook
Prospect Press
P.O. Box 3069, Diamond Farms Branch
Gaithersburg, MD 20878
(Out of print, but it can be found in many career libraries.)

Song Writer's Market
Writer's Digest Books
1507 Dana Ave.
Cincinnati, OH 45207
Website: www.writersdigest.com
E-mail: wdweb@fwpubs.com

Sports Marketplace
Sportsguide
P.O. Box 1417
Princeton, NJ 08542

Standard and Poor's Industry Surveys
Standard and Poor's Register of Corporations
Standard and Poor's Corp.
25 Broadway
New York, NY 10004

Standard Directory of Advertising Agencies
Reed Reference Publishing
P.O. Box 31
New Providence, NJ 07974

State Executive Directory
Carroll Publishing Co.
1058 Thomas Jefferson St. NW
Washington, DC 20077

State Government Research Directory
Gale Research Inc.
P.O. Box 33477
Detroit, MI 48232

Strong Interest Inventory
Consulting Psychologists Press, Inc.
3803 E. Bayshore Rd.
Palo Alto, CA 94303
Website: www.cpp-db.com

The Tough New Labor Market of the 1990s (video)
JIST Works, Inc.
720 N. Park Ave.
Indianapolis, IN 46202
Website: www.jist.com

Upper Valley Teacher Training Institute
106 Hanover St., Ste. 202
Lebanon, NH 03766
Website: www.uvti.org

U.S. Industrial Outlook
Superintendent of Documents
P.O. Box 371954
Pittsburgh, PA 15250
(S/N 003-009-00618-0)

U.S. News and World Report
2400 N St. NW
Washington, DC 20037
Website: www.usnews.com/usnews/home.htm

The Video Register & Teleconferencing Resources Directory
Knowledge Industries Publications
701 Westchester Ave.
White Plains, NY 10604

Ward's Business Directory of Corporate Affiliations
Gale Research Inc.
P.O. Box 33477
Detroit, MI 48232

What Can I Do with a Major in . . . ?
Lawrence Malnig with Anita Malnig
Abbott Press
P.O. Box 433
Ridgefield, NJ 07657

Where the Jobs Are: A Comprehensive Directory of 1,200 Journals Listing Career Opportunities
S. Norman Feingold and Glenda Hansard-Winkler
Garrett Park Press
P.O. Box 190
Garrett Park, MD 20896

Who Audits America
Data Financial Press
P.O. Box 668
Menlo Park, CA 94026

World Chamber of Commerce Directory
P.O. Box 1029
Loveland, CO 80539

Writer's Market
Writer's Digest Books
F&W Publications
1507 Dana Ave.
Cincinnati, OH 45207
Website: www.writersdigest.com
E-mail: wdweb@fwpubs.com

Y National Vacancy List
YMCA of the USA
101 N. Wacker Dr.
Chicago, IL 60606
Website: www.ymca.net/employment.htm

INDEX

About the Authors

Julie DeGalan is a project leader at Geographic Data Technology (GDT), Inc., in Lebanon, New Hampshire. GDT is a leader in the business geographics industry, providing data for various geographic information systems. Previously, Ms. DeGalan worked as an administrator and career counselor at Plymouth State College. Ms. DeGalan's degrees include an MBA in management information systems from Plymouth State College and a bachelor of science degree in geography/cartography from Michigan State University.

Stephen Lambert is director of career services at Plymouth State College, where, in addition to counseling students and developing year-round career workshops, he directs experiential education programs for a number of departments. Dr. Lambert's degrees include an MBA in marketing, a masters of education in counseling, a Certificate of Advanced Graduate Studies (CAGS), and a doctorate in education.